Fantastic
Antone
Grows
Up

Success has no single definition.
Success does not necessarily mean
attending college or
finding a full-time job.
Success may mean finishing things
some of the time.
It means hitting a punching bag
instead of a person.
It means remembering you forgot
your homework at 4:30, and
getting your mom to drive you
back to school.
Success means knowing who you are,
accepting yourself, and understanding
that everyone has handicaps.
For someone with FAS, success means
knowing that these are goals worth
striving for, not someone else's
unreachable line in the sand.

— Jan Lutke, "Works in Progress:
The Meaning of Success for
Individuals with FAS/E,"
in *Fantastic Antone Grows Up*

Fantastic Antone Grows Up

Adolescents and Adults with Fetal Alcohol Syndrome

Edited by
Judith Kleinfeld
with **Barbara Morse**
and **Siobhan Wescott**

University of Alaska Press
Fairbanks

Library of Congress Cataloging-in-Publication Data

Fantastic Antone grows up : adolescents and adults with fetal alcohol syndrome /
edited by Judith Kleinfeld, with Barbara Morse and Siobhan Wescott.
   p. cm.
   Includes bibliographical references and index.
   ISBN 1-889963-11-9 (pbk. : alk. paper)
     1. Fetal alcohol syndrome--Case studies. 2. Alcohol--Physiological effect--
Case studies. 3. Fetus--Effect of drugs on--Case studies. I. Kleinfeld, Judith.
II. Morse, Barbara. III. Wescott, Siobhan.

RG629.F45 F36 2000
618.3'268--dc21

                                           00-022765

Publication coordination and production by Pamela Odom, University of Alaska
   Press.
Book design by Paula Elmes, Publications Center, Center for Cross-Cultural
   Studies.
Cover design by Dixon Jones, IMPACT/Graphics, Rasmuson Library.
Index by Paul Kish, Kish Indexing Services.

The illustration on the cover is from a painting by Cindy Gere
entitled *The Art Door Opens*.

To the courageous young people coping with FAS/E

To the parents and their wisdom

Contents

ᔇ

PART ONE
WHAT IS SUCCESS FOR ADOLESCENTS AND ADULTS WITH FAS?

A birth mother tells the story of how her son Ryland created a good relationship with her, his family, and the community. He has a job and is living on his own. "Ryland is doing very well, thank you, and so am I."

An adoptive mother who is also a college professor describes the techniques she used to prepare her daughter Cindy for college and to help her succeed during her college years. Cindy, an accomplished artist, offers strategic knowledge about how to succeed in college, including coping strategies for such problems as difficulties with mathematics, spelling, and remembering.

A mother describes how she prepared her daughter Sidney for adulthood and how she dealt with the crises of adolescence, especially a wild boyfriend who was getting Sidney into trouble.

A young woman with FAS describes her life with her husband and the responsibility of living on her own. She explains the importance of her husband in creating structure for her life and the kind of work environment that is best for her.

↪

PART TWO
STRATEGIES THAT WORK: EDUCATION, COUNSELING, SEXUALITY, TROUBLE WITH THE LAW, LIVING SKILLS

When Devorah starts talking about not wanting to live, her mother knows she has to get her daughter out of the standard school program that was destroying her self-esteem. Like many other adolescents with FAS/E, Devorah thrives in a school emphasizing projects, activities, and group work.

Focusing on the case of Sarah, a psychologist discusses her success with insight therapy, long considered an ineffective approach for people with FAS/E. She shows how to adapt the therapeutic techniques, for example, using visuals to represent troubling interpersonal problems.

When her 21-year-old son gets arrested for sexual touching, Marie Jones' world collapses. Her son had never before been in trouble. He was working and taking courses at the community college. Drawing on her own mistakes and experience, she suggests effective strategies for other parents of children with FAS/E in dealing with the criminal justice system.

A social worker and psychologist describe ways to understand and handle the emerging sexual needs of adolescents with disabilities like FAS/E.

An adoptive mother who started a newsletter for families describes the concerns that emerge at adolescence such as sexual modesty. She highlights the charm of many young people with FAS/E.

An adoptive father discusses common issues for young people
with FAS/E as they reach adolescence. He emphasizes sex education and how to prepare young people to live as independently
as possible.

Two researchers use information about other disabilities to understand why young people with FAS/E often have such severe
difficulties at adolescence and how to provide them with the best
opportunities for the future.

↩

PART THREE
WHAT FAMILIES NEED FROM THE COMMUNITY

Hanging out with his mentor for a few months teaches Janet
Adam's son far more about appropriate social behavior than he
learned from four years of social skills training in school.

A psychologist describes how Native American communities help
individuals with FAS/E find useful positions in tribal life based
on their strengths and ability to contribute.

To get her adoptive son the services he needs for his inappropriate sexual behavior, Ann Michael has to relinquish him to state

custody. She works with state agencies to create a supervised program that enables him to control his sexual urges, support himself, and stay close to his family. When the agencies stop the supervision, disaster strikes.

In their commitment to caring for young people with FAS/E, many caregivers forget to take care of themselves. The founder and developers of the Family Empowerment Network describe how to get beyond the guilt that saps the energy of both birth and adoptive parents.

A noted researcher describes the breakthroughs in research on FAS/E and applies these new findings to practical questions such as how to get a diagnosis at adolescence and what the future may hold.

The wisdom of practice, together with research on FAS, offers useful answers to the questions on the minds of parents and practitioners: What does success look like for young people with FAS? Why is adolescence so difficult? What strategies help? What do parents and people with FAS most need?

⌐

Foreword:
Fantastic Antone is Growing Up
SALLY CALDWELL

Sally Caldwell is the adoptive mother of Antone, the title child of this book, Fantastic Antone Grows Up, *and of the earlier book,* Fantastic Antone Succeeds. *Her son was adopted at birth and diagnosed at three years with fetal alcohol syndrome, severe expression. Sally is completing a Masters in Education and she makes presentations on FAS to social service agencies and schools, bringing both a professional and parental perspective to the field.*

MY SON ANTONE, THE TITLE CHILD OF *FANTASTIC ANTONE SUCCEEDS*, IS growing up. No longer does he drench himself from head to toe in honey, just for the pleasure of feeling its sticky sweetness. No longer does he slump tearful into the snow, refusing to walk into a preschool too stressful. Today, Antone is 15 years old and hormones surge.

Since *Fantastic Antone Succeeds* was published,[1] Antone has grown beyond my height, his voice has deepened, and peach fuzz shadows his upper lip. But not all things have changed. He still responds best to hands-on, experiential teaching methods. Concrete explanations, tied to a visual cue or related to familiar experiences, still communicate more clearly than do abstract verbal explanations.

When I first held this baby in my arms and dared to dream a future for him, an overriding hope flooded my heart that he

---

[1] Sally Caldwell, "Nurturing the Delicate Rose," in Kleinfeld and Wescott 1993, 97–129.

be known for the quality of his character. The issue of a conscience in individuals with FAS/E has been raised in the dialogue among professionals and among parents. Some question whether children with FAS/E can be taught such qualities as empathy and trustworthiness. Since I have been so concerned with character, this is something I have paid particular attention to in raising Antone. As a youngster, he revealed the nobility of his character in small, random acts of kindness done in familiar and safe settings. At 15 his compassion, honesty, and conscience is as strong as when he was a young child. He is still, in his relationship with his Dad and me, concerned about "what is the right thing to do." He is still trustworthy.

But what of the future? Though Antone is an honest, sensitive person, one of the effects of FAS that we confront daily is that his comprehension level is younger than his 15 years. He cannot keep up with childhood friends who have moved on to grapple with adolescent demands like homework, weekend jobs, and career planning. So far, one foot rests securely in the value-directed world of his family, his school, and religious community, but the other taps to the luring rhythm of corruptions that are within his reach. Peers who now are more accessible to him are teens whose direction is less focused. Many are experimenting with drugs, alcohol, and sexual relationships. Some of these new friends make easy money selling drugs and establish and maintain a pecking order through intimidation and violent acts.

Will Antone follow them, as do so many adolescents, especially those with fetal alcohol syndrome? Will he continue his effort in school? What does his future hold?

School remains an overwhelming source of stress for Antone. Teaching methods in high school center on lectures and texts that abstract the curriculum from real life experience. The community and family atmosphere so purposefully nurtured in neighborhood elementary schools can disappear in larger secondary schools. Moving from teacher to teacher, from room to room, and encountering unfamiliar faces with each class change undermines his sense of order, predictability, and security.

The daily demands of school leave him completely exhausted. During Antone's first year in high school, he continued to experience the shut downs he had experienced in elementary school but now they lasted for days, even weeks, at a time. This resulted in frequent and extended absences from school and the need for special accommodations from his teachers.

Parental intervention at adolescence is more complicated than before and is not always an option. My son's choices are influenced by friends and the entertainments and advertisements that appeal to adolescents with messages of sex and violence. His emotional response to increased responsibilities and expectations is more complex as well. Mild depression and lack of motivation are new factors in Antone's life.

Adolescence and FAS—this situation of mixed hope and worry—inspired me to ask for this book: Where are the stories about teens with FAS who are succeeding? Where are the stories about parents sustaining nurturing relationships, and what are their parenting strategies for the budding adolescents in their lives? Where are the stories about high school teachers discovering ways to accommodate these students in the more complex and faster-paced high school curriculum?

Fantastic Antone Grows Up addresses these questions. As I read the stories found in this book, I realized that adolescence means Antone has moved beyond my abilities to create a safer world for him and beyond my own goals for him. Defining himself, establishing some autonomy, and working toward competence in areas he chooses are his goals, the goals that focus his attention. My requests must be framed within his adolescent world, and compromise is an important part of our communication.

I explore new experiences with him, listen to his ideas, and celebrate the victories. I adjust my dreams and try to confront with courage a future in which my son may always need some external support. Antone's battle with FAS is different from mine, and I have learned it is best not to confuse the two.

Though children with fetal alcohol syndrome differ from each other in temperament and in the degree of their prenatal exposure to alcohol, they are bound together by similar experiences. As their parents, we, too, are bound together by similar experiences. In *The Siege*, Clara Claiborn Park expresses most succinctly my feelings about living with fetal alcohol syndrome:

> This experience we did not choose, we would have given anything to avoid it. Yet, it has made us different. It has made us better. Through it, we have learned the lesson that no one studies willingly, the hard, slow lesson that one grows by suffering.[2]

Each night, I try to reflect on the day's happenings, even wax sentimental, to search for personal meaning. Out of my experience with Antone has come an unimagined and enriched life.

Sally Caldwell
Fairbanks, Alaska
October 1999

---

[2] Clara Claiborn Park 1990, 320.

Acknowledgments
JUDITH KLEINFELD

MANY PARENTS AND PROFESSIONALS HAVE A WISDOM BORN OF EXPERIENCE but not all are able to put into words what they know. To unlock this wisdom took many, many hours of collaboration. I am grateful to the authors of the chapters who worked so hard without any monetary compensation, and to the professional writers who worked so hard with them.

I would especially like to thank the authors of those chapters who wrote anonymously, without credit, so that others might have the benefit of their painful difficulties and what they learned. I wish to express great appreciation both to them and to all the authors—birth mothers, adoptive parents, professionals, and, most important, adults with FAS/E themselves.

Cindy Gere, an adult with FAE, contributed the painting on the cover of this book as well as the paintings inside, and the image used to create the motifs which separate chapters. She has given so generously of her artistic talents without compensation. Her self-lessness in itself demonstrates the generosity and strong moral character of so many young people with FAS/E.

Many chapters required the expertise of professional writers to reach fruition. I would especially like to thank Sherry Simpson, journalism professor at the University of Alaska Fairbanks, for her fine eye for detail, drama, and imagery. Pam Odom, the editor of both *Fantastic Antone Succeeds* and *Fantastic Antone Grows Up*, not only brought fine writing skills to these chapters but also a most valuable ability to see what was missing—the information that we needed but had forgotten to ask. I can not thank her enough for her professionalism and dedication to this project.

For his creative talents, I thank Dixon Jones who designed the cover of the book, title page, and section dividers, adapting Cindy Gere's painting, *The Art Door Opens*, to each section.

I also wish to thank the FAS/E parent groups in Alaska and in Boston who guided this project, suggested the questions that needed answering, reviewed chapters for sensitivity to parental concerns, and suggested ending the book with the type of humor that got parents through the times of troubles.

The Licensed Beverage Information Council gave us a small grant to help with this project. None of the authors or editors, however, received any financial compensation from grant funds or other sources.

All royalties from *Fantastic Antone Grows Up* will be donated to FAS/E parent groups in the United States and Canada, as we have previously done with all royalties from the earlier book, *Fantastic Antone Succeeds*.

Fairbanks, Alaska
November 1999

Introduction:
The Roller Coaster Ride
of Life with FAS/E

JUDITH KLEINFELD

Judith Kleinfeld is professor of psychology at the University of Alaska Fairbanks. She pioneered the idea of "wisdom of practice" studies to glean the wisdom of experienced parents and other people who work with FAS/E. Professor Kleinfeld won the Emil Usibelli Award for Distinguished Research for her work on fetal alcohol syndrome.

"I SURE WOULD LIKE TO HEAR ABOUT A YOUNG MAN WITH FAS WHO IS doing well." Even though I was talking to the mother on the telephone, I could see the expression on her face—wistful, yearning.

So let me tell you about Ryland, a big, cheerful guy with FAS. Ryland left home after high school and went to Wyoming with his girl friend to live with her grandparents. He got a job in a body and paint shop doing car detailing. He thought it was a great job, so great he decided to go in and work without pay one weekend to scrub down the walls which he thought looked dingy.

Ryland has FAS, and he also has a job and a girl friend. Maybe he should be giving advice to my own 24-year-old son, who right at the moment has neither.

His mother says "there is a hole in our home" without him, but she held her breath and let him go. Mary Lou Canney is his birth mother, and she tells her story in this book. It is not only a story of good parenting. It is also the story of the way she learned how to be a good parent—from Ryland, who taught her how to bond with him.

I did not know Ryland Canney had FAS when I first met him. Ryland was the guy I always looked for at a gas station where I went to put fuel in my car. I never could remember how the pump worked at the self-service island. Was this the gas station where you pushed the red button to start the gas flowing or was this the gas station where you pulled back the black lever? I always felt so foolish messing around with the pump that I put off getting gas until the last moment.

Ryland never made me feel stupid. He just made the pump work. Then he cleaned off the dirt and dead insects from my windshield, even though I hadn't asked and even though I wasn't entitled to any service at the self-service island. You can see why I always looked for Ryland.

I first learned that Ryland had FAS when I heard his mother speak at an FAS conference about her son who worked at a gas station. I wondered if this was the good-hearted guy who always helped me out. Yes, he was.

Mary Lou had done some heavy drinking when she was pregnant with Ryland. She would drink a case of beer in one evening, she says, and then down some goat's milk for the health of her baby. She was, she says, "out of my mind...."

Now Mary Lou knows a lot about how to raise a son with FAS. She knows Ryland imitates the people around him so she took care to put him near people she would like to have him imitate—like the hard-working mechanics at the gas station. Work experience at places like that became the centerpiece of Ryland's high school education.

Mary Lou let Ryland have his independence even though she knew he would run into trouble and he did, even before he got off the plane to Wyoming.

"So how is Ryland doing?" I asked his mother after he had left home.

"Just fine!" she told me. "Of course, he lost not one but two sets of travelers' checks on the plane trip. But he made a phone call and a whole new set of travelers' checks was waiting for him when he got there.

"He still loses things. But he is learning to cope."

Ryland is coping in large part by relying on his girl friend. She helps him structure his life, just like dear old Mom used to do. Finding a partner who provides structure is one of the ways we see young adults with FAS/E successfully organizing their lives. The noted FAS researcher, Ann Streissguth, pointed out the potential of this "get-married" strategy long ago when she did a follow-up study of French women who had been diagnosed with FAS. Some had married, she said, and were doing well. Their husbands managed the household tasks that they could not.

DEALING WITH FETAL ALCOHOL SYNDROME AT ADOLESCENCE

Many young children with fetal alcohol syndrome live happy lives within their families and can deal with the stress of school and with learning to assume greater responsibility for themselves. Using structure, supervision, routines, visual methods of presenting information, relaxation techniques, and other strategies, parents and teachers can create environments where children thrive.

As biological changes and cultural demands escalate, however, strategies that worked for young children are no longer enough. Many adolescents with FAS/E cannot cope with the independence and new responsibilities they are expected to assume. As a result, we don't see happy endings very often when we follow these adolescents and adults. What we see are roller coaster rides, with ups and downs.

But we also see courage. We see adolescents and adults and their families who are coping, often magnificently, with the problems life has dealt them. Having FAS is "like having a broken spider web in my brain," says one young woman. Whenever she tries to do something, she feels like she is trying to walk through the spider web. Sometimes she gets it right and other times she drops through the holes in the web, unable to do something she knew she could do only the day before.

We also see inventions. Many families, teachers, and the young people themselves have devised ingenious ways to cope with the problems of FAS/E. This book includes their strategies for dealing with memory losses, with lapses of attention, with the pounding emotions that threaten to overwhelm them and other people.

We also see wisdom. We see parents thinking about the meaning of success. In doing so, they remind us of what really matters in our lives, what matters more than going to college or getting a good job. They remind us that we don't have to accept other people's standards for success. As Jan Lutke puts it in her chapter:

> I define success for each of my children quite differently. Success may mean finishing things some of the time. It means hitting a punching bag instead of a person. Success means knowing who you are, accepting yourself, and understanding that everyone has handicaps. For someone with FAS, success means knowing that these goals are worth striving for, not someone else's unreachable line in the sand.[1]

Why We Wrote Fantastic Antone Grows Up

Our purpose in this book is to undermine an accepted but destructive myth—that people with FAS/E don't have a chance of getting a good job or of living on their own or of going to college.

The image of young people with FAS burned in people's minds is the picture of a young man looking out through prison bars. This is the face of FAS that looks out on us from the newscasts and documentaries on our television screens. It is a powerful image. The image is real and the message is true—for some people with FAS/E. But not for all of them. Ryland communicates another image and another message, just as real and true.

Our images of people with disabilities matter. One of the mistaken stereotypes about people with Down syndrome, for example, is that they never progress beyond the mental age of an eight year old. The stereotype is false but its effects have been profound. In one celebrated case, Sandra Jensen was refused a heart-lung transplant because she had Down syndrome. Two

---

[1] See chapter 1, "Works in Progress: The Meaning of Success for Individuals with FAS/E," by Jan Lutke.

California hospitals refused to give her the transplant that would save her life on the grounds that she lacked the intellectual ability to follow the post-operative regimen. Yet, Sandra Jensen had been living independently for 14 years. After a public outcry, she got the transplant.

As our image of people with Down syndrome has changed, so have our public policies. Before, people with Down syndrome used to be warehoused in institutions. Now, many get the education they need to marry, hold jobs, and live on their own.

We are writing this book because we want people to realize that the possibilities for young people with FAS/E go far beyond the young man in prison. The possibilities go far beyond the most famous FAS poster child of all, Michael Dorris's son Abel, dead at age 23 because he could not remember to wait until the light turned green to cross the street.

Cindy Gere's experiences, for example, demonstrate the variable nature of individual outcomes for people with FAS/E and what a young person can accomplish. She, too, has had many dark periods in her life. But Cindy completed a two-year college program at the Institute of American Indian Art. Then, with special assistance and approved alternatives to meet course requirements she could not fulfill, she got a four-year degree in art from the University of Alaska Fairbanks. After she graduated from college, she managed to complete a teacher certification program. I watched her doing her student teaching:

> Cindy turned off the classroom lights, a technique that quieted seventh graders hungry and agitated just before their lunch period. Shining a flashlight on a can of soda pop, she showed her art students where the shadow would fall.
> She switched on the lights and gave the students an assignment—to draw the soda pop can and its shadow. Some students complained that they didn't know what they were supposed to do, but Cindy held her ground.

"I have more compassion for students who have learning disabilities," she told me later. "I realize that it isn't their fault. I feel that when I am in the classroom I want to make absolutely sure that those students succeed and that has to do with my own experience and what I have gone through."

In their joint chapter, Cindy Gere shares strategies she developed to succeed in college, and her mother, Anne Ruggles Gere, discusses how to establish a support network at a distant university and how to find creative alternatives to meet college requirements. For example, Cindy substituted a computer art class for a math requirement.

Cindy's accomplishments are exceptional. She represents and sees herself as representing what it is possible for people with FAS/E to accomplish. But we cannot avoid the stark fact: She has diagnosed neurological disabilities as a result of prenatal alcohol exposure. I worried about Cindy's ability to take full responsibility for students in a classroom. But she managed to find a teaching position where she did not have to take full responsibility. She worked as one member of a teaching team, the art teacher in a Native American charter school. The charter school failed, but Cindy succeeded until the end, working without pay.

We wrote *Fantastic Antone Grows Up* to tell you about young adults like Cindy and Ryland, to offer images of success and to describe what success looks like for adolescents and young adults with FAS/E. Our previous book, *Fantastic Antone Succeeds*, focused on young children. We wrote it to challenge the stereotype that children with FAS/E are doomed, that they are without conscience or caring. We can be thankful that this stereotype has receded. The real Antone, as we showed in our earlier book, tucks a blanket around his mother because he worries that she may be cold. The real Antone worries about injustice in the world. We have acquired a wealth of information, from parents and practitioners, about how to work with young children with FAS/E.

But the territory of adolescents and adults with FAS/E is still uncharted. The pioneers are the parents and practitioners. Theirs is the "wisdom of practice," the lessons of experience. They try with everything they've got to help their children—every flash of imagination, every particle of analysis, every fiber of the will, every prayer of the spirit. The people writing these chapters are not only experienced. They have thought about their experience, conceptualized it, developed new strategies as a result of it, and tested these strategies in the laboratory of daily life. These are not just people with stories. These are practitioners with expertise. Scientists have much to learn from them.

In making the point that some people with FAS/E are able to deal well with their disabilities, we are not implying that others who are alcohol-affected would do fine if only they had tried harder or if only their parents had raised them right. We are not implying that for some, their FAS/E has gone away; FAS/E does not go away.

Some people with FAS/E do better than others for many different reasons. One is the amount of neurological damage. Prenatal alcohol exposure has a wide range of effects, and some children with FAS/E have experienced far less damage than other children. Ironically, children who in one sense are less damaged, whose faces do not reveal the signs of FAS and whose IQs lie in the normal range, from 90 to 110, can fare worse than others. The people around them so often do not recognize their disability and give them the understanding they need.

Some people with FAS/E do better than others because of qualities that have little to do with prenatal alcohol exposure— their temperament, physical beauty, and personality. We know from research on resilience[2] that children who have warm and engaging personalities are more apt to draw others to them and to get the help they need. The young people with FAS/E who are doing especially well as adolescents and adults, I have noticed, also are particularly attractive and sociable young people. Nonetheless, the road to success may be bumpy. One mother said that her 17-year-old daughter with FAS sometimes seemed like "an accident waiting to happen":

---

[2] The classic research on resilience describes how some Hawaiian children, raised in poverty and in homes where alcoholism and abuse were a way of life, nonetheless became competent adults. See Emmy E. Werner and Ruth S. Smith 1992. For a popular account of resiliency, see Steven J. Wolin and Sybil Wolin 1993.

> She is very pretty, physically affectionate, flirtatious, and too friendly with strangers. Last week she broke her curfew, but informed us it was 'All right, because I'm so much in love.'

The most loving and intelligent and dedicated parents cannot overcome the damage of prenatal alcohol exposure, but they can do a lot. Nothing matters more in the development of alcohol-affected children than committed and caring parents. "Living in a stable and nurturant home" indeed turned out to be the most powerful protective factor in the lives of adolescents and adults with FAS/E in Ann Streissguth's research.[3]

Parents of children with FAS/E can take comfort in knowing that, but for their care, everything would have been so much worse. Nola Barry, who adopted a boy with FAS so difficult to handle that he went through ten homes before he was five years old, puts it this way:

> Reflecting back, I now realize that, although I made normal parental mistakes, I did not cause the disabilities my son has. I have learned to understand that my good parenting is what kept him out of trouble as long as it did.
>
> • I no longer feel responsible for my son's behaviors and know that I cannot fix them.
>
> • I have learned that other people's judgments can not hurt me when I am strong, focused, and comfortable with my own values.
>
> • I have learned to ask for help and to know that some struggles are too big to handle alone, and there is no shame in that.

WHY WE PIONEERED "WISDOM OF PRACTICE" WORK IN ALASKA

Alaska has exceptionally high rates of FAS/E, and state and federal agencies have devoted substantial attention and funds to prevention and intervention. The Alaskan Fetal Alcohol Syndrome Prevention Project carefully monitored the prevalence of FAS in the state during the 1990s. Over 20,000 Alaskan women of

---

[3] Streissguth et al. 1996.

childbearing age acknowledged that they were heavy drinkers, and seven percent of new mothers said that they drank alcohol during the third trimester of pregnancy.[4]

Alaska parents of children with FAS/E have organized active support groups to educate themselves and have placed enormous pressure on school systems and state agencies to assist alcohol-affected children. In 1990, one parent who had adopted a baby boy with FAS came to me, in my role as a psychologist at the University of Alaska, and asked what he could do for his baby, how he could prevent the terrible future that he saw staring at him from the television screen. At the time, virtually no scientific research had been done on how to educate children with FAS/E. Prevention was the target.

We wanted to learn a lot and we wanted to learn it fast. His baby boy was growing up. We decided to hold a conference in 1991 at the University of Alaska Fairbanks and invite parents, practitioners and researchers from all over the world to discuss what they had learned about helping alcohol-affected children. To our amazement, we learned that parents and teachers from many different places, who had never talked to each other, had spontaneously invented similar educational strategies—such as hanging photographs on the wall of children with FAS/E doing a chore. That way a child who forgot what to do next could check the photographs. So many people wanted to attend the conference that we had to turn them away at the door—from a hall that seated over 250 people. Collaboration among researchers, parents, and practitioners proved exceptionally fruitful. Often parents knew something worked but didn't know why. The researchers often could explain the reason. In *Fantastic Antone Succeeds*, we offered to others what we had learned, the "wisdom of practice."

Alaska offers many examples of young people with FAS/E who are doing well. Antone, of *Fantastic Antone Succeeds*, comes from Fairbanks, Alaska, as does Ryland Canney, the young man we

---

[4] DHSS Report # 1, 1997, page 5. The report correctly notes that the especially high rate of FAS in Alaska may be partly due to extensive case finding by the Indian Health Service. Other populations are not screened with comparable intensity.

describe in this chapter. Cindy Gere graduated from the University of Alaska Fairbanks and did her student teaching in a Fairbanks school where her cooperating teachers were aware of her disability and took care to give her close supervision. We sought examples of success not only in Alaska but across the United States and in Canada, where parent advocacy groups are particularly vigorous. We wanted to see what success looked like for adolescents and young adults with FAS/E in different places and what parents and professionals had learned about how to deal with the difficult problems of this stage of life.

A CAUTION: CASES OF CONVENTIONAL SUCCESS ARE FEW

We had hoped to find many examples of young people with FAS/E who looked like Ryland Canney and Cindy Gere—young people who were holding ordinary jobs or going to college. The plain truth, we are sad to report, is that we have not found many such young people. We have found a few.

Fetal alcohol syndrome is a roller coaster ride, we have realized from working with the authors of these chapters for close to five years. There are highs and lows, ups and downs. In these chapters, we caught some of these families and their children at a peak. Since these chapters were written, some have hurtled downward; others have gone full cycle, hurtling down and climbing up again. Where significant change has occurred since the chapter was written, we note what happened in an epilogue.

A DILEMMA: SHOULD SOCIETY CHANGE ITS STANDARDS?

One reviewer of this book in manuscript, reading the parents' accounts, raises a question that must be dealt with:

> I have one problem with the book's contents. The book too often says, in effect: To h— with society and other people, all that matters is what's best for my kid. If that means lowering academic or behavioral standards, fine.
>
> Candidly, if a group residence for alcohol-affected adolescents were planned for my neighborhood, I would be concerned. And if a child of mine were attending classes with an FAS child, I'd

want my kid to have counseling to prepare her to deal with possible problems and to understand what's going on. Acting out?
Inappropriate sexual touching? These are serious matters.

These are indeed serious matters. Many of the parents know
full well how serious they are because they are the ones who most
often deal with them, in the courts and in the schools and in their
own families, over and over again.

The social naivete of young people with fetal alcohol syndrome,
combined with the explosive feelings surrounding sexual touch-
ings, makes this area particularly difficult. Many parents worry that
their children's sexual exploration will result in charges of sexual
assault and even rape. This was the nightmare of Ann Michael who
describes her feelings when her adopted son was arrested and
convicted of sexual molestation.[5] One of the children he molested
was her own young son:

> He calls and says, "I'm sorry."
> I said, "I need to tell you something. YOU made the choices.
> YOU stopped taking your meds (to lower his testosterone level)."
> When he is in jail, he can't get out. He can't hurt anybody else.
> I feel relief. There is always the tension, the fear. When he is in
> jail, it's like a holiday.
> But there is no way I can abandon the child. We will talk to our
> priest tomorrow. We will reconnect.

Ann Michael had established a support system where her son
was given medication to control his sexual drives and was
carefully and continually supervised. The strategy worked until
her son's very success led agencies to believe that a network of
support was no longer necessary, so it was removed. Without that
support, he regressed and the consequences were devastating.

So this is how I answer this reviewer, who thinks that parents
of children with FAS do not care about the larger society: With a
diagnosis and appropriate intervention, it is possible to protect young
people and their communities. But once a support network is in
place, don't remove it. Let the children with FAS have their advocates. Let the parents be their advocates. Who else will be? The

---

[5] See chapter 19, "Relinquishing Our Christmas Child So We Could Reclaim Him," by
Ann Michael.

parents realize the risks and they are far from oblivious to your justifiable concerns.

The Questions We Are Asking About FAS/E in Adolescents and Adults

Early in life, so many children with FAS/E seem to respond well to a structured environment and specific educational strategies. Why do problems become so pronounced at adolescence? Why do our earlier strategies no longer seem to work so well at adolescence?

These questions, like the others we address in this book, grew out of collaboration between FAS/E researchers and parent advocates. We began by asking parent groups to identify the questions that troubled them as children with FAS/E entered adolescence and adulthood, the questions they most wanted answered. We then searched the United States and Canada for researchers, parents, and practitioners who had experience with these issues and could offer an informed response. Each chapter was reviewed by a researcher noted for her work on the education of children with FAS/E, Dr. Barbara Morse, to make sure that the information was consistent with what we know from the scientific literature. Parents of children with FAS/E also reviewed the chapters to make sure the chapters spoke to their concerns in sensitive ways. Scientific research moves onward, and parents differ from each other. We have done our best, and we apologize for unwitting errors or offense.

We have organized this book around three issues that parents emphasized:

1. Can we find examples of adolescents and adults with FAS/E who are doing well? What is the best we can hope for at this point? What does success for a young person with FAS/E mean?

2. What specific, concrete techniques help in dealing with high school, emerging sexuality, employment, entanglements with the law, and independent living?

3. What do families of children with FAS/E need from their communities and from researchers?

The three sections of *Fantastic Antone Grows Up* address each of these three issues. We have taken care to include in this book not only the knowledge of parents and practitioners but also the knowledge of alcohol-affected people themselves. Many have come up with personal inventions: one young woman describes how she visualizes each step beforehand when trying to navigate through the "broken spider web" in her brain. We celebrate their home-grown inventions, as well as those of people who are trying to help them.

In these chapters, parents and practitioners describe the problems they are facing and the concrete solutions they have found. Vivid detail is the virtue of cases. Parents take us to their homes and show us the breathing techniques they use to help adolescents with FAS/E calm down. Therapists take us to their offices and show us how they use baby books to convince adolescents that they really do have a loving family. Educational consultants take us to their schools and show us how to use color coding to organize class materials in a student's locker.

In sidebars which accompany some of these chapters, we present variations on the author's idea. The sidebars show how the same basic strategy worked in another situation. The sidebar on page 14, for example, offers an ingenious solution to a common problem—teaching young people with FAS/E how to tell time. Reading a circular clock is just plain difficult—as anyone knows who has tried to explain to a child why the hands of a clock go around two times during one day. We live time in a line, not in a circle. So why not use a linear clock, that looks like a ruler, to represent time during a day? Richard Laplante's linear clock is typical of the inventions people come up with for coping with the problems of FAS/E. We know that young children with FAS/E need visuals; so do adolescents and adults with FAS/E. The linear clock is visual, simple, practical, and plain delightful.

Let me add a word on terminology. In the scientific literature, consensus does not exist on diagnostic labels, especially the use of the older term "fetal alcohol effects (FAE)" to refer to people without all of the diagnostic criteria for "fetal alcohol syndrome (FAS)": a maternal history of alcohol abuse, characteristic facial features, growth deficiency, and central nervous system impairment. New diagnostic systems have been suggested but no single system has as yet become established. To avoid confusion, we use the hybrid term "FAS/E"—commonly used by parent groups—to describe the general condition of alcohol-related birth defects. Where a particular person has received a medical diagnosis of fetal alcohol syndrome (FAS) or fetal alcohol effects (FAE) and prefers to use this term in a chapter, we follow this wish.

THE STORY OF THE LINEAR CLOCK

Richard Laplante worked in a residential facility. A young man with FAS would wake up in the middle of the night and not realize that he needed to go back to sleep or he would be bad-tempered the next day.

To show him that it was nighttime when he could not read a clock, Laplante invented a linear clock. The night hours are labeled "Sleep Time" and colored dark blue with a cartoon of the moon. A marker shows the young man where he is in time and what he should be doing. When he wakes up and sees his marker in deep blue, Sleep Time, he knows he should close his eyes and go back to sleep.

The linear clock is sectioned into four parts and color coordinated:

- Light blue is used for morning and progressively darker shades of blue for afternoon, evening and sleep time.

- Green marker is used to indicate when it is time to leave.

(continues next page)

MORNING   AFTERNOON

6^{00}.. 6^{30}.. 7^{00}.. 7^{30}.. 8^{00}.. 8^{30}.. 9^{00}.. 9^{30}.. 10^{00}.. 10^{30}.. 11^{00}.. 11^{30}.. 12^{00}.. 12^{30}.. 1^{00}.. 1^{30}.. 2^{00}.. 2^{30}.. 3^{00}

CONCLUSION

Young people with FAS/E will almost always need assistance and support for the rest of their lives. They will need help from the outside. The noted University of Washington researcher Sterling Clarren has coined a term for this need: an "external brain." Adolescents and adults with FAS/E still need the structure and support they needed as young children. They still need concrete, visual guides. But this assistance must be offered to adolescents and adults about new matters—how to use a checking account or how to locate the boundaries in romantic relationships—and in new ways.

• Amber marker is used to indicate transitional activities (get ready mode).

• Red marker is used to indicate time to stop.

• Personalized pics (mini pictures) are used to identify specific activities.

The linear clock has a magnetic backing so it will stick on the refrigerator or other convenient places, e.g., on a metallic dry erase board.

For more information contact Richard Laplante at 8298 Cook Road, Vernon, B.C., Canada V1B 3M7. Telephone/fax: 604-549-3877. E-mail: laplante@mindlink.bc.ca.

EVENING   SLEEP TIME

30 .. 5⁰⁰ .. 5³⁰ .. 6⁰⁰ .. 6³⁰ .. 7⁰⁰ .. 7³⁰ .. 8⁰⁰ .. 8³⁰ .. 9⁰⁰ .. 9³⁰ .. 10⁰⁰ .. 10³⁰ .. 11⁰⁰ .. 11³⁰ .. 12⁰⁰ .. 12³⁰ .. 1⁰⁰ .. 2⁰⁰ ..

But who among us does not also need assistance and support from those around us? Good parenting matters, effective programs matter, and the resources of the spirit matter most of all. These chapters show what good parenting, effective programs, and the resources of the spirit look like.

Part One

What is Success for Adolescents and Adults with FAS/E?

1

Works in Progress: The Meaning of Success for Individuals with FAS/E

JAN LUTKE

Jan Lutke is the mother of 20 adopted children, 11 with FAS/E, of whom 8 are teenagers or adults. She is also the director of the FAS/E Support Network of British Columbia, a provincially funded agency providing information, education, consultation, and advocacy support services to individuals with FAS/E and their families as well as to the professionals and agencies who work with them.

WHEN I LOOK AT MY CHILDREN, I AM REMINDED OF THE VARIABILITY of outcomes for children with FAS. Instead of believing that the possibilities for my children are limited, I think of FAS in terms of what they can do now. I look for seeds of ability and help them build on their interests and strengths. The result is that my children have accomplished many things that were not thought possible.

Good self-esteem has allowed them to continue trying long after others would have given up, buffering them against frustration and allowing them to accept, with grace and equanimity, things they cannot do. Conscience, empathy, and compassion exist in all my children, when circumstances allow them to understand the situation. When they do not understand, the problem is not personal lack of integrity. Over and over again, my children have shown themselves to be young people of character who have much to teach us if we are willing to see with different eyes, hear with different ears, and feel with different hearts.

We measure the accomplishments of the alcohol-affected adolescents we have adopted in many ways:

• Karen takes immense pride in her job as a dog groomer and her contributions as a public speaker on FAS.

• Ken is a hard worker who has a new job installing automatic garage door openers.

• Mandy is overcoming her shyness and learning to play the keyboard with the help of a friend.

• David's lack of judgment has led him into a dangerous lifestyle, but he has entered a new school program where he thinks he can finally learn.

• Patsy, despite numerous alcohol-related birth defects and an IQ of 47, is learning basic sign language to help a friend who is deaf and autistic.

• Katie spends hours drawing pictures and writing stories and was elected to represent her class on the student council.

Each of my children is different, but they all need an invisible guidance system to help them navigate their passage into adulthood. When the innocence, activity, immaturity, and poor judgment of FAS merge with the hormones, autonomy issues, and just plain pain-in-the-ass behavior of adolescence, difficult situations arise. These test our commitment, flexibility, and willingness to grow with the child. Allowing an alcohol-affected teen to do the work of adolescence in an unsupported manner assumes they have the intellectual and social maturity to become independent. This is a crucial mistake. What's critical is recognizing the need for the creative use of unobtrusive support systems that foster success, defined in terms of each child's abilities and not some generic ideal.

DEFINING SUCCESS

Success has no single definition. I define success for each of my children quite differently. I frequently must redefine success for a child based on his or her needs and functional abilities at that particular point. Success does not necessarily mean attending college or finding a full-time job. Success may mean finishing things some of the time. It means hitting a punching bag instead of a person. It means remembering you forgot your homework at 4:30 and getting your mom to drive you back to school. Success means being able to stop, with help, a behavior when asked rather than never starting it in the first place. It means paying attention, remembering, and accomplishing tasks for four hours in the workplace instead of eight hours. It means asking question after question about things everyone else already knows, and more important, understands. It means knowing who you are, accepting yourself, and understanding that everyone has handicaps. For someone with FAS, success means knowing that these are goals worth striving for, not someone else's unreachable line in the sand.

For a parent, success means knowing, valuing, and working within the limitations of your child, and it means knowing your own limitations as a parent. I remind myself of this daily. I work to avoid taking my children's misbehavior personally or taking ownership of problems that are not mine. I have learned to accept that my children's behavior does not reflect on my abilities as a human being. As long as I understand what is really happening, I can maintain my sense of worthiness as a mother. One of the hardest things I had to learn as my children grew up was that I could not, and should not, be all things to all people, all of the time. There will always be times when I must accept that I, like my growing child, am doing the best I can at that moment. I am not superhuman, and that is okay.

In fact, this may be one of the most valuable lessons I can teach my children: that I have limits. I, too, can make mistakes, even fail, and *even so*, I survive, and I still have value to those who love me. I have always taught my children that the outcome is not nearly as important as how well one tries, that I don't care about a grade, for instance, as long as I know they have done their best. I finally learned to apply that to myself as well. I cannot always control the outcome, no matter how much I might like to. I can control how well I try. That is also success.

When I make the mistake of measuring the successes or failures of my children against those of their chronological peers, when my own sense of frustration or despair causes me to lose sight of the magnitude of their actual accomplishments, I remind myself that for every frustration there has been effort, for every negative a positive, and for every failure, an equal success. My job is to keep this knowledge always before us, for we are now together, the keepers of the faith, and that is a most remarkable thing.

SUCCESS STORIES AND WORKS IN PROGRESS

Learning how, when, and where to relinquish control while continuing to offer guidance has been difficult, especially given the wide range of abilities among my children. My job is no longer to walk in front of them blazing the trail, but to show them how to do it for themselves. Over the years, my children have grown in many different directions—not always the ones I would have chosen but ones I can live with.

Karen

In the late 1970s, Karen was diagnosed at age three with fetal alcohol syndrome. She had been removed from her mother's care shortly after birth and placed, along with an older birth sister, with a succession of relatives unable to provide adequate care. Multiple foster homes followed, with each shift attributed to her unmanageable and disruptive behaviors. In retrospect, she displayed the classic signs of the young child with FAS—hyperactivity, appearing to be bad and out of control. At age four, she entered a resource facility. We adopted her a year later.

Today, at 21, Karen is typical of many young adults with FAS. With an IQ of 90, she speaks and reads much better than she understands. Her social and emotional functioning resembles that of a young teenager and varies widely depending on the circumstances. She spends hours talking on the phone. The spats and disputes of her younger friends and siblings easily embroil her. Her favorite television shows remain Walt Disney movies. With minor provocation, she can sulk like a ten year old.

But Karen is also a self-assured young woman with a part-time job, a boy friend, and a social life that includes her family, a former social worker, her birth sister, and a few loyal friends. Her daily living skills are relatively strong and continue to improve. She cares entirely for herself, her hygiene is now immaculate, and she can prepare basic meals, do laundry, and accomplish other household chores. Time and money management remain a problem, but alarms, strict schedules and joint signatures on bank accounts help. She swims, plays pool, goes to movies, likes to bake, uses the computer, and creates arts and crafts.

For the last two and a half years, she has made weekly visits to a three-year-old niece in foster care, the child of her older biological sister. She participates in all aspects of this little girl's life, including helping to select a preschool program. Karen sees herself not only as an aunt but as a role model for this drug- and alcohol-affected child. She wants her niece to know what people with FAS can do. For Karen, FAS is a hugely irritating inconvenience but not necessarily an insurmountable handicap.

Over the years, Karen maintained a close friendship at home and in school with a neighborhood girl, Kelly, who accepted her as she was. By the time they attended junior high school, their friendship was solid even though Kelly had pulled ahead of Karen socially and academically. All through high school, Kelly was there for Karen, explaining to, advocating for, supporting, and protecting her. Most important, Kelly truly liked Karen. She saw her spirit, her joy of living, her compassion for others, and her innocence not as qualities to be exploited but as traits to be protected and admired.

Throughout her life, and especially during adolescence, Karen has been unobtrusively supervised by responsible people, including peer mentors, older unaffected siblings, adult friends, and program staff. We found such supervision key to keeping her safe and protecting her from a vulnerability to bad judgment. Indeed, we regard supervision as a teaching tool.

For instance, Karen is susceptible to perseveration, or repeating a stereotyped behavior over and over. She calls it "hyping." She winds herself up physically and emotionally until she becomes semihysterical with laughter and unable to stop. Anyone acting in the supervisory capacity steps in immediately when these signs appear. That person gets Karen's attention and asks, "Karen, what is happening?"

Karen has reached the point where she can see when she is starting to "hype." She knows she needs to remove herself from the situation for at least ten minutes, close her eyes, and concentrate on breathing deeply. Headphones and serenity tapes help as well. This rest allows her to return to a normal state and rejoin an activity without losing control. Without the unobtrusive support that supervision provides, this behavior would become an entrenched and socially isolating problem for Karen. The goal is for Karen to learn to recognize and take charge of this behavior without someone else bringing it to her attention. Occasionally she can do this, and the day is not far off when she will be able to monitor herself.

Despite her frustrations with abstract learning and reading for content, Karen has succeeded in school largely because a vice principal let us design a program for her. Based on her strengths and emphasizing living skills, the program used community-based learning and peer tutors. We arranged a schedule that did not require her to shift classrooms every hour or to change areas in the school. She studied the same subjects at the same time each day. We dispensed with social studies, sciences, and a second language. Instead, she learned activities she could handle well with direction, such as cooking, sewing, art, and woodworking.

Our educational program emphasized her abilities. For example, Karen learns best through visuals and hands-on experience, so in sewing class, she teamed up with another student who handled the more abstract components, such as understanding patterns. Karen did the actual sewing. Together, they completed two garments and received a combined grade of A. While Karen could not handle the pressure and fast pace of a factory assembly line, her mechanical sewing skills are good enough for her to secure a job in a home-based cottage industry doing slower-paced, piecework garment sewing if she collaborates with a pattern cutter who directs her about what to sew next. Her work is slow, but it is meticulous.

In school, Karen focused on life skills, math, and English requirements. With peer tutors she practiced such skills as grocery shopping, banking, and reading labels. Most important, she emerged from school feeling competent.

Her first love, however, has always been animals, and she is very good with them. A pre-employment vocational skills program capitalized on that strength. In high school, she spent two six-month periods in job training at a combined veterinary clinic and dog grooming business. Her teachers helped employers and workers understand her learning styles, needs, and capabilities. Teamwork between home and school convinced the veterinarian that he could depend upon Karen to do her job.

This successful approach led to part-time paid employment for Karen after she completed school, and she continues to work at the clinic approximately 15 to 20 hours a week, which she can comfortably manage. When she works longer hours, migraine headaches appear. She needs enormous energy to pay attention, think, process, and remember on a level required to maintain employment.

But Karen loves her job, and she is good at it. She particularly enjoys comforting sick and injured animals. Her workmates treat her much as a younger sister and frequently go out of their way to accommodate her. They use charts and lists to help her and patiently explain things until she understands them. She has been trained so well in grooming animals that friends of the family occasionally bring their animals to our home for her personal attention and pay her for it. Her success is a tribute to her courage, tenacity, and determination.

Public speaking has been one of the most important tools to develop Karen's self-esteem. She wants people to know about FAS and to hear about it from someone with FAS. She emphasizes her strengths, but she also talks about the difficulties life presents her and the things she is unable—not unwilling—to do. She stresses what those in the helping professions can do to support her, starting with accepting her as she is instead of encouraging her to be more. Her talks vary widely and may include laughter and tears.

Karen sees herself as a role model for other people with FAS so they'll understand that even with limitations, they can do many things well with support. She emphasizes that without support, she is unable to do many things those of us without alcohol effects take for granted.

No matter how many times she delivers that message, I am struck by the number of well-intentioned but sadly ill-informed teachers, social workers, therapists, probation officers and the like who insist on believing, "Yes, she can," as if an act of will could change the way her brain works. Frequently, someone in the audience who is impressed by her speaking ability, always a professional, asks about Karen's plans for further education, as if there is something intrinsically wrong with her work with animals. One of my proudest moments as her mother occurred the last time someone asked that question. Karen straightened her shoulders, looked directly at the speaker (a mental-health therapist), and said, "For me, FAS means I can't do college work, but I am a very good dog groomer."

Ken

When Ken was removed from his birth family at age seven, he had been parenting himself and a younger half-brother for some time, had witnessed serious violence between his parents (including the shooting of his mother), had survived a deliberately set house fire, and lived a nomadic hand-to-mouth existence that did not include school. He joined our family through adoption at the age of ten and was diagnosed with FAE at 12.

Ken, now almost 21, graduated 18 months ago from the same pre-employment program Karen attended. After completing school, Ken spent about eight months without any work before obtaining employment through a family friend as a drywaller's assistant. Since then, he has had several temporary jobs, such as working for a roofing company and a garbage collection company. He recently found a job as an assistant in a company that installs automatic garage doors. If things work out, his employer will train Ken as an installer.

Ken works very hard, and as long as he understands clearly what is required, he performs his job as best he can. His employment problems, as in other areas of his life, remain his inability to see the bigger picture and to make necessary connections.

The key to Ken's adolescent successes were creative supervision through our invisible guidance system, sports, and the role modeling of older brothers and friends. Like Karen, he had at least one good friend at any time who provided direction and protection. We did not always like everything about these friends, particularly the lack of home supervision and some of their attitudes towards school. However, they were not bad kids, and we recognized the importance of these friendships to Ken. They meant he had someone to talk to and hang out with. He listened to their advice, and since they were not into illegal activity or drugs and alcohol, that had to be good enough. If he was with one of these kids, he wasn't with the ones I *really* didn't want him near.

While never quite fast enough for team sports, Ken could always play in pick-up games, and he spent many hours mastering the school's climbing walls. He thrived on casual camaraderie. Well aware of Ken's diagnosis of FAS, his teachers attributed his slow processing of thoughts and words to shyness, and we capitalized on their interpretation and response: his teachers spent extra time with him "to draw him out," as they put it.

His quiet good looks and gentle nature attracted girls, but his problems reciprocating such relationships meant they didn't last long, a problem that continues. After ten years in our family, Ken has formed a fairly sound degree of attachment to his father and me (depending on who defines it), but his ability to understand the give-and-take of human interaction limits his capacity to form bonds. I realize this may be the pattern of his adult life. However, he is happy with his life the way it is, and he does not miss the connections. I understand the loss. He doesn't. I need to remember that.

At 19, Ken decided to move into a room-and-board situation with an older brother. Freedom beckoned! While I wanted him to remain at home for another couple of years, it had become obvious that he was going to leave, one way or the other. A compromise seemed in order. Living with his brother's family provided some of the support he needed in a way he could accept. He still has trouble managing money and understanding what things are worth. With some unobtrusive guidance, we have prevented people from taking advantage of him.

About a year ago, for example, Ken wanted to buy an old car for sale in the neighborhood. Among many other problems, it had no left turn signal and no reverse gear. He reasoned that he would only turn right, so the turn signal wouldn't matter, and he would only park where he didn't have to back up, so reverse didn't matter. No amount of discussion could unseat his thinking, and we quickly realized we were simply making the situation worse.

We changed tactics, doing what we should have done in the beginning. Recognizing that as parents we had no credibility where a first car is concerned, we called on one of our oldest sons who works as a department manager in a car dealership. Ken considers this brother to be an expert and would hear him when he wouldn't hear us. When Paul dropped by, Ken took him to see the car. After an expert opinion regarding the significant number of costly problems, Ken quickly agreed with his brother that this was the wrong car for him. They worked out a deal where Paul would act as Ken's consultant for other potential purchases.

Ken recently returned home (again) after moving to Saskatchewan with a friend from school. His dream was to live in a particular small town where his friend had extended family. He had listened to his friend talk at length about how great things were, how cheap stuff was to buy, and how easy it was to get a job. They planned to move there, find jobs, and get rich. So, with a bus ticket and about a hundred dollars, he left his brother's house and made the trek.

This time we said nothing, only insisting he call us every other day. We let him know we would pay his way back if he decided this wasn't for him. After six weeks, Ken came home disillusioned but at least a little wiser. We were glad he chose to live at home once more, and he seems to accept that it just isn't yet time to fly.

Structure, routine, order, simplicity, and consistency have worked well to teach Ken the fundamental things in life. He can take care of his daily hygiene and nutrition. He prefers to have someone else cook so he doesn't have to think about what to make, but he knows what a balanced diet is and can follow and prepare simple meals from a menu plan if necessary. He puts all of his clothes in the laundry every day or every time he changes so he doesn't have to sort out dirty from clean clothes. He does his laundry as soon as he has no clothing left except what he's wearing. He manages banking with a savings account that allows in-person withdrawals only. That significantly limits the availability of impulse buying and undue influence by other people, especially since our credit union does not have extended hours. He uses public transportation without difficulty, and he has obtained his driver's license.

The big problem for Ken is not what he does or doesn't do, but his judgment. He lost a job at a car dealership because, when asked to back up a vehicle, he did just that—backed it up straight into the car behind it! Ken's lack of critical thinking will continue to make him vulnerable. He will always need some degree of external support. Over the next few years, we'll continue finding creative ways to help him solve problems. In adolescence, we surrounded him with a safety net. In adulthood, he needs the same net but at a more acceptable distance.

Mandy

When Mandy joined our family as a foster child at age ten, she arrived with a history of such severe abuse, neglect, and difficult behaviors that we questioned whether a family was the right place for her. Her IQ is 60, but we don't know how much of this is due to FAS (diagnosed at age 14) and how much to the extreme emotional deprivation she suffered. A dedicated social worker who had placed three other children with us over the years convinced us this child would have a chance with us. She made no false promises, guaranteeing only headaches and hard work, which have occurred in abundance. Taking her in was one of the better decisions we have made.

Today, at 20, Mandy is a full, contributing member of our family. She bonded well to all of us. The transition from a severely disturbed, extremely dysfunctional child with FAS to a young adult with FAS who used to be disturbed and dysfunctional has been remarkable. Screaming, swearing, violent temper tantrums over the slightest things once occurred daily, even hourly. Physical assaults on other people were common. Refusing to eat or gorging to the point of vomiting made her physical health precarious. She destroyed everything she was given, stole whatever she could, was sexually provocative, refused to cooperate, couldn't remember a thing, and shut down* when she didn't throw tantrums.

Labels suggested for her behaviors included oppositionally-defiant, passive-aggressive, conduct disorder, and post-traumatic stress disorder. They were accurate to a point. However, they didn't explain her short stature, small head, facial dysmorphia—the fact that she resembled my other children with FAS. No history was available when we first took her into our family, so no diagnosis could be made. Nonetheless, we decided to treat Mandy as if she had FAS, which allowed us to view her actions not only in the light of a child who has been severely abused, but as those of a child with a neurological impairment. After termination of parental rights, we obtained the history of her birth mother's pregnancy, and Mandy was diagnosed with FAS.

The combined efforts of home, school, and social and mental health services allowed Mandy time to heal as much as possible from the effects of her past. Although she will never function as well as our older children, what she can do is perhaps an even greater accomplishment. There are no more temper tantrums, only slammed doors; no more physical assaults on people, only rude, sarcastic remarks when she is stressed. Diet will always be a problem, as she rarely feels hunger or fullness, but eating can be managed with care, coaxing, and encouragement. She takes pride in her possessions, and although she is very careless, she is not deliberately destructive. She no longer steals and only borrows with permission,

---

* "Shut down" is an expression used to describe a person's reaction to overstimulation.

but she must still be reminded to return things and that borrowing means for the occasion, not for an unlimited time.

Mandy will not try anything if she thinks she will fail, a lasting legacy from her past in which she was told constantly she was stupid. She is still extremely sensitive to the way people ask her to do something, and the wrong approach provokes total refusal. The trick is making people understand how to give her comprehensible instructions and how to approach her so that she feels competent or at least able to chance trying. Mandy still shuts down when stressed or overstimulated. To minimize this, we strictly regulate her activities outside the family and make sure she takes lots of catnaps, which seem to help.

In the past four years, Mandy has probably made the most progress of all our children. Academically, she functions at about the third-grade level. Socially, emotionally, and behaviorally, her progress has been astounding. At school, she moved from a highly structured, tightly supervised program for seriously behaviorally disordered teens into one for adolescents without behavioral disorders but with borderline to mild mental handicaps. The program emphasizes life and job skills while providing academic studies.

Her success, indeed, created new problems for us. This program expects to place students in unsupervised community jobs, and Mandy is simply not ready for this experience. Last spring, a work placement in the school cafeteria provided a good example of the risk to Mandy. After six weeks of suddenly aggressive and angry behavior, Mandy revealed that her teacher in the cafeteria program was touching the girls inappropriately and grabbing them by the neck. An investigation ensued and subsequently cleared the teacher of any criminal wrongdoing. However, he was found to be yelling, insulting, and threatening toward his students. The investigating officer believed this man had no business teaching students with special needs. If this can happen in a school, how much more likely is it to occur on an unsupervised, unaccredited job site with employers who have undergone absolutely no training or criminal record check? We have been firm with her school program: Mandy cannot be placed in an unsupervised setting.

Mandy is learning slowly how healthy relationships work. Outside school, she continues a friendship with a 13-year-old girl from a supportive family in our neighborhood. They are teaching Mandy to play the keyboard, using a system of color and letter symbols to translate sheet music onto the appropriate piano keys. This relationship has encouraged Mandy to take chances with other young people her own age. Watching the process is excruciating. For every ten phone calls she makes, she receives one. I consider it a godsend that she doesn't understand rejection that is not brutal. Invitations to go skating or swimming come infrequently, as she often does or says something to put others off, especially in a mixed crowd. But this is progress; two years ago no one at school would even talk to her.

Her siblings have been enormously patient with her and present essential role models for negotiating boy-girl relationships, especially since Mandy's early life was based on sex as the medium for human interaction. She asks them questions and takes their advice; they take her in hand, wiping off the excess make-up and redoing her hair. Even they, however, have limits, and if she strays too far into their space or becomes provocative in an effort to attract a friend, they quickly put her in her place or exclude her until she gets it together.

Mandy has begun developing her own strategies for dealing with her problems of perserveration, memory, organization, and abstract thinking. She writes lists of things to do, follows a schedule every day, and uses a calendar. She has festooned her bedroom with her own line drawings—placing symbols on dresser drawers and cupboards showing where things are. She uses a system of colored and clear containers to store her belongings.

Mandy is doing so well that I believe she may experience a measure of supported independence in her future, something completely unthinkable even a year ago.

David

We adopted David (with his brother Ken) just before his eighth birthday. At age ten he was diagnosed with FAE. During the first six weeks and final three months of pregnancy, his mother drank about a case of beer each day. Forced incarceration during the second trimester of her pregnancy likely reduced harmful physical effects to David. He was also physically abused by his mother's partner and later in a foster home.

David has been a challenge from the moment he walked into our family. He lied a lot, was a worse thief, and had no understanding of consequences, even though he is over average intelligence. He did everything at full force and top volume, all of the time. He also had the most wonderful grin, liked everybody, and would do anything for anyone, traits which continue to this day.

At the end of second grade, David already lagged academically more than a full year. To us, it seemed obvious he was alcohol-affected, and we did not wait to institute the structure and supervision he so desperately needed. He made significant progress with absolute consistency, unvarying routine, and the use of every trick I knew to help him see the abstract, such as a symbol code placed on items to denote ownership, a concept he had great trouble with. Medication might have helped, but David's one enduring memory of his birth family was their drug and alcohol use, and he refused to take drugs at that time, rejecting even Ritalin as a medicine because he knew it could be abused.

When he shifted from elementary to secondary school, David entered the same program for severely learning-disabled and behaviorally disordered students where Mandy had succeeded. As long as he was supervised and received immediate intervention, his problems with impulsiveness, language processing, cause-and-effect relationships, and generalizations were managed well. Students in this program were integrated in regular classrooms on various occasions.

Trouble emerged during his third year when we relaxed his noon-hour supervision, which we ourselves had been providing as there was no other relief for the child care worker. Soon, one situation after another occurred, leading to suspensions. Other students took advantage of his gullibility and used him to steal for them; he was encouraged to harass and make inappropriate sexual comments to a girl from a regular classroom; he was caught with a "found" knife which another student accused him of using as a threat (David said he was showing it to him); he smoked; he lit matches in school; he was chronically late from lunch, sometimes by as much as an hour; he cheated. We began to feel on intimate terms with the principal and the school's police liaison officer. Though we always succeeded in returning David to the program, we no longer had his cooperation to re-institute lunch hour supervision. In effect, we knocked out a bearing wall in the structure we had built around him over the years.

When he was required to leave to make room for a child with greater needs, he entered into an alternate program where the staff treated his neurological disabilities and diagnosis of FAS as secondary to his problems with "compliance." The new program staff downplayed our concerns and made us feel inadequate as parents, something we had not experienced in many years.

An opportunity arose almost immediately to demonstrate to his new teachers exactly where some of David's problems existed. During the initial meeting, the program staff read the rules to David and required him to repeat them to make sure he understood. Two days later, David was suspended for breaking one of these rules. His teacher was angry at what he considered to be deliberate behavior. After David finished his suspension, I asked the teacher if I could try something. I sat David down and read the rules to him, only this time, in front of each rule, I added David's name to make it clear and specific. When I came to the rule that he had broken, David simply stared at me, then looked at his teacher, and said, "I didn't know you meant me."

I used that point to make the case to his teachers that David simply does not understand the things other people do. However, accommodating his learning style was not in their mandate, and he was not allowed to continue in the program. After plans for other programs fell through, David left school entirely.

The past 18 months have tested the very limits of our commitment to him. His inability to make sense of the world frustrates him, and the right and wrong of things is a mystery. He is now $17\frac{1}{2}$ years old and, until very recently, heavily involved in a lifestyle dangerous to himself and others, resulting in probation for car theft, shoplifting, breaking and entering, probation breaches, and, most recently, assault. He returned home after spending six months on the street and four months in a juvenile jail.

Even with his antisocial behavior, however, David understands that some things are just plain wrong. He left a living situation where drug dealing took place because, even though he was using drugs himself, he felt strongly that dealing was wrong and he wanted no part of "doing bad things to little kids." If he can make that connection, we hope he will eventually understand the effects of his other behaviors on himself and those around him.

I will always regret allowing David more freedom than I knew intuitively he could handle. I wish I had not taken no for an answer, or been swayed by his desires. I wish I had insisted on exceptions to policies. Hindsight is a wonderful thing, and I have come to realize that one reason I made these mistakes is because I was tired and burned out from the constant parenting that FAS demands, particularly in adolescence. If I could do one thing differently, I think I would have taken better care of myself so that I could have taken better care of my son's needs.

David now has an extremely strict probation order that we hope will give us the support to hang on to him. He's been accepted into a school district program that exists in the garage of a house in our own neighborhood, of all places. There he will have no access to the kids we want to separate him from. The class is almost identical to the one that had worked so well for him before. In fact, at his intake interview, David's first comment was that he could "learn here."

David remains a difficult young man. He is also one of the sweetest people I know. There is an unextinguishable spark in David, and we may yet fan it back into flame.

Patsy

Patsy is the second child of a middle-class married woman who had severe alcoholism. At birth, she weighed just over three pounds, arrived three weeks early, and had multiple physical problems, including a severe cardiac defect. Patsy has an IQ of 47 and 14 other alcohol-related birth defects. She was not diagnosed with FAS until she joined our family at age five.

Patsy will be 15 this year. By all professional accounts, she cannot function without supervision and support. These reports do not convey, however, that with minimal support she is completely functional and independent in our home. She needs no help and only the occasional reminder when she forgets something. She appropriately chooses her own dress for the occasion and the weather; takes care of all her personal hygiene without problem; keeps her room neat, clean and organized; gets herself up, makes her own breakfast, and organizes her coat and shoes to catch a 7:00 A.M. school bus (everyone else is just getting up as she is going out the door); uses a calendar to keep track of her orthodontic appointments; and lets me know when she needs a haircut. A willing worker, she always performs her assigned chore (currently the recycling) without complaint and when asked. She can set the table, make beds, and vacuum. In fact, I wish a whole lot of Patsy would rub off on her siblings!

Most rewarding is how well Patsy relates to people. In spite of the severity of her FAS, she is polite and well-mannered. She entertains herself and makes simple choices about what she wants to do. She is learning to stand her ground with her siblings and to say no.

Her single biggest drawback socially is her incessant talking—a sort of random audible thinking that people find highly irritating. We are working slowly to improve this. Whoever is with her says, "Patsy, you are thinking out loud. What do you need to do?" She has learned that this cue means she must put her top lip on her bottom lip, keep it there, and think quietly inside her head.

Last fall, she moved to a special high school program for significantly mentally handicapped teens. This program has a high ratio of support staff to students and provides individual support whenever necessary. Instead of handicapped students struggling to function and fit into a regular class, students from the regular classes join the special class. For the first time in her school career, Patsy feels comfortable and not on display. She explained, "When the other kids come, I'm not different."

Patsy has emerged as classroom leader who supports other students. She is learning basic sign language to help a friend who is deaf and autistic. She serves as the fingers on the computer keyboard for a young man in a wheelchair. She uses her good visual memory to help others find what they cannot, and she prompts other students.

Patsy understands FAS, its causes, and its diagnosis. About a year ago, she participated as a demonstration patient for the national Royal College of Physicians Pediatric Residency Exams for Canada. In one scenario, a pediatrician was asked to evaluate her current cardiac status, since Patsy has undergone five major cardiac surgeries. Primed for this exercise, she knew she was not to volunteer any information he did not request. After he finished his exam, an examiner asked if he noticed anything else about her. Patsy sat there and beamed at me, her lips pressed tightly together. She knew what he was supposed to notice.

When the doctor could find nothing else, the examiner asked if he noticed anything unusual about her face, which is still very dysmorphic. Still, he could not answer. Patsy grinned at me over his head, and I nodded at her to answer the question. She reached over, tapped the doctor on the shoulder, and said, "See this face? It's FAS!" As the examiners exited hastily to muffle their laughter, my daughter, who is supposed to be very low-functioning, gave a very high-functioning doctor a crash course in the causes and diagnosis of FAS.

Katie

Katie, diagnosed with FAS at birth, was the last child born to her mother, who was intoxicated at delivery and later died because of her alcoholism. Katie spent the first five months of her life in the hospital with many medical complications and physical problems, including the inability to eat. At the time, we seriously considered whether we had the stuff to take on a child who needed as much help as we were told she would. After considerable soul-searching, we decided Katie should be with her two older siblings, whom we had already adopted. We have never regretted that decision.

At 13, Katie, who is four feet, five inches tall and weighs just 54 pounds, is a red-haired, freckle-faced dynamo. She is a remarkably successful young person with FAS. What is most remarkable is that she is not remarkable at all! Apart from her size, she does not noticeably stand out from her peers.

She (and our youngest daughter, April, who is ten) have reaped the benefits of everything we learned about FAS in raising their older siblings. Programs, equipment, attitudes, and expectations have been modified or designed to meet her needs at home, in school, and in the community. When writing appeared impossible, a government program assigned her a computer. The school electrician installed electrical outlets in her classroom near her desk so she and her computer could remain in the circle of her classmates. Her current teacher is seeking funds for an optical recognition stylus notebook computer that can take her distorted squiggles and translate them into typed script as she writes.

Most important, a wonderful part-time aide, "Ms. G.," has worked with Katie for five years. Although originally assigned to address Katie's medical needs, her job description was expanded to include her educational requirements as well. Working under the resource room and classroom teachers, this aide has single-handedly ensured that Katie learns, succeeds, and joins classroom life. Ms. G. previews all of Katie's work and rewrites it to her comprehension level, simplifying and shortening things. She breaks projects into chunks before Katie can become overwhelmed. With endless patience, she teaches and reteaches and reteaches math. She keeps Katie organized and on track. She finds unobtrusive and supportive ways to remove her from the classroom when her stress level starts to climb (i.e., running an errand for the teacher, or accompanying Ms. G. to a quiet place because *Ms. G.* can't stand the noise).

In particular, she monitors Katie's social relationships with other students. She serves as a mediator, always explaining, interpreting, modeling, and helping her practice. When problems arise, Ms. G. is always there, and she informs us of things we need to know or address.

Katie has two close friends who accept her as she is, and in return Katie is fiercely loyal, protective of their feelings, and unfailingly happy to be with them. Her joy for living is infectious, and she makes people feel good. Her friends help her when she needs it, but she also provides a role model for them.

As the second-youngest child in a family with siblings well into their thirties, Katie receives a lot of adult support. She acted as a junior bridesmaid, complete with formal gown, for her 30-year-old brother's wedding. She was so excited to be asked and immediately started working on "how not to be hyper," as she put it, for such an important occasion. Her solution was to take along some track pants and running shoes, change clothes, and go running between the ceremony and the picture-taking. She made this decision after working through why she couldn't wear running clothes under her dress, a process that took about an hour from the time she started talking about it to the time she figured out the reasons.

Katie also has an adult brother of 25 who shares her passion for cats. He gave her a kitten for Christmas, her first teenage responsibility. She is proud that her brother feels she is mature enough to care properly for a pet, and she keeps a journal in which she documents the ups and downs of pet parenthood. Like her older siblings, Katie is so aware of what she can do, she seems largely unaffected by what she cannot do. Her motto could best be described as "If I can't do it today, I'll get it tomorrow, and if I don't get it then, there's always the calculator!"

These experiences have given Katie the excellent self-esteem she will need entering high school. Developing a transition plan will be crucial to her continued success. We also are working on ways to establish some safeguards and to reduce some of her anxieties about being physically smaller than her peers. Fortunately, the school district supports transferring her aide with her to the new school.

Even though Katie has an IQ of 85 and excellent spoken language, she is still completely unable to tell time, do multiplication, or distinguish left from right without the consistent use of structural crutches. She finds social studies and science beyond her comprehension. She cannot spell. She frequently perseverates, and memory often fails her. Socially and emotionally much younger than her years, she cannot always handle peer relationships.

In spite of this, Katie has many strengths. She adheres strictly to her system of values and beliefs. She is wonderfully creative and artistic, spending many hours writing stories and drawing pictures. She knows how to conduct research by using the visual model of a spider web, with the topic as the spider in the center, the main pieces of information as big flies in each quarter of the web, and little flies as interesting bits and pieces filled in. She uses this method to prepare a report from information she has gathered, or to organize what she might like to discover about a particular topic. She uses books, computers, and the Internet to find what she wants.

Her biggest problem is overstimulation—recognizing it is happening before she becomes highly argumentative, obnoxious, and completely unable to focus. Katie uses several techniques to control herself. When she is overwhelmed, she tells the adult in charge that she needs to leave. She has places at school, home, and at her friends' homes where she can sit quietly in dim light and take deep breaths. When she becomes agitated from too much noise, she wears headphones or ear plugs. To reduce fidgeting, she likes to run in open spaces with natural boundaries, such as along hallways, between the lines on a basketball court, or across our yard. When there is no such place nearby, she does jumping jacks or runs in place.

Katie is caring and compassionate about those less able or less fortunate than herself. When she plays basketball with the nonjocks at lunch time at school, she insists that everyone who wants to play be included. She serves as an unofficial advocate for a smaller handicapped child and a child whose previous head injury causes him behavior difficulties. Because of her fairness to others, she was elected as her class representative to the student council. She found the job mentally exhausting, but she finished her six-month term.

Katie believes in herself, and we are determined to see that Katie continues to flourish. She has overcome obstacles that would have daunted many a lesser person, and she continues to defy her prognosis.

SELF-ESTEEM

Karen, 21, and Katie, 13, often speak in public about FAS.What I find most fascinating about hearing them speak is the way they draw respect for their persons, not sympathy for their disabilities.

In November 1996, Karen and Katie joined a panel of five young adults with FAS at a national conference. After their powerful presentation, a young man with FAS said that for the first time, he felt it was okay to have FAS. Then a mother who had adopted a Russian child eventually diagnosed with FAS spoke with tears running down her face about how this panel offered the first positive things she had ever heard about FAS. She came to the conference feeling hopeless for her daughter, and she left with hope for the future.

Patsy, who is significantly mentally handicapped, asked to be included in this public speaking. We sat down with her and walked through what would be involved. When we asked her what she would want people to know about FAS, she said: "I would tell them that I am mentally handicapped, but that mentally handicapped doesn't mean I am stupid. It just means that my brain works differently."

Children with good self-esteem are not limited by their diagnosis of FAS. It represents only one piece of who they are, much like having blonde hair or brown eyes. Patsy knows that FAS does not mean you are stupid. It does mean your brain works differently, and that needs to be respected.

CONCLUSION

I take each day as it comes, treasuring small successes. In the end, what matters is belonging to each other and finding a place where we are safe, accepted, and loved.

Every night, my husband and I try to settle our teens in bed by 11 so we can watch the late news and discuss the day's events. One night in late spring, as we sat talking on our bed, we heard footsteps upstairs, moving up and down the hall between rooms. After a few moments, I called up to Karen, then 17, and asked her what she was doing, to which she replied, "Nothing." Now, any competent parent knows that "nothing" means "something," but I accepted her answer.

The footsteps continued, along with the sound of closet doors opening and shutting. I repeated my query and received the same exasperated answer. Then we heard the sound of running water in our bathroom. My husband and I bolted off the bed and into the bathroom to find water cascading from the ceiling as if from a shower head.

I raced up the stairs to meet my daughter emerging from the bathroom with a final armful of towels. Losing my practiced cool, I demanded to know what was going on. I was greeted with a huge sigh, rolled eyeballs, and a patient repetition of the assertion that nothing out of the ordinary was occurring. Sputtering, I followed her into her bathroom to discover every towel from the linen closet and racks piled high around the toilet. Water, overflowing from a plugged toilet, also gushed from a broken pipe. We had taught our daughter what to do if the toilet was plugged: get some towels, clean up the water, then come and get one of us—obviously, much too general an instruction!

Meanwhile, my husband called me downstairs in the urgent voice he reserves for "situations." I hurried down into a haze of drifting blue smoke. Water running between the walls had hit the fuse and sparked an electrical fire. We called 911 and herded the 11 children at home outside as the screech of fire sirens approached. Naturally, all the neighbors were interested in the latest goings-on at the Lutkes.

The firefighters punched holes in my ceilings to release all the water after they turned off the valve to the toilet. Just after they had coiled the hoses and put away the axes, I noticed smoke billowing out of my laundry room. Karen had tried to help by collecting the wet towels, stuffing them all in the washer, and turning it on. The motor caught on fire. I ran after the firemen, and in front of my neighbors, had to ask them to come back in and put out another fire before they left.

When they finished cleaning up for a second time, one of the fireman said, "Lady, if you don't mind me asking, what kind of a place is this?" Karen looked him straight in the eye, and said, "It's a family, stupid!"

2

Ryland's Gift: How My Son Taught Me to be a Good Mother

Mary Lou Canney

Mary Lou Canney has lived in Alaska for the past 21 years. She is the parent of two boys, ages 20 and 11, and three girls, twins who are 12, and a 14 year old. Ms. Canney has been in recovery from alcoholism for 15 years. Her 20-year-old son was diagnosed with fetal alcohol effects and attention deficit disorder in the fifth grade. Living with a child with FAE and his siblings helped her develop skills in observation and problem solving. She applies these skills in her position as a Family Preservation Outreach Counselor at the Resource Center for Parents and Children.

WHEN MY TEENAGE SON, RYLAND, BOUGHT HIS NEW PICKUP TRUCK, he asked me to drive it after he had set up the stereo. "I've got this song I want you to hear," he said. When I saw that the album was by the late rap musician Tupac Shakur, I was a little surprised. The song's title was "Dear Momma." The lyrics describe a mother's struggle to raise a son right and the son's gratitude for her love. "I just want to thank you," the musician sings.

What 16 year old would think of playing a song like that for his mother? My son, my firstborn child, would. Many people believe that children with FAS/E cannot bond with their parents. But Ryland taught me, a recovering alcoholic, how to bond with him. He reached out for me when he was a young boy, when I didn't know how to reach out to him. Because of his efforts, we became allies. Together we figured out ways to help him through the turmoil of school. We didn't do this alone. An understanding high school teacher, counselors, family members, and friends cared about Ryland's success, too. He discovered what he was good at, and he found a job he liked through high school. We forged connections in the community. We became a family.

Facing the Truth About Alcoholism and FAS

By the time Ryland was born, I had been drinking for 14 years. Early in my pregnancy, I tried not to drink after I heard that the first two trimesters were fragile periods for fetuses, but I would end up bingeing.* My bingeing continued through the third trimester, especially during the weekends when I would drink as much as a case of beer in an evening. At the same time I ate health foods like yogurt, goat's milk, and concoctions of brewer's yeast. I was thinking with the mind of an alcoholic.

During childbirth, I told the delivering obstetrician that I had been drinking while I was pregnant. Was he sure the baby was okay? I was afraid for my newborn son—afraid to see what he looked like, afraid I had really damaged him. I thought Ryland appeared un-healthy at birth, but he was a big baby and the doctor seemed to think he was fine. From the time Ryland opened his big blue eyes and started absorbing everything around him, I knew he was a special person.

I continued drinking during the first five years of his life, working during the weeks and bingeing especially hard on the weekends. I could not handle being a parent. I didn't know how. I was a single mother until Ryland was two, and then I lived with a partner in an alcoholic family system for the next eight years. When Ryland was six, we entered a family recovery program. The next year, I gave birth to my daughter, followed by three more children. During the next four years, we tried to make our family emotionally healthy.

Everyone improved except Ryland. His behavioral problems had appeared when he started school. In preschool, they said he was a little rambunctious. In kindergarten, they said they were

---

* Bingeing is when a person consumes five or more drinks per occasion. See chapter 21, "Diagnosis and Thereafter: What We Know Now and Where We are Going," by Barbara Morse.

starting to get a little worried. In first grade, they said he was terrible. The teacher said he never finished his work, bothered the other kids while they worked, and didn't have any manners. She told other parents not to let their kids play with him because he was so bad. Ryland would come inside the door at home and collapse in tears on the floor, exhausted and hurt.

He didn't seem to make progress in therapy like the rest of us, and he was even kicked out of a support group for the children of alcoholics. The counselor said he needed to be in a group home. This was the worst advice for me—knowing that I had caused his problems by being an alcoholic, and hearing that those problems were so severe he should live away from me. That's when I woke up and started looking for more information from agencies, counselors, and anyone who would see him and tell me something useful. I still find it sad that rather than being supported and guided towards help in the first place, my search for help was driven by crisis and fear.

Then I saw an announcement in the paper for an FAS support group. The ad said, "Does your child have problems with organization? Attention span? Fighting with kids? Trouble in school? Doesn't like to be touched? And did you drink during your pregnancy?"

Oh, I said, this is it!

After I attended the FAS support group and we got a diagnosis for Ryland, I knew that what had looked like a behavior problem for all these years was actually a medical problem. He was ten years old. I can't erase the grief of knowing that not only did I cause his problems by drinking while pregnant, but that I wasn't a complete parent during the years I spent recovering. But learning his diagnosis was crucial to our recovery, an important piece in facing what happened, beginning to grieve, and then learning as much as I could to help me deal with the diagnosis constructively.

HOW RYLAND TAUGHT ME TO BOND

Some parents are afraid that their alcohol-affected children won't bond with them. That did happen when Ryland was a baby.

We didn't bond well at all. But Ryland changed our relationship. Over the years, I had worked hard at my own recovery, at trying to become a good parent, and at making our family healthy and happy. This was slow work, and it was hard work. When Ryland was in junior high, I joined a support group called Codependency Anonymous (CODA) and attended a 12-step writing workshop on codependency, where I began learning about intimacy and relationships.

For the first time, I recognized Ryland's attempts to bond with me. He put his arm around me, looked me in the eyes, massaged my feet—touches that made me feel so uncomfortable that I would stop them. I was terrified of his desire to bond. Connecting with other people is something you should learn in childhood, but I never had. I was afraid to trust others with my love. I was beginning to learn that this trust was something I had lost at nine months old when my father had died. As a baby, I didn't know that he had died. I just knew that one day he didn't come back. In CODA, I began confronting my fears of abandonment and then moving through the process of growing close instead of stopping it. Now that I was sober, I had to face relationships rather than escaping them through alcohol.

That was the beginning. Then I became capable of loving my child. I started becoming a real advocate for Ryland. I began to believe in him as much as he believed in me. We really opened ourselves up to each other, and that changed everything.

What happened between me and my son, and what I learned from my own experience of abandonment, makes me wonder about bonding problems between parents and children with FAS. Bonding with children with FAS simply may be different from what we expect with other children. If I had not been in recovery and examining my own inadequacies, I would have blamed our lack of attachment on Ryland.

Becoming Ryland's Advocate

As we grew closer and as I listened to Ryland more, I started thinking about his viewpoint when it came to his school problems. He hated school. Teachers blamed him for most of his troubles, but

I realized things were more complicated than that. The district had a policy of completely mainstreaming students from the emotionally impaired class when they entered junior high. The school had a sink or swim philosophy.

For Ryland, then 13, entering junior high meant big changes. He had a different teacher for every class, different expectations in each class, a different schedule every day, and three different combinations to memorize—one for his hall locker, another for his gym locker, and a third for his bicycle. Between classes students jammed the hallways, which upset Ryland, who is extremely sensitive to touch. The system set him up for failure.

Ryland worked hard to please his teachers and did exceptionally well for the first few weeks. Some days were great—all synapses firing, open windows, open lines of communication. This fooled his teachers into thinking he could sustain that level of work when he couldn't. Doing everything well all the time became so exhausting for him that at home he pestered his brother and his sisters verbally and physically, became agitated, fought with neighbor kids, and couldn't focus on anything.

I told Ryland's teachers that he was unraveling at home and he would unravel at school next. They said I was being ridiculous because he was perfectly capable. I insisted that it couldn't last. Then, when he failed to finish his schoolwork, began fighting in the halls, and talked back to the teachers, they held a meeting to tell me what a terrible kid he was, that he'd stopped trying and had become disruptive. The result of the mainstreaming program was failure, and yet they wanted to blame someone else—Ryland or me. We were easy targets because I couldn't explain his disability well enough to them, and they didn't know enough about FAS to understand what works and what doesn't. At that time, nobody really knew much about FAS.

The meeting was devastating to me as a parent and dangerous to me as a recovering alcoholic. Instead of reacting to the turmoil by getting drunk, I called the lead counselor and told her how damaging the meeting's tone had been to someone who might have chosen drinking as a way to handle the problem.

As the expression goes, Ryland "blew out" of the mainstream program at junior high. In other words, he used an explosive way of trying to communicate to teachers and family that they could no longer continue with the way things were. In the school's sink or swim program, Ryland sank. He returned to the special ed class for all of his subjects.

In my growing role as Ryland's advocate, I began wondering why school was so difficult for him. When outbursts occurred, what happened beforehand to spark them? Instead of working on changing him, why couldn't we change the way the school dealt with him? How could I communicate better with his teachers?

Since I didn't know how to make things at school work for him, I visited the Disability Law Center of Alaska. This advocacy group intervenes for people with disabilities whose rights are being violated. I explained our story—that I had a child who was not learning anything in the school system—and Ryland became their client. I also met with the head of the school district's special education department because I didn't know how to approach Ryland's teachers. Ryland's advocate from the law center and the head of the special ed department began attending his Individual Education Plan (IEP) meetings and looking out for his interests.

Failing at junior high school had been terrible for Ryland's self-esteem. We worked at ways to repair the damage. We arranged for him to tutor kids in math and reading at elementary school. He took a cab so we could be sure he arrived for his tutoring, and that made him feel special. Teaching others also reinforced his own skills.

When Ryland had a bad day in the special ed class, the teacher called me and I picked him up. The school believed he would manipulate this arrangement to get out of school, but Ryland really did prefer to be at school with other kids, not at home with his mother. I also asked the staff and teachers not to touch him but instead to use their arms at a distance to herd him wherever they wanted him to go.

I also became more realistic about dealing with people in authority. When Ryland encountered difficult people, we talked about the need to look past the person toward what you want to accomplish. Life is full of difficult people, I told him, and your family's survival might depend on getting along with them. He still struggles with this.

TEACHING RYLAND TO HELP HIMSELF

Ryland and I began looking at problems together and trying to figure out how to navigate through the world so he would prevail with his spirit intact. I started teaching him how to advocate for himself. I wanted him to learn how to tell people he didn't understand what they were saying or that he couldn't listen any more. We started at home. He would stop me in the middle of my directions and say, "Mom, I can't hear anymore. That's enough words." It was terribly hard for me to stop talking and start listening. I made myself learn that eventually I would be able to return to the subject, but that I couldn't do it right then or he would simply shut down to stop the bombardment of meaningless words.

We also worked on ways he could tell people he did not understand what they said. He learned to say that he learns differently sometimes and words were not working. He asked, "Can you find another way to teach me?"

When he rose in the morning I could tell if it was going to be a good day or a bad day. I watched for signs of difficulty. Did he answer questions by saying he didn't know or didn't care? Did he seem tense, defiant, or volatile? There were other cues. His forehead would wrinkle and his eyes would look cloudy and troubled. He would be physically and verbally intrusive, and he would make repetitive annoying noises. He tipped me off if he had problems sleeping or talked excessively. Any combination of these cues signaled me that he was deteriorating. When I noticed these signs, I backed off—one of the most important and one of the hardest things a parent can do.

On these days, I would keep him home from school because he could not focus on his studies. He was also prone to get into trouble, which was discouraging for him, frustrating for the teachers, and scary and sad for me.

My goal was to teach him to recognize these signs and do something about them himself. I would say something like, "Your energy is getting way out of line. Do you want to go to your room?" There he had art supplies to relax with. Then later I would ask, "Do you want to come down for dinner, or do you want dinner in your room?" I was careful to be non-judgmental and never to indicate that I was mad or that he had been bad.

He absorbed what to do through this process of our both paying attention to cues about his mood, looking at the problem together, and then discussing ways to deal with it. Knowing that I also had a responsibility here helped him feel as if we were partners. (He loved knowing that my role might be to stop talking.) Eventually he learned that when he had that extra-uncomfortable feeling, he could go to his room or, when he was older, play basketball, take a drive, or play cards.

I also tried to keep the mood in our home calm and under-stimulating. At night he slept with a radio playing on the pillow next to his ear as white noise. The house had bare white walls and few knick-knacks, because he was uncomfortable if the walls were cluttered. His room contained a bed, dresser, and bedside table. Ryland chose not to decorate his walls with posters or art. If I noticed Ryland seemed distant and was not participating with the family much, I would look around the house. Too many papers and artwork posted on the kitchen walls or refrigerator door would make him uncomfortable, so I would clear them off. Soon Ryland would join us again.

I separated school and home as completely as possible. I didn't force him to prepare for the next day by organizing books and clothes because it only made him anxious. I didn't want him to do homework because he came home already exhausted from his day at school. Instead of focusing on academic success, I tried to surround him with people who understand FAS/E. We socialized with other families with alcohol-affected children. Our parent support group started meeting informally as families on Friday nights for skiing and skating.

We expanded these sessions into annual three-day summer camps and invited families from around the state to participate. Originally we thought that in an understanding environment, our kids would do well. They did, but other benefits emerged, too. The siblings without FAS didn't consider the children with FAS as disabled, so everybody formed friendships at camp more easily. This is not often what children with FAS experience in daily life. As parents, we were all surprised at the bonds we created with each other—bonds that sustain us from year to year, until we see each other again. We found that we learned from each others' experiences, sharing new insights into the disability and how to handle certain behaviors. Meeting in remote places also contributed to the success of our camps. There was no television or similar distractions, and we concentrated on out-of-door activities like playing in the water, fishing, climbing, hiking, riding horses and bikes, and enjoying time with each other. We came together each night to cook and eat dinner. We shared stories and songs around camp fires. The result was a community of adults who understood our children and our lives.

EXAMINING SCHOOL PROBLEMS

The school staff continued to wonder if Ryland's problems at school were linked to problems at home, but as I explored these parenting techniques, I knew we were doing okay at home. I tried hard to explain to the school staff that Ryland's problem was brain damage, not willful misconduct. I stressed that his behavior was his form of communication. His teachers became discouraged that what had worked for them with other students did not work for this child. They looked at our family situation and concluded that a single parent plus alcoholism plus poverty equals behavior problems. Each time they tried to make a connection with home life, I'd repeat calmly (in the spirit of problem-solving, of course), "We're doing fine at home. What's going on at school?"

We looked at what had changed in the special ed classroom: rearranged furniture, new students, substitute teachers, a different location, school vacations, and holidays. Were teachers trying to develop new skills, switching subjects, or making other changes in the curriculum? Was the behavior of other kids in the class noticeably different? Any of these things could affect Ryland. The teachers' observations were important because I couldn't know what was happening in school. I wanted the whole picture.

Finding a friendly adult at the school offered Ryland a refuge. For him, this person was the janitor who stored his bike, gave him a soda, or just let him sit in his work space. In years past, it had been a nurse, a librarian, a counselor, and a choir teacher. They were also willing to speak on Ryland's behalf with other professionals. This was helpful because they were often the only ones who had anything positive to report about him.

Connecting With the Community

I began to realize that school might never be a good experience for Ryland, but I wanted him to have at least good community experiences. I wanted other adults to know him as a good kid, not always as a problem. I volunteered him or myself for projects at the Resource Center for Parents and Children so he could be around people who treated kids with respect. We helped remodel their building, he helped put up a reception tent, and we chipped in at other tasks. Employees at the center and other parents and kids who volunteered liked him, and he liked feeling valuable, useful, and *important*. His work there acquainted him with people he would see around town. I worked for other organizations that support families, such as Head Start, the FAS/E Parent Support Group, the Fairbanks Native Association, and the Resource Center for Parents and Children, where I work now. Ryland often accompanied me to work or got involved in projects. He was treated with respect. When he's treated well, he responds well.

When Ryland was in seventh grade, the Big Brothers-Big Sisters program started in Fairbanks, and he applied immediately. Big Brothers-Big Sisters matches children with an adult who becomes their friend and spends time with them. The program gave my son a chance to get away from his siblings and have one-on-one time with a responsible adult. It offered an opportunity for him to practice talking on the phone, to set up activity dates, or just to chat. Ryland learned how to use the answering machine, to display manners, and to express appreciation.

The program allows parents to help pick the right person for their child, and I looked for someone who was kind, had experience with children, and would be able to see my son for the good person he is. I told his prospective Big Brother about his diagnosis and how to identify when he needed time to himself. He was matched with Jeff Cook, who remained his Big Brother until Ryland turned 18. The program's age cut-off ended their official relationship, but they remain friends. As a successful businessman, family man, and hard worker, Jeff was an excellent role model. His strong values also gave me an opportunity to point out to Ryland that although Jeff simply could have donated money to the organization, instead he contributed his time and attention to someone else in the community.

Their relationship made Ryland feel special and gave him a greater sense of responsibility. He realized that his decisions reflected not only on himself but on our family, and on Jeff and his family as well. I think this knowledge prevented him from being disrespectful of others or trying illegal activities. Ryland's relationship with Jeff was another good bonding experience for him.

JOINING THE WORK WORLD IN HIGH SCHOOL

Ryland wanted to work a lot more than he wanted to go to high school. His new special education teacher, Mike Jamison, found a great solution: Ryland could work in the community for academic credit. He took a job at the state Department of Transportation assisting the diesel mechanics in the maintenance garage. He changed oil, helped move vehicles in the yard, and did other tasks. Mr. Jamison wanted Ryland to see if he liked this kind of work, which could be a good trade for him.

A stipulation was that Ryland was required to attend school in the morning in order to work in the afternoon. If he missed school, he missed work, and if he missed work, he would lose the job. They depended on him at work, and they weren't happy if he couldn't come. He learned to call his supervisor at work to let him know when he was sick, a responsibility he dreaded.

Ryland arrived at work during lunchtime and ate with the men before his duties started. Mr. Jamison wanted him to hear responsible adults talking about everyday life and family matters— bill-paying, recreational pursuits, and work. He earned a minimal wage of a few dollars a day, and my family matched his earnings to encourage him. Money is a great motivater that I've used in other situations when nothing else works.

The next step for Ryland was finding an after-school job. At school he polished his resume and practiced job interviewing. The work study program had a pool of potential jobs available to teenagers, and Ryland chose a gas station. He interviewed for a position as an attendant and was hired to work part-time after school.

The job was not easy at first. He had a hard time getting used to an atmosphere where he was the low man on the totem pole. Until he could get a feel for how to act around his older coworkers, he didn't seem like himself. He was always at a loss for how to behave and what to say, so he filled in the gap with repetitive and artificial expressions, such as "You betcha." Often the others hurt his feelings, but he wasn't able to say anything.

He might have quit impulsively without my support. I encouraged him to keep trying by reassuring him that work becomes more comfortable once you stick it out and get to know people better. I pointed out that he needed money to buy a car or clothes. We talked over situations that made him mad, and this gave him a chance to get things out of his system. For years we had worked on naming feelings like "humiliated," "hurt," "satisfied," "frustrated," and "proud." Through his experience at work, he really started to understand the connection between the names and the feelings. He may also have been developmentally ready to process these abstract concepts.

I stayed connected with Ryland at work, providing transportation to and from work, taking him his lunch, and sending friends over to the station so he could pump their gas or help with mechanical problems. His Big Brother checked in with him frequently. I wanted the people he worked with to know he was part of a community, that he was a person with a good life. And I wanted him to feel both supported and responsible. One day a customer saw me talking with him and came over to me. "Is that your son?" she said. "He is the greatest kid. He's so good to me when I come here."

Another customer said, "I'm always needing help at the gas station with the pump or the credit card. When Ryland sees me, even when it's cold and windy, he comes right over, fixes my problem without saying anything, and starts cleaning my windshield—without even being asked!"

That's Ryland. He has his own style, and he's a good person to have around—a good friend, neighbor, and family member.

LEARNING TO DRIVE

By the time he was 15 and became comfortable at work, Ryland thought he was like everybody else—a grown-up employee. When I thought I glimpsed him driving cars in the station's lot, I mentioned to him that he was not old enough to drive. He assured me that he only drove the trash truck to the back of the station and his supervisor knew he did not have a driver's license. Then one day I called up the station and asked for Ryland. His coworker said, "He just went to do a drop-off." He had driven a customer back to work. I said, "He's driving? He doesn't even have a license." The person on the other end was shocked.

Ryland liked driving and was a responsible driver. His coworkers made him feel like one of the guys and recognized how capable he was. It seemed natural to them that he should assume driving duties as well. It did not occur to them that he didn't have a license. Ryland conformed so completely to his surroundings and was so used to his driving duties on the lot, that he forgot he didn't have a license. When he learned that he shouldn't have been driving, he was so upset that he didn't want to return to work. We talked about all the different things that might happen when he went back to work and how he might respond, but his supervisor never said a word to him. It was a good example of how closely children with FAS/E have to be monitored and supervised.

Ryland stayed in this job for almost three years. After he got his license, driving became a big part of his life. He prepared for the written exam by taking the test and seeing which answers he got right and wrong, not by studying the manual. The learner's permit allows parents and teenagers to practice driving and to rehearse potential situations for a long time. The license also becomes a huge motivator for teens and valuable leverage for parents.

Ryland loves cars and has already bought and sold five. He's using his earnings to pay off his second car loan, making ownership of a car a wonderful reason for working. When somebody hit his first real car, he called the insurance man at home at 11 P.M. to ask how he could have his car fixed or buy a new one.

Conclusion

Ryland spent four years in high school but did not graduate. Schoolwork was difficult his last year because he was more interested in working for pay at the gas station. He met a young woman at the end of his senior year, and they moved to Wyoming to live with her grandparents. He has been working most of the time while his girl friend attends college. He took a couple of classes in community college. A study skills class gave him the chance to look at his goals and direction. He decided to enroll at Wyoming Technical School for a nine-month course in diesel mechanics.

Ryland applied for funding his education with the Department of Vocational Rehabilitation (DVR). A decision to provide support is pending. In the meantime, Ryland is working on his relationship with his girl friend. In my conversations with him, I can tell when he is frustrated and close to shutting down. The problems of FAS are difficult for him, and he drifts in and out of denial of the disability.

There's a vacuum in our home without Ryland. Even though his brothers and sisters wanted his room, it took a long time before one of them moved in. We were sad that he left, and we miss him. But I'm also glad for him. I've always felt he would do well in life because he is so earnest and good-hearted. I want to see what he can do. We'll always be close, but I don't think I'll have much to do with helping him succeed in life. I think he does much better when he's in an independent and responsible role instead of that of a struggling kid.

I'm also proud that Ryland has found a caring relationship with someone. He's working hard at being a good partner. It's not that he doesn't still have trouble controlling his anger occasionally, but he's certainly learning a lot more about it.

When I took Ryland his lunch at the gas station, he always kissed me in front of all the mechanics. He possesses all those qualities we so often miss in the world today—a sense of loyalty and sweetness, the ability to be nonjudgmental and accepting. I wouldn't want him to be any other way. I'm glad I've gotten to know who Ryland is. We have a close mother-and-child relationship that's really quite special. I didn't know how to make that happen. Fortunately for all of us, Ryland did.

3

The Graduate: College for Students with FAS/E

ANNE RUGGLES GERE AND CINDY GERE

Anne Ruggles Gere teaches at the University of Michigan where she directs the Joint Ph.D. Program in English and Education. She has published widely on topics in education, and her most recent book, Intimate Practices: Literacy and Cultural Work in U.S. Women's Clubs 1880–1920 *(Illinois 1997) received the National Women's Studies Association Manuscript Prize.*

Cindy Gere studied painting at Detroit's Center for Creative Studies, received her AFA from the Institute for American Indian Art in Santa Fe, and her BFA and teaching certificate from the University of Alaska at Fairbanks. During the 1997–98 academic year she taught art at the Turtle Island Learning Circle, a Native American charter school in Detroit, and in 1998 she spent several months with her birth family in the Yukon. She and Anne Gere are collaborating on a mother-daughter memoir about living with fetal alcohol syndrome.

ON THE AUGUST DAY IN 1990 WHEN OUR DAUGHTER CINDY BOARDED a plane bound for the Institute of American Indian Art (IAIA) in Santa Fe, I managed to remain dry-eyed until she turned and walked down the jetway. As I watched her bounce with anticipation, her long, dark hair dancing, I wept with the realization that our family would never be quite the same, that there would be an empty place at the dinner table, and that I would have to walk past a vacant room filled with the stuffed animals and books she couldn't fit into her trunk. At the same time, I felt a tremendous sense of accomplishment that we had come this far, that Cindy was ready to begin a more independent life.

This child who joined our family when she was three and a half had developed from a clinging toddler into an attractive young woman who wanted to learn more about her American Indian heritage. A friend had always said that her goal as a parent was to work herself out of a job, and as I watched Cindy make her way down the jetway at Detroit Metro, I felt as if a major piece of parenting was behind me. Concerns mixed with that feeling of accomplishment as I thought back to my own college days and remembered all the potentially dangerous and self-destructive things I had done during those years. Recalling my own experiences reminded me of the pitfalls that come with the freedoms and responsibilities of college life. In the midst of all this, I felt a sense of liberation as I realized that the phone and the bathroom in our home would be more available than they had been in years.

Most parents probably feel a similar set of mixed emotions as they see a child off to college. For us parents of youngsters with FAS/E, these feelings assume an extra layer of complexity because we know all the special needs and vulnerabilities these young people take with them. In addition to grief, delight, worry, and liberation, I felt an enormous sense of uncertainty and fear as Cindy left. I knew how difficult high school had been for her, how much she had needed my help both with homework and with educational bureaucracies. I also knew how fragile her self-confidence was. Most of her school experiences had made her feel, in her words, "dumb," and I had a hard time imagining how she would handle setbacks two thousand miles from home.

Partly, Cindy went to college because I pushed her in that direction. High school sapped her self-confidence, but I persuaded her that an art school wouldn't be like high school. She could do more of what she is good at and leave courses like government and basic math behind. But Cindy also wanted to go to college. She spent her junior and senior years listening to friends in chorus—the one class she shared with the college prep group—talk about applications and acceptances. She yearned to be part of that world.

Cindy was especially anxious to go to IAIA where she would, for the first time in her life, be among a majority of Native Americans. Despite her motivation and enthusiasm, I worried.

Thankfully, most of my fears were unfounded. Cindy not only graduated from the Institute of American Indian Art, but she also earned a bachelor's degree in art from the University of Alaska Fairbanks. She later studied to become a secondary school art teacher. In the process, she faced but managed to overcome the difficulties of handling college on her own, and I learned strategies for long-distance support. In this chapter I share some of my experiences in the hope that they can be helpful to other parents of college students with FAS/E.

Many of the things I learned grew from parenting a child with FAS/E over the years. Each new strategy was an extension of past approaches. Cindy's test results have always been spiky—she has some areas of real strength and some of enormous deficit. Her sense of direction, for example, has always been outstanding, but computational math has been a continuing area of weakness. Overall, she tested within the normal range on IQ tests, but that was because her lower verbal and mathematical scores were balanced by her very high scores on the performance section that asked her to solve spatial problems and find her way through mazes. When we adopted Cindy, she was a highly active child who seemed very interested in her world, but even in preschool she showed little ability with school-like tasks. Her Montessori teacher observed, for example, that Cindy excelled in creative activities of any sort, but she showed only sporadic interest in letters and numbers.

When Cindy entered elementary school after an extra year of kindergarten, she had great difficulty with reading and math, and we began a long search for both a diagnosis and a strategy. The diagnosis of fetal alcohol effects was relatively easy to obtain because we happened to live in Seattle where Dr. David Smith was doing his ground-breaking research on the effects of alcohol on the fetus. Both what we knew of her birth mother as well as Cindy's small, close-set eyes and her short crooked pinky fingers confirmed that her mother's prenatal consumption of alcohol was responsible for her learning difficulties. The harder task was figuring out how to deal with those difficulties.

One strategy I developed when Cindy was still in elementary school was *to help her identify and focus on her strengths.* It was crucial to keep her from giving up on herself, and I knew she needed to feel successful at some things or her difficulties with academic courses would overwhelm her. As she struggled through elementary and high school, I kept telling her that college would be different, because she would be able to do more of what she really enjoyed, that she could choose a major in which she excelled.

In one way, it may have been unrealistic to encourage Cindy to think about college, but three of the four grandparents in our family were teachers, so our family saw higher education as very important. From the time she understood that she had another, Native American, family, Cindy wanted to "help my people," and education seemed a good way to accomplish that goal. Furthermore, I knew that Cindy did have talents. Art always came easily for her. Not only did she test high in spatial ability, but she could draw well and had a keen sense of color. Throughout her elementary and secondary school years, I tried to insure that Cindy took an art course or participated in some creative activity. In high school, for example, she enrolled in the visual merchandising course offered by the vocational program. Cindy showed a real flair for creating store windows and other displays of merchandise.

By taking a mixture of regular (but not necessarily college preparatory) offerings along with music and art courses, Cindy managed to graduate from high school with a *B* average. Her high school counselors had given her no encouragement to attend college, and the psychologists who tested her when she was nine had stated categorically that she was not college material. I knew that Cindy would have great difficulty with a traditional college curriculum, but I knew she had real gifts as an artist, so I encouraged her to apply to an art school where she could avoid some of the subjects that had been most difficult for her in high school, like math.

Thus Cindy began a series of moves, each requiring more independence, from a local college near our Detroit home to the Institute for American Indian Art in Santa Fe, New Mexico, to the University of Alaska at Fairbanks, 2,000 miles away.

Over the years I learned that Cindy needed *help with transitions* to make any move. When she was a toddler, I had to allow lots of extra time for her to shift from one activity to another. If I wanted her to stop playing and put on her coat to go home, I had to prepare her to make that move rather than simply bark, "Put on your coat. Let's go." When Cindy graduated from high school, neither she nor we felt she was ready to move to a residential college, so she commuted from home the first year. Living at home with all the familiar structures helped her adapt to the more open schedule of college where classes meet two or three times a week rather than daily. During this year she learned how to deal with longer-term projects rather than the day-to-day work of high school. Driving to the local park-and-ride, taking the bus to Detroit, and finding her way around the campus of the Center for Creative Studies, a four-year art school, she developed a greater sense of independence and became ready to make the transition that led her to the Institute of American Indian Art. Going to art school in Detroit whetted her appetite for more drawing and painting, but she also hungered for more Native American experiences. IAIA offered both.

"The next best thing to a good education is a pushy mother," wrote some wag, and Cindy taught me to be a pushy mother so that she could have a good education. Even with the best-intentioned teachers, I had found that Cindy needed special intervention. Too often, particularly because Cindy was a quiet and well-behaved student, teachers would not attend to her special needs unless I made a fuss. I learned to intervene to make sure she sat in the front of the classroom, that she received written instructions as well as verbal cues about what was expected, and that she was allowed extra time for tests.

When Cindy began at the Center for Creative Studies, she was scheduled to take a placement test for English. I didn't know much about this school's testing program, but I knew enough about my daughter to predict that Cindy's test results would place her in the most remedial class where she would be consigned to workbook drills on parts of speech. Having watched her struggle with long and short vowels and sentences like "The dog dug the mug," I knew she would never be able to complete the worksheets of a remedial English class successfully, and her hard-won confidence in her own ability as a writer would wither. Thanks to a gifted teacher who worked with her in high school, Cindy learned writerly skills of developing ideas, organizing her material, and thinking about her audience. She needed time for multiple drafts and a computer with a spell checker; I knew she'd never succeed on the timed placement test.

We took a risk and proposed that Cindy be allowed to enroll in a regular composition course that focused on writing about art. I reasoned that Cindy, like most people, would write best about something she knew and cared about, that her visual ability would inform her compositions, and that she had a chance of succeeding here whereas she faced certain failure in a remedial class that focused on language drills, with no connection to anything concrete.

Watching Cindy over the years taught me to *question hierarchical views of learning* that assume one must learn in a certain fixed order. I knew Cindy had capacities for relatively sophisticated thinking and writing, even if she could not demonstrate mastery of certain skills like correct spelling or flawless sentence structure. The many journals, letters, and papers Cindy had written demonstrated her ability to communicate.

We discussed various alternatives before we settled on this plan, but I was the one who approached the administrator. At this stage in her development, Cindy was not ready to be her own advocate. The administrator in charge agreed to exempt Cindy from the placement test in English and allow her to enroll in the art-based composition course with the understanding that if she could not succeed there she would drop back to the remedial course.

The gamble worked. Cindy wrote papers comparing paintings and discussing styles of art during different historical periods. With the help of a tutor and a computer, she transformed her invented spelling and unorthodox syntax into acceptable compositions. Together Cindy and I explained her difficulties to her instructors, and they responded with compassion and understanding to her in-class writing, looking past her unconventional spelling to the ideas she conveyed. By the end of the year, she had completed the college writing requirement successfully.

When I approached the administrator about the placement test, I struggled, as I have many times, over whether I was helping Cindy too much. I wondered if I was teaching her a kind of help-lessness so that she would not be able to act on her own behalf. I have continued to ask myself that question each time I am tempted to intervene, and if there is a way for Cindy to accomplish her goal without my aid, I happily back off, as I did when she made it clear she was ready to travel to IAIA on her own. At the same time, I feel it is entirely appropriate to help her when she requests and needs my aid. All parents help their young adult children—some by find-ing them a place in the family business, some by introducing them to influential people, some by teaching them a trade. In addition, what I've read about disabilities suggests that neither complete independence nor complete dependence represent a good goal. Rather, *interdependence* seems the best approach. I have tried to find that middle ground in my relationship with Cindy where teamwork accomplishes what individual effort might not.

I contacted many of Cindy's college instructors during her first college years. In addition to developing a way for her to meet the composition requirement, I checked with her instructors at the Center for Creative Studies when I sensed that she was having difficulties in a course. Later, such intervention became much less frequent.

When Cindy went to the Institute of American Indian Art, I had a harder time maintaining telephone contact with her profes-sors, so I sent a *progress form* to each of her instructors at the middle of the semester. Cindy had agreed that this would be a good way for both of us to have a sense of how she was doing. By keeping it short—usually three or four questions—I got a nearly 100 percent return. My questions usually included some version of these:

"What is Cindy doing well?" "Where does she need improvement?" "What is her approximate grade at this time?" "Do you have any suggestions or advice?"

I saw these forms as the college version of the parent-teacher conferences I'd participated in when Cindy was in elementary and secondary school. When I received responses (in the stamped, self-addressed envelopes I'd enclosed), I relayed the information to Cindy. Often, as is true for many students with FAS/E, she had not been able to monitor her own performance well enough to know how she was doing. When Cindy followed up by talking with instructors, they frequently made specific and useful suggestions that Cindy could implement before the semester ended, and this procedure helped her learn to become better at keeping track of her own performance in classes. Not surprisingly, my progress forms became unnecessary by Cindy's second year at the Institute for American Indian Art because she had learned to track her own work.

During her first year at IAIA, Cindy lived in a dormitory where meals were provided, but as she entered her second year, she wanted to live in an off-campus apartment with two other friends. Her father and I felt some serious reservations about this plan because we knew from our own experience how time-consuming it can be to shop, cook, clean, and do all the other things that dormitory living makes unnecessary. But we decided that we had to *avoid being too protective* and let her try the plan out for herself.

During a summer visit to Santa Fe, we saw the new apartment, helped move some things in, and established a joint checking account where we could deposit and Cindy could withdraw money. We developed a budget for her monthly expenses and rehearsed the checkbook management skills we had taught Cindy in high school. That semester was an especially difficult one for Cindy because she fell and tore ligaments in her ankle and had to be hospitalized for several days. Shortly after that, her boyfriend, one of the threesome in the apartment, moved out. Hobbling on crutches, she discovered that living some distance from campus without the services of a dormitory made for a complicated life, and her experiences with roommates were not particularly positive. During the next and every other semester, she elected to live in a dorm in a single room.

Although I was prepared to let Cindy try things out for herself, I also knew from years of parenting that she almost always needed *extra time*. When she was little, we had a favorite book, *Leo the Late Bloomer*, and when it seemed as if she would never learn to tell time or to name colors, I would read *Leo* aloud, reassuring both of us that Cindy would eventually learn these things. An extra year of kindergarten helped prepare her for elementary school, and another extra year made the transition to high school easier. She received her high school diploma when she was nearly 20, but, like Leo, she finally made it. I had to remind myself of Cindy's need for extra time as she worked her way through undergraduate education. It took Cindy seven years to complete her bachelor of fine arts degree, and she took courses both semesters of each of these years.

To be sure, she transferred twice, from the Center for Creative Studies to the Institute for American Indian Art where she received her associate's degree, and from there to the University of Alaska Fairbanks. But even if she had remained at the same college the whole time, she would have needed more than the customary four years. Like most students with FAS/E, she can focus on a limited number of things at any one moment, which has meant that she cannot comfortably take more than 12 credits per semester, and she sometimes needed to take less. Some colleges allow students to retake courses in which they have received low grades, and the second grade, if higher, either replaces or is averaged in with the first. This system has served Cindy well, particularly in dealing with a math requirement when she transferred to the University of Alaska at Fairbanks (UAF). It has also meant, of course, that she has needed more time to complete the work required for her degree.

Like most FAS/E parents, I knew that Cindy needed help breaking projects into component parts. Asking the six-year-old Cindy to go upstairs, take off her clothes, put them in the hamper, put on her pajamas and come downstairs, was to set an impossible task. She needed to be given one or two steps at a time. Although her skills increased considerably as she grew older, I knew that the college-bound Cindy could find herself awash in the details of registering for classes, particularly after she transferred to UAF, which was far away and considerably larger than her previous schools. Cindy wanted to go to UAF because she wanted to understand her Kaska Athabascan heritage, but I also knew she would need extra assistance at this university.

For the first couple of semesters I made up a packet of typed sheets at the beginning of each new semester. I listed each step necessary to register and enclosed the documentation for each step, attaching Post-its with special instructions when necessary. When Cindy registered for her fifth semester at UAF, I happened to be on campus visiting her, and I watched with great pleasure as she moved confidently through the maze of halls and offices to register and buy her books. I knew I had worked myself out of another job.

Whenever Cindy entered a new school, whether fifth grade or the junior year of college, I knew that I needed to establish a *support network*. Because of her special needs, I had to identify the people in the system who could help her. Usually this required contacting the special education department, but it also meant discovering which teachers were likely to be understanding of Cindy's use of invented spelling, affirming of her abilities, and willing to modify course requirements by giving her extra time for tests or allowing her to substitute an art project for a paper, so she could accomplish these tasks successfully.

Even before Cindy enrolled in the fall of 1992, I began making preliminary inquiries at UAF to determine what special services would be available to her. I called the admissions office and ordered a copy of the university catalog so I could learn the names of relevant people and offices. Every college must, in compliance with federal law, provide some facilities for students with learning disabilities, and I decided it would be good idea to meet some of the people involved in this work.

Because it serves a relatively large percentage of Native Alaskan and Indian students, UAF has, in addition to the usual office for students with disabilities, an Office of Rural Student Services. A counselor in that office provided a lifeline of communication during the spring before Cindy enrolled, answering my questions about everything from dormitories to diagnostic tests required by the university for students with learning disabilities. Through a friend, I learned that a faculty member had done research on FAS/E, and I contacted her because my intuition told me Cindy might sometime need a faculty advocate who thoroughly understood FAS/E's implications for students.

When Cindy went to UAF for the first time, I flew to Fairbanks with her. I needed to make Alaska more familiar in my own mind so that I could deal with having my daughter so far from home, but I also wanted to do everything possible to set Cindy up for success at her new university. In addition to getting her settled into her dorm, I extended the support network a bit. Friends offered to fill in as Cindy's local parents. I left Fairbanks with a list of peoples' names and phone numbers that I could call upon if Cindy needed help. Later, as Cindy took courses and needed tutorial assistance, I became acquainted with other staff and faculty who offered guidance, answered questions, and provided the support Cindy needed along the way.

Although much of what we know as parents of children with FAS/E can be extended into higher education, college does require some new forms of parental involvement. First, parents need to become intimately acquainted with the *college catalogue*. It's not thrilling reading, but it contains essential information about courses, graduation requirements, and programs offered by the college. By reading the catalogue carefully and keeping a record of which courses Cindy had taken or transferred from her other postsecondary programs, I was able to help her move smoothly through UAF requirements.

Like many students with FAS/E, Cindy finds logical thinking and considering consequences difficult, and I knew planning sequences of courses across several semesters would be daunting for her. Even with the help of very good advisors, I found that Cindy needed my assistance in making decisions about courses each semester. We supplemented the class schedule with advice from faculty and staff about which professors might be most sympathetic and responsive to Cindy's needs. We drew grids listing the days of the week on one axis and the hours of the day on the other so that she could construct a schedule that distributed her classes throughout the week.

Another useful skill for parents is learning to read course descriptions, particularly if students transfer from one college to another. Transfers require the registrar's office to evaluate the transcript and decide whether classes taken at the previous college will be granted credit at the new college. Even if your child does not transfer, it's a good idea to read course descriptions carefully to assess whether your child can do the required work. Advisors who do not know your son or daughter as well as you do may, with all the best intentions, guide him or her into an impossible learning situation. This happened to Cindy when advisors recommended that she take a basic math course. I knew that Cindy would not be able to succeed in this course, but her advisors were convinced that their outstanding instructor could teach her. After a semester when Cindy called home in tears every week, her instructor and advisors agreed that Cindy really couldn't do math.

Becoming familiar with course requirements and descriptions prepares parents to write petitions with or on behalf of students. Just as colleges must, by federal law, provide some facilities for students with learning disabilities, so they must provide reasonable alternatives to requirements students are unable to fulfill. We used petitions to make creative substitutions for course requirements Cindy could not otherwise fulfill.

To satisfy a foreign language requirement, for example, Cindy studied the language of her Kaska heritage. During the summer of 1993, Cindy worked with a linguist in Whitehorse, Yukon Territory, her birthplace. With his help, she interviewed elders, studied archival photographs, visited fishing camps, and became familiar with the culture as a means of learning the

CINDY'S STUDY TIPS*

↪ *Focus on basic skills.*

Take a class in study skills. Learn how to write well. The work load for one semester might be taking a study skills class, taking an English class, and taking a math class. Those things are very important. Then take a research skills class. It's imperative to know how to write down what you have learned.

↪ *Sit in the front of the classroom.*

Paying attention is incredibly important. Research shows that 90 percent of the kids who sit in the front of the class get As, according to my mother. Someone with FAE might not get an A in class but might get a B. If you're sitting in the front of the class, the teacher is interested in you. You're on a first-name basis. The teacher will say, "Wow, this person really wants to learn!"

↪ *Take notes and review them each day.*

In class, you take notes. Then you go home and you read the notes. You get up early in the morning. You read the same notes. Then you've got it in your brain a little bit. Next time you take more notes. You read the first set of notes. Then you read the second set of notes. The next day, you take and read the third set of notes plus the first two. You are training your brain to grab information and to hold it.

↪ *Meet with your professors for additional help.*

If you don't understand the material in class and are too embarrassed to ask, write down your questions on a paper. Go and see the teacher privately. Say, "I have a little list of three things I don't understand." This can help the teacher know that you are really interested in the class.

The professor will also help you focus and zero in on what you should study for a test.

↪ *Use visual ways to learn.*

It's easier to learn when information is presented through visual stimulation rather than lectures. Go to the public library or video store and find a video on the topic at hand.

↪ *Learn in a group.*

Find someone in the classroom that you feel comfortable with, get with your partner, and work together.

↪ *Call on family members for expertise.*

Let's say someone is into engineering, and you are interested in that. You might call the person up and say, "We are hitting on this topic and I need help with that. Can you recommend books for me?" He might say, "There's a wonderful book out there. And this book describes the subject very concisely."

---

* Dictated by Cindy Gere; transcribed and edited by Judith Kleinfeld language. This experiential learning made it possible for her to learn the Kaska language, whereas it would have been impossible if she had had to memorize vocabulary and verb forms in a traditional classroom where language was decontextualized and not part of a culture. Cindy completed her independent study program with a paper about Kaska salmon fishing, but I thought the best demonstration of her learning came when she honored her father, speaking Kaska, at his birthday later in the summer.

Finding experiential learning alternatives offers one way to deal with college requirements, but students with FAS/E often need other alternatives as well. The UAF core curriculum also requires two courses in mathematics, and given Cindy's long history of difficulty with math, I knew that even experiential learning would not get her through that requirement. During a painful struggle with her remedial math course, Cindy depicted her frustration in a painting. One of the large canvases for her senior show features a tiny figure in the fetal position with enormous numbers and mathematical symbols looming overhead (see this painting, *College Trials*, and other examples of her artwork in Cindy's Portfolio beginning on page 79).

After she had suffered through the basic math course and her advisors agreed that she should be allowed substitutions for the math requirement, Cindy herself suggested computer work as an alternative. An introduction to computers satisfied the first requirement, and for the second Cindy took a course in computer art. Doing math-related work in the context of art seemed like a good idea. This turned out to be only partly true. Cindy received a *D*, the first of her college career. Even though she liked the artistic dimensions of producing computer art, she found the technical aspects of working with computers very difficult. This was an occasion when the option to retake a course became a lifesaver. In fact, I recommend that parents determine whether a college allows this option before choosing that college. Needless to say, everyone rejoiced when Cindy earned an *A* on the retake.

Even with our careful monitoring of requirements, Cindy's graduation was not assured until the final weeks of the 1996 spring

Navigating Through College*

College presents hurdles for all new students, but those with FAS/E may face additional challenges. Cindy Gere developed several successful strategies for overcoming problems at school.

Seek out people who will help you. Find people who are willing to be your advocates. Use them as much as you can. If you are having problems with teachers, send another teacher who is willing to stand up and argue for your side. Find an incredibly good advisor. Most crucial of all is getting good tutors.

Learn to tell people you have a problem. Inform your teachers that you have FAS or FAE but do it in a way that you feel comfortable. You should say, "This is a very private matter. I want to keep this problem between you and me."

If you're going to forget it, wear it. I have a problem with losing things. Losing keys is the biggest problem. I tie my keys on a string around my neck or put them on a long line and keep them in my pocket so they don't interfere with jewelry. Use a fanny pack for your important cards: driver's license, student identification card, bank card, and traveler's checks.

Make a schedule and keep track of appointments, but allow room for personal time. Between Friday and Sunday, I give myself bigger breaks in my schedule, such as time to go to the movies, things to do with friends. Once Monday gets here, I'm back in the saddle. I have to continue the study skills.

I have a little black calendar, maybe as big as my hand. I write down what I need to do that day. I make sure that once someone wants me to do things, I write it down immediately. Then the night before and first thing in the morning, I take out my calendar and look at the day.

---

* Dictated by Cindy Gere; transcribed and edited by Judith Kleinfeld

semester. She had not made much progress on her senior project for the art department during the previous semester, and her painting instructor expressed real doubts about her ability to finish her work in time. In addition to producing a dozen or so big canvas paintings, Cindy was required to write a thesis describing her project.

As I helped Cindy prepare her thesis, I was reminded of how important using technology can be for students with FAS/E. Cindy already knew the value of the computer spellchecker, and she also knew it was much easier to revise a neatly printed text. Writing the thesis posed special challenges both in length and conceptualization because Cindy needed to offer a detailed explanation of the planned theme and to describe the techniques for her senior project. We discussed the project on the phone until Cindy was able to articulate what she wanted to accomplish with the project. Then she dictated while I listened on the speaker phone and typed up a rough draft of what she had said. I faxed the copy to her so she could make changes. Then I printed a draft of the first three pages, sent it by express mail, and Cindy completed the required ten pages on her own with help from the University's writing lab. Throughout her years in higher education, Cindy has found computers, fax machines, and the speaker phone essential to her work.

As often happens with creative projects, after a long period of very slow progress, Cindy began to paint rapidly during her last semester, and her advisor indicated she might be able to complete her senior project after all. However, two more petitions remained to push throughout the system. During this period, I realized the importance of *initiating and maintaining communication* with major advisors, along with other members of the faculty and staff. These individuals can help students navigate through the bureaucracy required for graduation.

With commencement scheduled for May 12, I waited until the end of April to order plane tickets for Fairbanks because so many final details remained unresolved. Even Cindy's graduation application was a last-minute endeavor. With so many uncertainties attached to her case, Cindy had to wait until the very day of the deadline to see if her various petitions had cleared so she could actually graduate.

Not only did Cindy graduate, she also received an award as the outstanding student of the Rural Student Services Program, which provides counseling, advocacy, and academic support to Native students. Commencement happened to fall on Mother's Day, and Fairbanks, with sunny 70-degree weather, had never looked better. I glowed throughout the graduation exercises. Choosing to wear traditional Native American regalia rather than a cap and gown, Cindy looked stunning as she walked across the stage to receive her bachelor of fine arts degree.

In addition to taking enormous personal pride in her accomplishments, I saw that moment as a historic one. Afterward, at a party hosted by friends, most of the support team along with many of Cindy's friends joined us in celebrating. Sitting on a deck that looked out over the hills toward Denali, I thought about the beginnings and endings woven into this particular day. Without doubt, the most moving moment came at the party when Cindy received a gift from a member of the art department who was himself part Kaska and who knew many of the elders, including Cindy's grandparents. Throughout her years at UAF, Cindy received a great sense of affirmation from him because he provided her with information about strong and upstanding members of her birth family and other Kaska people. On this day, he gave Cindy a moosehide bag designed and beaded by her Kaska grandmothers. There was not a dry eye in sight as Cindy accepted this tangible symbol of her Athabascan heritage.

Even as I rejoiced at this marvelous gift to Cindy, at her accomplishments in higher education, and at the meaning of her graduation for other students with FAS/E, I reminded myself not to minimize the real pain and difficulties that Cindy had endured throughout her years in school, from kindergarten through college. This sunny day did not erase the many times Cindy had sobbed out her anger, frustration, and sadness; the numerous occasions when she had been dismissed or belittled by thoughtless others;

the complicated situations Cindy encountered as a Native American woman in higher education.

Most of all, no amount of sun could obscure the dark truth that FAS/E is a lifetime sentence. Regardless of her accomplishments, Cindy will always have to deal with the unreliability of her brain's retrieval system. She cannot count on being able to recall something she knew perfectly well yesterday. She will face humiliation when she cannot process multiple-part instructions, when she cannot do simple math computations, or when she cannot spell so-called easy words. Cindy will never grow out of the disabilities imposed by FAS/E.

With these sobering thoughts in mind, I recalled the need for maintaining a creative tension between honest acknowledgment of the limitations imposed by FAS/E and never underestimating potential when thinking about what individual people can accomplish. The strategies outlined here provided some of the practical support that helped Cindy toward her goal of graduation, but the most important factor was a belief, not a strategy. I remained convinced that Cindy was a person of considerable potential, and she, in turn, believed in herself.

That belief, which she frequently articulated as wanting to help her Athabascan people, may take concrete form. During the spring of her graduation she was accepted into, and in June of 1997 successfully completed, the UAF Teachers for Alaska program. Cindy now joins a small number of certified Native American teachers in Alaska.* I can think of no better way for this graduate to carry on the traditions of both our family and her Kaska grandparents.

---

* A videotape is available which shows Cindy Gere doing her student teaching with success. In this videotape, she explains her strategies for dealing with FAS/E and how her experience helps her understand students with learning disabilities. *Painting a Future: A Young Adult Succeeding with FAE* is available through the University of Alaska Press, P.O Box 756240-UAF, Fairbanks, Alaska 99775-6240. E-mail: fypress@uaf.edu.

Portfolio
Cindy Gere:
A Success Story

Editor's Note: Cindy Gere's thesis for her degree in fine arts from the University of Alaska Fairbanks included a gallery show of her artwork. Cindy called her show "On Deaf Ears: An Athabascan Perspective." The paintings on the pages that follow were in the show. They provide a poignant and candid expression of what FAE means to her.

College Trials

CAN'T BREATHE

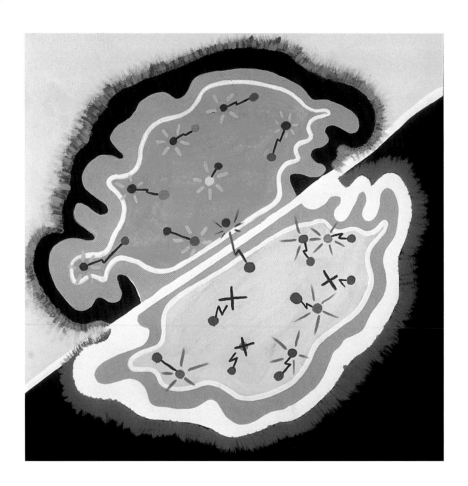

LIVING PROOF

MY PHILOSOPHY
by Cindy Gere*

I love my traditional name, woman of the king salmon, because what does a salmon do but start at the mouth of the Yukon and swim all the way up with all these obstacles? And it's like my life. My life is a bunch of obstacles, but I have conquered each and every one of those obstacles.

And that's how I've tried to conquer FAE, to deal with each and every one of these obstacles as they come and to jump over them.

I say to myself, "Yes, you are going to make it. And you are going to conquer these obstacles.

"Obstacles of psychological abuse in my own mind, what I do to myself.

"Obstacles of what people say to me when they find out that I have FAE.

"Obstacles of, unfortunately, the pressure of my parents that are put on me.

"Obstacles of employers who feel I will not be as good simply because they find out about FAE."

Through it all, I want to say to people, "I've made it this far, why not continue on?"

---

* From the videotape, *Painting a Future: A Young Adult Succeeding with FAE*

4
Living Independently:
A Mother's Tale

MARCEIL TEN EYCK

Marceil Ten Eyck is a psychotherapist and counselor in private practice in Kirkland, Washington, and a staff member of the FAS diagnostic clinic at the University of Washington, where she provides counseling support. Ms. Ten Eyck helped found the Fetal Alcohol Syndrome Information Service in Washington State, and is a FAS consultant to alcohol and drug treatment agencies, schools, social service agencies, and other counselors. She is the mother of two daughters, one diagnosed with FAS, and the other with FAE. Ms. Ten Eyck has been in recovery from chemical dependency for over 19 years.

WHEN THE DOCTOR AT CHILDREN'S HOSPITAL DIAGNOSED MY daughter Sidney with fetal alcohol syndrome, he did not give me much hope for her future. His words were:

> *She will probably never graduate from high school.... She will never be able to support herself.... She will probably need parental support for the rest of her life.*

She was 14 years old and beginning the seventh grade. I was devastated. Sidney was not. Her response was, "What a relief!"

She had been doing all right at school until that time, but Sidney was something of a lost child, always on the edges of the action. She was trying her hardest, but her grades were erratic. I kept telling her, "Just work harder! You are not working up to your potential." We began to think she had a learning disability, and decided to find out for sure. The diagnosis finally gave her some proof that it wasn't her fault that she couldn't perform in the ways her teachers and I thought she should be performing.

THE DIAGNOSIS AND WHAT IT MEANT TO ME

Faced with a diagnosis of FAS, I went into denial. "If that doctor had seen me," I said to myself, "he would not have diagnosed Sidney as having FAS." I am fully aware that my viewpoint made no sense at all. I had been an alcoholic. My father was a well-known physician, and my mother was a pharmacist who stayed home to take care of us children. They were both alcoholics. My own alcoholism grew worse and worse after college. Two years after Sidney was born, I was diagnosed with a supposedly terminal case of cirrhosis of the liver.

Even though I was in a state of denial about Sidney's diagnosis, I began to act as if it were true. I took her scores from the university's diagnostic tests to her school counselor. He looked carefully over the results and said, "Oh, this is how she learns." His way of shifting from the negative to the positive was an enormous relief.

He had said, "She learns."

THE DIAGNOSIS AND WHAT IT MEANT TO SIDNEY

Sidney's diagnosis did not qualify her for special education, and she attended regular classes throughout high school. But the diagnosis got people's attention. She was was no longer labeled a lazy kid and we could direct all our efforts at helping her deal with her learning disabilities.

The counselor put her in classes with teachers who emphasized a visual learning style that was best for Sidney. She also did well in hands-on courses, such as science classes that included a lab, movies, and videotapes. Because of her learning disability, teachers were willing to spend extra time helping her in class. With the special attention, sometimes she even went to the top of her classes.

The diagnosis helped Sidney put her learning problems in perspective, and she stopped believing she was stupid when she needed help. She realized, and her teachers realized, that she had a disability and that she must compensate. Sidney wrote a letter to her high school teachers explaining how she learns best (see sidebar, page 88). One teacher who read the letter gave Sidney a secret signal—putting her finger on her forehead and tilting it down—to let the teacher know she was getting lost. Then the teacher could choose either to slow down or to help after class. Because Sidney had a validated disability, the teachers usually took special care.

At age 14, Sidney had an average IQ—a score of 100—but her IQ test displayed unusual peaks and valleys. When she was tested at 19, her IQ measured 84. She seemed to stop growing intellectually. While other young people her age developed the ability to reason in an abstract way, she didn't. Her verbal abilities, on the other hand, led people to believe she was quite capable, and often they developed unreasonable expectations.

Without the diagnosis of FAS, I don't think she would have graduated from high school.

THE PLAN

I believed then, and still believe, that people need to be in charge of their lives to the extent they can. Sidney needed to be taught how to run her own life as much as possible. I also believe that part of the process of being in charge means participating in the planning, so Sidney and I sat down together and drew up what we called *The Plan*.

The Plan established a systematic way to teach Sidney how to ask for help. All her life, Sidney would have to be able to ask for assistance: *We developed The Plan to teach her how to advocate for herself.*

The Plan had four steps. If she used it at school, the steps would go as follows:

1. Go to the teacher and ask for help if you are having any trouble in class. The trouble could be big or small. The important part is being willing to ask for help. We worked on how to ask for help in an assertive manner.

How I Learn Best*
by Sidney Guimont

When I first found out that I had the symptoms of fetal alcohol syndrome, I was confused and angry. I thought that I was different from everyone else and that I would be known for what I have.

Since then I have learned that the symptoms of fetal alcohol syndrome vary from individual to individual, due to what stage of the pregnancy the mother drank and the amount of alcohol she consumed. My symptoms are very small compared to some of the other symptoms I've heard of.

Some people find it impossible to believe my problems when I explain them, since I don't show the [physical] signs of fetal alcohol syndrome.

Following verbal instructions sometimes confuses me. When I'm asked to do something like take out the garbage, I won't understand or the words get all mixed up in my mind. For example, my stepfather gives me a command to do something, and it's like I don't hear him clearly, even if he is in the same room. It's like I block out words and phrases.

Visual contact is a very important way of learning for me. When a teacher shows a topic, I can understand it.

I am not able to focus on reality if disaster strikes. I am acting on excitement. Most of the time I worry a lot and make problems seem impossible to handle. When I worry, I make myself sick.

This letter is to help me guide myself and others.

---

* Sidney wrote this letter as a ninth grader, when she was 15, for her high school teachers. Her junior high school counselor suggested she write it to help her teachers understand how she learns best.

2. If the teacher does not or cannot help you, go to your school counselor. We talked about how to make an appointment with the counselor, and how to be assertive in the school office.

3. If the school counselor will not or cannot help, go to the school principal and vice principal and ask for help.

4. If the principal can't help you, then come to me and together, we will find someone who can help.

Sidney used The Plan the first time after her school counselor mistakenly placed her in an advanced math class. For three days, she came home from school in tears, unable to understand anything in the class. I suggested she put The Plan into action. She asked her math teacher if she would help her transfer to another math class. When the teacher said "no," Sidney went to the counselor for help.

Later, I asked the counselor if Sidney had used assertiveness skills in her request for help. He laughed as he said, "Yes, you could say she was assertive. She stormed in here, furious, and she told me I had to get her out of that math class." We were both pleased because she had taken care of the problem herself, and she felt very proud of herself for having done so.

We discussed The Plan many times, and we altered it to fit other situations as they came up—for example, in her Girl Scout troop. Fortunately, it always worked on steps 1 or 2.

Sidney did well in the seventh and eighth grades, especially in those courses where visual learning aids were used, such as in science lab. She is a talented musician, and playing keyboard for the school jazz band and clarinet in the school concert band gave her a base. She had taken piano lessons since the fourth grade. Although learning to read music was not easy, once she overcame that hurdle she blossomed with the enjoyment of playing. Music was the delight of her life and provided a refuge when she felt overwhelmed or frustrated.

For those two years, it was easy for me deny the FAS diagnosis because she was a good student and she was able to form two friendships. I continued to plan for her future college years, rewarding her for academic achievement as well as her use of assertiveness skills and the execution of The Plan when necessary. Sidney also had an ability to pick the adults at school and other places who were empathetic and willing to listen to her and to help her.

Larry and Sexuality

Then one day, a boy named Larry showed up on the junior high school grounds with his gang and noticed Sidney, who was petite, slender, very pretty, and had long blonde hair. Within two weeks, before I had a glimmer of what was happening, Larry gathered her into his gang as his girlfriend. He made demands, I was soon to discover, that prompted her to take drastic measures.

At the end of those two weeks, her school principal called and said, "Sidney is missing from school. She was last seen in the parking lot with some kids, and her friends said she has taken a handful of pills."

After a frantic search, I found Sidney. She had taken eight Benadryl tablets in an effort to kill herself, then spent the day with some kids who had called poison control and followed instructions about how to care for her while she reacted to the overdose.

We got past the crisis, but for the next several months, Sidney refused to leave Larry and the gang, despite her mixed feelings. They were active nightly, although I didn't know this for a few months. The kids would sneak out of their homes in the middle of the night, roam the neighborhoods, and be back home before dawn. Needless to say, she did not have a lot of energy left for school.

After school, Sidney had always needed either a nap or quiet time because she said the stimulus of her "brain working all day" exhausted her. Now she could barely get out of bed in the morning, and she slept after school until dinner. Her grades dropped, and she seemed depressed and irritated.

More trouble developed. Our neighbors had asked Sidney to feed their dog for them while they took a vacation. They came home early, in the middle of the night, to discover Sidney, Larry, and the gang having a party in their house. There was drinking and sex going on all over. The gang and Larry jumped out windows and ran out the back door, leaving Sidney alone to face the neighbors. She was devastated. I was devastated. Her stepdad was furious.

I felt helpless and powerless. Her stepdad grew more and more frustrated and angry as he became more and more determined to take control of the situation. He refused to believe that Sidney was unable—not unwilling—to control her impulses, and he punished her by yelling at her when she did something he did not like. Home life was awful, but her relationship with Larry provided no greater stability. Thus began a cycle of abuse and rescue of Sidney that escalated until I ended our marriage a year later.

SENSE OF RIGHT AND WRONG

Even though Sidney used extremely poor judgment, had little or no impulse control, and had the active hormones of puberty, she had a sense of right and wrong and wanted very much to do the right thing. Her inability to turn down the excitement, the sex, and the acceptance from Larry and his gang conflicted directly with her desire to meet her responsibilities at home and at school. She has a strong conscience, but she also wants to please the people she is with.

This was the time I finally emerged from the denial that had protected me from accepting the impossible truth. Sidney's diagnosis of FAS was indeed accurate, and I began to take the focus off academic success and place it on basic survival.

Fortunately, the day after the incident with our neighbors, Sidney was scheduled to visit her father for two weeks. When she returned, we had all cooled down and were better able to deal with the whole affair.

FACING SEXUALITY

This situation brought up some very strong issues with me. I painfully realized that my 15-year-old daughter had not only been lying and sneaking out at night, she was sexually active as well. It was difficult for me to accept that she was exploring her sexuality. When I could take some deep breaths and gather myself to think, I realized that my difficulty was related to the powerful messages I had learned in the past: sex was dirty, sinful, and unforgivable before marriage. I examined my own guilt and shame, and recognized that I had been projecting my mother's beliefs onto Sidney. I was deeply saddened at these insights and was determined to handle things differently with my daughter.

Reversing my feelings about Sidney's sexuality took the full two weeks she was visiting her father. After her return, we attended a class for mothers and daughters about sexuality and birth control. This was not the first time we had discussed the subject of sexuality, but it was the first class we attended. We both learned a lot, including how to put on a condom, using a banana. I improved at being matter of fact and nonjudgmental about sex, not to mention the use of condoms. Now she takes birth control pills, and she's upset if she does not take them exactly at seven each night.

While we learned about sexuality, Sidney told me she wanted to stay away from Larry and the gang. With mixed emotions, we settled on changing schools, but the separation was more difficult than she expected. After about three days Larry and Sidney tracked each other down. One day Sidney's principal called to say she had skipped classes. By the end of the day, I had talked to police about Larry and was told, "He has a record as long as your arm. He transports girls over state lines. You can't let your daughter be with him," etc., etc., etc. The police also told me they had an agreement with Larry that if he reached age 18 without getting in trouble again, they would erase his criminal record. But if caught, he would be prosecuted as an adult and keep his record.

When I picked up Sidney from school that day, I told her, "You can't ever see Larry again!" She looked at me, stopped speaking, and became catatonic. Her eyes were glazed, and she did not move any part of her body. This complete shut down lasted several hours. By way of the hospital emergency room, she was admitted to the psychiatric hospital with a diagnosis of severe depression.

At $1,000 a day, she was finally in a safe place. Her hospital stay lasted for three days and became a turning point, due to the help of a psychiatrist who understood FAS and teenagers. Following her discharge from the hospital, Sidney continued to meet with him for a year. The counseling was very helpful. The focus of the counseling was decision making, self-esteem building, and how to use good judgment.

GETTING LARRY TO HELP SIDNEY

When I got home from the hospital after Sidney's admission, I found a letter from Larry taped to my front door. He wrote that he was "deeply in love" with Sidney and that it was "unfair" to keep them apart. As I read the letter, I knew exactly what to do, a certainty that gave me a great sense of calm. I called Larry and made a date for coffee at the hospital cafeteria.

We talked. I told him that Sidney had some brain damage due to my drinking when I was pregnant, which caused her to have problems with impulse control. We talked about how my family was predisposed to alcoholism and addiction, that drinking and drugs were dangerous for Sidney, and that I knew he would want the very best for her because he loved her so much.

I also told him I had been unfair to him because I had given Sidney a set of rules, but had not told him what these rules were. We talked about what rules would be right for them. First, I insisted that he not ask her to skip school, and that she not be allowed to leave school at any time, even if she begged him to do otherwise. The second rule involved curfews. On school nights, she needed to be in the house at 8:30 P.M. because she needed extra sleep. I pointed out that Sidney needed time to calm down after excitement. She listened to music, for example, to calm herself down after school. The curfew was negotiable on weekends for dances and movies.

As long as they observed the rules, Larry could date Sidney. Needless to say, I thought of about a hundred other rules I could have insisted on, but I didn't want to diminish the power of the two rules we had agreed on.

I also told him that I knew about his problems with the police and would find a reason to turn him in if he goofed up.

Larry agreed to my conditions. After Sidney left the hospital, he and Sidney became an item. He asked her to marry him at the homecoming dance a couple of weeks later. She was in the tenth grade, and he had been in high school for four years and was far from graduating. Larry told me with great dignity that they would wait to marry until after she graduated. I restrained myself from asking, "How about after you graduate, Larry?" Instead I managed to say, "Congratulations," and worked hard at my 12-step program, which dictates that I let go and let a higher power take over.

Over the next three years Larry became a part of the family— a mixed blessing. He stole money from me, but he never broke our rules. On a couple of occasions, he made sure Sidney listened to me and followed suggestions I made. One difficult day, Sidney ran out the door screaming, "I'm running away. I will never see you again." I sat for about ten minutes crying, angry, frustrated, helpless, considering all the options, and finally accepting that I might never see her again. Then the front door opened and there was Larry carrying a very angry, howling Sidney. He put her down on the floor and said, "You stay with your mother. You are not old enough to leave home yet!"

LOOKING FOR THE RIGHT JOB

Sidney graduated from high school with a GPA of over 3.0. She had a diploma in hand but no plans for the future. After breaking up with Larry in her senior year, she fell in love with another young man, only to have him end the relationship after graduation. Both her brother and sister had recently married and before long, each had a son with their respective partners. Without a boyfriend, these joyful family events made Sidney painfully aware of her loneliness. She was grieving and depressed, and not in a frame of mind to seek a job, much less a career.

In her senior year, she had worked for about a month at a local hotel, turning down the sheets on the beds and placing a chocolate on the pillows each evening. Interviewing, being accepted,

punching a time clock, arriving at work on time, and carefully following prescribed tasks did build her confidence. But she quit
after an incident in which she could not understand the supervisor's
instructions: the supervisor got angry with her, and she felt
overwhelmed. So, what to do next?

Cats and kittens were among Sidney's favorite pets, so I
thought about a career for her with animals. At an early age, she
had decided she wanted to become a veterinarian, but I worried
about feelings of failure once again, knowing she would never be
able to satisfy the requirements. I turned her focus to related voca-
tions, and we began searching. We found a school with a veterinary
technician program, but the curriculum included chemistry, advanced animal anatomy, and many other difficult courses. Sidney
looked through local technical college programs and picked the
dental assistant program as a possibility. She failed the required
placement test. A visit to the school counselor revealed she could
have taken the test with extra time and help if she had disclosed
her FAS before the test, and now it was too late to retake it.

The counselor gave her a vocational interest and aptitude test.
Sidney was not interested in anything much, the counselor said,
and she was such an introvert that she didn't think Sidney could
do much in this world.

A career counselor who was a friend of mine agreed to look
over Sidney's tests and spend an hour with her. In that hour, the
counselor and Sidney agreed that she would do best in a job using
her hands. My friend talked to Sidney about how an introvert and
extrovert were just different from each other, each type being just
fine, and Sidney decided she would prefer a job where she was not
on the front lines and not working with people. She and Sidney
brainstormed about places where an introvert might be happiest.

With the counselor's encouragement, Sidney registered for
two computer courses at the vocational school. She could take these
courses until she felt comfortable enough with her skills to look
for a job using them. Sidney was pleased because she had felt
pressured to find work right away. She also decided to take piano
lessons to give her fingers a workout and to continue playing the

music she loved so much. The counselor also told Sidney it was a good thing she had not passed the test for dental assistant or enrolled in classes in veterinary technology because these classes were not organized in ways that help students who need to move slower or who need extra assistance. She completed her computer classes successfully, and her piano teacher told her that she was very talented. Though she has not used these skills in the workplace, her achievements enhanced her self-esteem, and this has been very important in her job searches and day-to-day living.

Soon Sidney found a job washing dogs and cats for a pet grooming shop. She and I felt much better. In fact, Sidney was smiling for the first time in two months.

Preparing Sidney for Living Alone

Sidney was happy. She had places to go at certain times, structure in her life, and she was doing what she was able to do with success. I felt it was time to prepare her for living on her own.

Learning to Drive

I had already agonized over whether she should be allowed to get a driver's license. After much thought, and working with my own 12-step program, I decided to let a higher power, the state of Washington, make that decision. Sidney had passed driver education classes with no problem. She passed both the written and road tests the first time.

Letting her drive was a good decision. She is extremely careful and pays close attention. Driving through traffic is difficult because so many stimuli are coming in, but she has not had any accidents and has received only two tickets. One citation was for driving 25 miles an hour in a 35-mile-an-hour zone. I accompanied her to court, and after she explained the circumstances to the magistrate, he halved the fine. The other ticket was for driving in a lane designated for car pools only. This time she went to court by herself to talk to the judge. She dressed in a businesslike fashion for the meeting, just as she would for an interview. She told her story to the judge, and he dismissed the case.

Sidney prefers to drive when the traffic is light. Her driving is excellent, and she can now get around on her own and feel good about herself.

Handling Money

Dealing with money has always been a big problem for Sidney. She can add, subtract, multiply, divide, and even keep a checkbook. She keeps track of her own bills, paying the living expenses first, such as the rent and the electricity. But she has no concept of what anything costs, and $3, $30, $300, and possibly $3,000 all have the same meaning for her. She will not buy a necessity for $3 but will spend $30 on something frivolous without worrying about it.

I helped her open a bank account and carefully taught her how to use a checkbook. For several months, we worked on the checkbook together until I thought she was doing fine. Some time later, Sidney revealed that she did not keep track of her account balance the way I taught her. Instead, she called the bank each day to find out what her balance was. Fortunately, her bank does not charge for the service.

I wish Sidney did not share my attitude about money. I always felt I needed to be able to support myself and my family, whether I was married or not. I talked about how we can't count on anybody else to take care of us. Now Sidney is determined to take responsibility for herself. She agonizes about not having enough money and being forced to depend on anyone.

Cooking, Cleaning, and Car Maintenance

Sidney needed to experience being alone and taking care of herself on a regular basis, so I arranged my work schedule to be away from home at dinner time so she could have a chance to prepare her own meal without me. I worked with her on how to comparison shop and choose better buys, made grocery lists with her, and let her shop by herself. We talked a lot about nutrition, which she had studied in high school cooking and home economics classes. Although Sidney does not routinely practice good nutrition, she can talk about the right kinds of food to eat each day, and she gets down on herself for not eating better.

I hired her to clean the house each week and taught her how to tidy the bathrooms and kitchen, change the beds, vacuum and dust, and do all the other chores. She drove a car I had provided, and I carefully taught her how to get the oil changed and the car maintained regularly.

Gradually, I left her home for longer and longer periods, first for a weekend, and then a week, and finally two weeks. I was careful to give her telephone numbers so she could reach me and to provide lists of things to do while I was gone—water the plants, empty the garbage, make her bed, clean the kitchen sink. She was so proud of herself that she had picked up the house and finished the lists by the time I came home.

I could not teach her how to motivate herself if she did not have a class or job to go to, nor could I figure out how to teach her to structure her time. When I was not at home to do this for her, she slept most of the time and watched a lot of TV. She was terribly bored when she did not have a job or something to do that someone else had planned for her.

UPS AND DOWNS: TRYING TO GET WORK

Sidney wanted to drive from Seattle to San Diego to visit her sister and go to school in preparation for finding a job. I gave my wholehearted support for making the trip, saying that she needed to find someone to drive with her, and that she could not come home until she had explored all her options, just as if she were going away to college. After much commotion and a few traumatic events, Sidney and a driver left Seattle with the car packed to the ceiling. The drive to San Diego tested her decision-making skills on more than one occasion, and she did very well.

Because of her experience washing dogs and cats, she decided to learn to groom dogs. When she reached San Diego, she found a dog grooming school. She investigated the school, gathered written materials, and called me. She had done a wonderful job researching schools and being her own advocate. I agreed to pay her tuition (directly to the school, of course) and to buy the equipment she needed. The school was 12 weeks long and, even though it was hard, she said she knew she could do it. She was very excited.

When Sidney left, she assured me she was moving away forever so she made sure to pack all her belongings. During the next three months, she called me three times and said, "I can't stay here. *I hate my sister* and this place. The car is packed and I am coming home!" On one occasion, she said, "If you don't let me come home, I'm going to stay in the navy barracks." I managed to keep my cool each time and told her calmly and clearly: "You can't come home until June. That was our deal." To her threat about the navy barracks, I answered, "O.K., honey, if that is what you want to do."

In May she graduated from dog grooming school with a certificate of completion. She was thrilled, and I couldn't have been happier if she had earned her diploma as a veterinarian. She was ready, she declared, to return home and look for a job. When she came home she went job-hunting right away and was disappointed that no one would hire her as a full groomer without having experience as an apprentice. She became awfully discouraged because she could not understand the concept of apprenticeship.

When she took a job as a "glorified dog washer," she remarked, "Why did I spend all that time in dog grooming school anyhow?" When she injured her back lifting a large dog and a chiropractor told her she should probably never work at lifting and washing large dogs again, she felt mixed emotions. Since she thinks in very concrete terms, she took this comment as the absolute truth, forever and ever. The dog grooming shop then assigned her "limited" work. Between trying to understand and fill out the forms for her work injury and learning to work the cash register, Sidney spent most of her time agitated. When she walked out on her job in a fit of hysterics, I was not surprised.

Sidney then volunteered at the fetal alcohol syndrome office at the University of Washington. Her supervisor said she did fine. "Sidney is so good to work with because she lets you know what she needs. I thought I was providing enough structure. But I wasn't.

She cued me in on when she needed breaks. She asked for help when I didn't realize she needed it." Sidney was still applying The Plan.

My friends told me that Sidney should apply to the Social Security Administration for benefits based on her FAS disability. I struggled with this path. Applicants must prove they will need the support for as long as they live. Will Sidney just give up and not even try? I couldn't stand to think about it. But what if something happened to me and I couldn't support her? After two years in the application process, the agency granted Supplemental Security Income (SSI) benefits.

Sidney Marries and Lives on Her Own

When Sidney was visiting her sister in San Diego, she began a relationship with a sailor; they fell in love and decided to get married. I was very pleased with the young man who chose Sidney and whom Sidney chose. He understood that Sidney had some limitations even though he did not appear to understand what that really meant. He loved Sidney just as she was, and she reciprocated. After calling the marriage off a couple of times, they held their wedding aboard his ship during a dependents' day cruise. They may be the first couple to have ever been married aboard a U.S. Navy ship while the ship was at sea!

While her husband is gone, Sidney lives alone in a small apartment. She has her difficulties, such as not eating right. But she is coping with one of the most difficult situations—a husband on sea duty. She does better than I did when her dad was at sea.

I know she cannot structure her time when she is alone. I know she gets depressed. At the same time, I believe and hope she is able to survive on her own. When I think back to the years when Sidney was at home and realize all the work that went into teaching her the skills to do just that, I wonder why I cried when she moved away. A big part of me wants to wrap Sidney in cotton, rescue her from the world, and keep her close to me so I can protect her from getting hurt. I will be there if she needs me, but Sidney is learning to live on her own. She is developing her courage and her confidence. Living on her own is working out, and I am proud of what she has accomplished.

ᕦ EPILOGUE ᕦ

Four years later, Sidney has had her ups and downs. But she is still happily married and happy in her new job as an assistant in a cat clinic. She lives not near me in Washington State but far away in Washington, D.C., with her husband and three cats. The move and transition were extremely difficult for Sidney. For several months, she suffered from depression and anxiety attacks and spent a lot of time sleeping.

Her husband called me for advice after he struggled with the need to do everything "on my own." Sidney got excellent counseling from advisors through the navy, but first she had to use The Plan. The psychiatrist originally assigned to Sidney said, "FAS? That shouldn't make any difference." Sidney let people know that this psychiatrist would not do! Her husband worked hard to get them into housing on the military base so Sidney would feel safe and he would be close to her should she need him. His commanding officer was very understanding and allowed him the time necessary to get Sidney stabilized.

Sidney has gained skills and self-confidence. She commutes with ease from Washington, D.C., to her job in Alexandria, Virginia. She adopted a kitten left at the clinic because it needed more care than the owners could give it. She has shown one of her cats in a cat show. Sidney is happy with her work, and her employers are happy with her. She has told the people at work about FAS, and they help her whenever necessary.

Sidney and her husband have chosen to remain in the Washington, D.C., area because jobs for him are so plentiful and because Sidney is so happy with her job at the cat clinic. I cried when they told me they were not moving back to the Northwest even though I knew the decision was a good one. Sidney is quite capable, with her very supportive and loving husband, of living on her own.

5

Why I Chose to Live Alone

SIDNEY GUIMONT[*]

*Sidney Guimont, the young woman in the previous chapter,
"Living Independently," was diagnosed with fetal alcohol
syndrome when she was 14. She has a high school diploma
and later earned a certificate in a dog grooming school. She
is married to a navy man and manages their household.
This chapter was written when she still lived near her mother
in Washington State. She later moved with her husband to
Washington, D.C, where she is employed at a cat clinic.*

I'M FINDING OUT WHO I AM INSTEAD OF STAYING HOME AND LETTING
my mother take care of me. If I were living at home, she would be
taking care of things.

I have always wanted to move out and take care of myself. At
first I was insecure about living alone. I didn't think I could handle
the finances, like taking care of bills. But I pay all the bills, including the rent, the phone bill, and the power bill—and I pay them on
time. I haven't missed one.

Paying bills is simple. But I haven't been balancing the
checkbook. My mom showed me how to do it, but my husband's
navy federal account is too confusing. This is how I handle the
checkbook: At the beginning of each month, I call to find out how
much money is in my account, and then I write the checks. I haven't
bounced any checks yet.

---

[*] This chapter is based on a transcription of a taped interview with Sidney Guimont
conducted by Judith Kleinfeld. Ms. Guimont edited the text and suggested changes.

When I visited my mother, I went back to my old bedroom, and it didn't feel like my house any more. I detached myself very well from my place. My mother and I have a wonderful relationship, but I never want to return home.

Getting Married

I married a navy man, someone who is used to a very structured lifestyle. When my husband is here, he provides structure for me. We constantly do things, and we sometimes battle to see who drives. We'll go to see our families. When we go to our families' houses for visits, my spirit completely cheers up. People say that my aura just glows.

Even when my husband is at work, he provides the structure I need. When he's at work, I get up and do things for myself. I get out of bed and clean the house and go to the store. We also work out together. He is a good instructor. At dinner time, we love to cook together. We love to sit down and talk. We do a lot of talking.

Right now he's out at sea. Keeping structure for myself is hard when I don't live at home. I find myself sitting in front of the TV a lot, and I'm depressed most of the time. Now when I go to the store, I feel so lonely. Little things like that will be more fun and more interesting to do when he gets back.

Soon he'll be home for a while. The next time he goes out, it will be a world cruise. He may get out of the navy, or he may go to a navy photography school. He's a great photographer. He may want to work with his father in Colorado. He has all these options. I've told him, "Whatever you want to do, I'll be at your side. If you want to move to Colorado, we'll move to Colorado. If you want to stay here, we'll stay here."

My Day

My day is pretty boring and lonely. Most of the time I don't even have the energy to get out of the apartment. Usually I get up at 11 in the morning and watch my favorite soap opera. If I don't feel lazy, I go down to the cabana in the apartment complex and work out for two hours. Then I come back up, have an apple and take a shower. I sit in front of the TV, take a nap, and get up again. Each night I record songs on Star 101.5; from 8 P.M. to 9 P.M., I listen to an hour of '80s music. It's a happy thing for me and cheers me up. About 11 P.M. I usually go to bed. I hate watching as much TV as I have been.

I can't have a lot of things coming at me. I have to do one thing at a time. If I have to clean the bathroom, I clean the bathroom. Every month I do a big cleaning. Every day I make sure the kitchen sink is empty or has just a couple of glasses in it. I hate things sitting around the counter in the kitchen. I don't let things pile up, except on the desk, where I have a lot of letters from my husband. On Friday I got two letters. Sometimes I write back the next day.

I write things down constantly: grocery lists, dates on the calendar so if my mom invites me to dinner I don't forget. Directions give me big problems, and I have trouble with street names and finding my way somewhere. I get lost and panic. Finding my way around the navy base is frustrating so I stay away from it. Navy wives like to gossip, and I am one of the few who shy away.

I do well in quiet situations without a lot of commotion. I don't even like going into a fast food place at lunch time—too many kids, too much noise, too much going on. When we got married on the ship, you could just see all the people coming in on the trip. I was overloaded and I got real sleepy, my way of shutting down.

My big thing right now is eating better. Last month I was eating pretty bad. I sat in front of the TV and ate ice cream. Now I'm getting the sweets out of the house. A couple of years ago, I didn't eat fruit and vegetables for a month. For dinner, I've taught myself how to make some things. Every once in a while, I cook up some pasta. I have my own little creation—Dinty Moore stew over the pasta.

About twice a week I call my mother for information—like about the car insurance. On weekends, I drive over there to see her and to visit a friend. I see my mother once or twice a week. I am trying to push myself to be more independent. When I first moved out, I was trying to cling.

Most of the time it's just me and my cat. My senior year in high school, I wanted to adopt a cat. A friend had a cat with kittens. I went into the trailer, and there was my kitten, sitting on the back of the couch. We sat for two hours, and the kitten fell asleep on my lap. She was the last kitten left, the runt of the litter. I named her Ashley because she is the color of ashes. Wherever I go, I'm not leaving my cat.

Problems with Paid Work

My vocational rehabilitation counselor called and said, "Be thinking about what you want to do." I need something to keep me busy. But it isn't so much a question of what job. It's more a question of the environment where I can work best. I need:

1. A quiet place.

2. Slow-paced work.

3. A workplace that is not too busy.

For two months, I did volunteer work at the Seattle FAS clinic. When we first started, we were mailing out New Year's cards. I folded the cards, printed address labels, stamped them, and mailed them. After that was done, I did copying. But that ended and there was nothing left to do. I'm just waiting now.

I love working with animals, but most of the occupations working with animals take at least four years of college. Some of these occupations are too fast-paced. For example, I worked bathing dogs. That sounds simple, but it's not. You may be working with one animal, but in actuality you are handling many animals at a time. Things come up—the groomer will ask you to answer the phone. Then you have to stop that and do something else—like clean up a mess or do towels.

I injured myself lifting a dog, which was very painful and upsetting. I told people I couldn't lift the dogs any more, so I answered

A SIMILAR EXPERIENCE TO SIDNEY'S:
HAVING A BOYFRIEND HELPS MY DAUGHTER SUCCEED
by Steve Williams*

My daughter Shannon,* who is 19, shows little outward sign of FAS/E. She may seem shy with anyone she doesn't know, but around family and friends she can be very outgoing. For the past three years she has been in a relationship with a man who is a year her senior and who is now in his fourth year of obtaining a computer science degree. Shannon worked through high school at a local pizza delivery restaurant. Now she takes various clerical, computer, and acccounting courses with the intent of obtaining an office job. I suspect this relationship has allowed her to be as successful as she has been. I would be concerned about her ability to live entirely upon her own resources.

_____

* Steve Williams and Shannon are pseudonyms.

the phone and helped customers pick up their animals. My problem was trying to communicate that doing too many things at once was difficult for me. I don't like asking for help. I ended up quitting abruptly. I wrote a note and said, "I'm sorry. I can't handle this any more." They were upset by that.

I need a job where I can do one thing at a time. Maybe I need a job that doesn't get paid by the hour but gets paid by the project.

ON MY OWN

My mother and I have a wonderful relationship. I was the baby of the family. When I was driving away, she was sobbing, and I was also choked up. She also had to detach herself from me.

As a 21 year old, my advice to parents of young adults with FAS is: "Don't smother us. Give us space. Let us know that you are there for us. Don't push us out. Give us stable ground, like my Mom did. I always knew she was there. But at the same time, she didn't hold me back."

6
How I Grew Up with FAE
Stef Pummell

Stef Pummell was diagnosed with FAE when she was a senior in high school. After she graduated, she joined the navy, where she met her future husband. After the birth of their son, Stef left the navy and now devotes her time to raising their child, working at a paid job, and managing the household while her husband is at sea.

Like my sister, Sidney Guimont,[*] I was affected by my mother's drinking while she was pregnant. I have been diagnosed as having fetal alcohol effects (FAE). Because my mother wasn't as advanced in her alcoholism when she was pregnant with me, my problems are not quite as severe as my sister's.

For most of my life, I have been angry about something or other, and when I wasn't angry, it was because I was too depressed or too happy. There was no middle ground and no warning about when my mood would shift or what would set me off. In the fall of 1987, after a suicidal episode, I visited a psychiatrist who discovered that the tremendous ups and downs I experienced were due to bipolar disorder, a chemical imbalance in my brain. I took lithium, and my life finally seemed to level out.

I wasn't diagnosed with FAE until I graduated from high school, so everyone assumed that I was smart but lazy. I earned *Bs* and *Cs*, receiving good comments about participation and attitude, usually followed by remarks about "not working up to potential" or "could make more effort." I did well in hands-on subjects like art

---

[*] Sidney Guimont tells her own story in the previous chapter, "Living Independently."

109

and architecture, but math courses seemed beyond me, supposedly because I never bothered to apply myself.

Then I had problems with men. I became sexually active at the age of 16 and then followed a self-destructive path of sleeping with guys I dated—no matter how long I had known them. All that was necessary was for me to be physically attracted to them. I never thought about consequences. The only thing that mattered was that they liked me. My attitude led to quite a few one-night stands, and, eventually, date rape.

I graduated from high school without much idea of what to do next. I began working in a series of jobs that never lasted, usually because of my anger. I was asked to quit my first job in the kitchen at a Bible camp when my hostility toward a fellow worker grew out of control. My mom told me that if I wanted to continue living at home, I would have to attend meetings at a 12-step program called Emotions Anonymous. Between the lithium and the EA meetings, I began to learn some control over this intense anger.

That fall I attended Bellevue Community College while living at home and working part-time at a day care center. I managed to earn a 3.6 grade point average the first semester, but because of the lack of structure, my grades slid downhill in the next group of courses I took. I chalked it up to bad teachers. I started a new job at an insurance company, working part-time after school and enjoying the new sensation of business clothes.

Around this time, my sister Sidney was diagnosed as having FAS. My mom involved me in the tests as well, even though I didn't appear to have the same learning difficulties as my sister. The physical tests proved negative, and because I didn't exhibit the more serious problem of FAS, the doctors could do nothing to help me understand why I did the things I did.

I moved out of my parents' home and moved into an apartment with a woman I'd met at school. I still worked part time, and Mom sent me additional money every month. I was responsible for my food, shelter, clothing, and transportation, as well as entertainment and massive car expenses from a faulty transmission problem.

After getting fired from a job as a nanny because I couldn't structure my time, I found myself looking in the newspaper at the want ads and discovered two horrible things: Nothing looked like something I wanted to do, and the only jobs that looked interesting were things I was not qualified to do. So when Mom suggested the military, I grudgingly agreed to call.

The recruiters were so enthusiastic and complimentary that it pulled me out of my apathy during the three days of academic and physical testing. Without stopping to think about the consequences, I became a member of the United States Navy. When the time to leave for the navy rolled around eight months later, I was not really ready to go anymore. I now had a life I didn't want to leave behind—friends who didn't want to see me go, a successful part-time job as a temporary office worker, and a position as a caregiver for kids who wanted me to stay. But I left for Orlando, Florida, where my new life would begin.

Boot camp was hell on earth. From the first day, I wanted to go home. Suddenly, I was confronted with my huge fear of failure—I had never succeeded at anything, and I was sure I wouldn't succeed at this. The only problem was, if I failed, I would be punished by the company commanders, and I was afraid of that more than anything.

This fear of failure actually motivated me to accomplish things I never thought I could do. I used to pass out when getting shots, but in boot camp, I didn't even wince. I hated to run, but I passed my physical readiness tests. I despised studying, but I always earned the highest scores on tests. As the weeks went by, I persevered, thanks to the encouragement of a company commander who gave me the best pep talk of my life during a particularly rough period. By the end of boot camp, I had painted our company flag, painted a mural on a wall, acted as mail petty officer for the company, and received the highest academic scores in a company of 65 women. I ran the final physical readiness test with bronchitis and passed that, too. I had actually finished what I had started, thanks to the structure and constant motivation provided in the navy.

With some ups and downs, school went pretty well, and I surprised myself by actually liking what I was learning. I found a formula: if I could picture the concept in my head—create a mental image—I got it just fine. I always did well on the labs because I could touch the concepts and put them into practice.

I was not on lithium at this time, and my mood swings returned—along with the anger. At times, I became so angry I was reduced to crying jags or even striking the cinder block walls with my fists. Once, my vision blacked out and my company commanders sent me to the psychiatric ward because they were afraid I would hurt myself. I argued with classmates and was generally known to be moody and difficult.

Eventually, I met James, who became my husband in April 1993. He is a good man—patient, kind, loyal, and smart, and he shares my sense of humor. He was also in the military, so we could commiserate on the daily stresses we endured. Two months after we married, I got pregnant. I requested a discharge from the navy, and we transferred to California.

Living on little money in a cramped apartment, we fought frequently, and my moods deepened. I returned to work after my son was born, and things improved between James and me for a little while. Unfortunately, working just cured some of the excuses for all that anger, and I soon found other reasons to vent it. The strange thing was, this anger was physically painful. I felt adrenaline running through my blood, and my arms and hands would tingle with it. When that happened, I had to either yell and scream, or sob uncontrollably. The cause could be anything from a car that didn't signal when it turned to watching the news on television.

I knew I needed help. My marriage was falling apart, and I was a wreck. I went through all the military health care red tape and saw a doctor who prescribed the medications I needed—not just lithium, but Zoloft and Prozac as well. Together they have removed the depression and the intense anger, and now I can think clearly again. I also became involved with a church group, where I learned that it takes a lot of work every day to make a marriage strong.

My husband is stationed on an aircraft carrier out of Norfolk, Virginia, that is out to sea for two months. When James is at sea, I'm a single mom with the full responsibility of working, managing a household, and caring for a two-year-old boy. It's not easy, but I have learned many things about myself over the past ten years. One is that planning for the future is impossible for me. Tomorrow is an abstract idea, whereas today is something I can work with. Second, I need to be on medications—always. Without them, I can't think properly, and I can't control my emotions. Third, I need to be held accountable for my life and that's why I attend the church I do. Not only am I accountable to God, but to God's family as well. At church I receive the advice, the support, and the friendships I need.

All this hard work has not been without reward. I have survived things that many people with FAS/E do not survive, and I am thankful for my life because of it. I don't drink or use recreational drugs, and I don't smoke. Best of all, I have a beautiful little boy who has been given a chance at a full life because of the choices I have made.

7

Creating an "External Brain": Supporting a Mother and Child with FAS

SUSAN DOCTOR

Susan Doctor is a consultant specializing in FAS/E. She works with service providers from various organizations— schools, alcohol/drug treatment, drug court, social service and health agencies. In addition to her work as a consultant, Ms. Doctor is also an assistant professor at the University of Nevada at Reno. She concentrates on alcohol-related birth defects and fetal drug exposure.

I FIRST HEARD THE EXPRESSION "EXTERNAL BRAIN" FROM DR. STERLING Clarren while observing at the FAS Clinic in Seattle, Washington. Dr. Clarren directs the Fetal Alcohol Syndrome Program in the Department of Pediatrics at the University of Washington School of Medicine and is head of the Division of Congenital Defects. I listened to Dr. Clarren as he gently and compassionately explained to parents that, to one degree or another, depending on how severely the mother's use of alcohol had affected the fetus, their child would always need an external brain—beyond childhood, through adolescence, and into adulthood. The external brain is another way of saying that individuals with FAS need more guidance and direction than they can provide for themselves. As the person ages, the concept remains but service providers shift.

A Life Dominated by Alcohol

Many women suffering with alcohol problems want to keep their children, and this desire often compels them to seek and stay in treatment. Prior to entering treatment, they often live in shelters or on the streets, searching for refuge in gangs or with abusive sexual partners, use alcohol and drugs, and give birth to babies they are unable to care for.

Kim exemplifies this life course. Alcohol addiction has shaped her entire life. Her mother's addiction had progressed dramatically by the time Kim, the youngest of nine children, was conceived. Kim's parents divorced when she was one year old, and she lived with her father and stepmother, who owned a bar. Kim and her siblings went to the bar every day after school, studying or playing in the back room. Kim's older sister, with whom she was close, introduced her to alcohol when Kim was just five years old. She drank from that time forward.

Until she entered alcohol/drug treatment at age 33, no one ever suspected that she might have problems connected to her mother's prenatal consumption of alcohol. Kim was born in 1963, ten years before FAS was first diagnosed in the United States. There was no reason for anyone to connect her learning and behavior problems with her mother's alcoholism. Kim found school fun and was popular with her peers, always out for a good time and willing to do almost anything on a whim. She reports that her academic problems did not begin until middle school, although I believe that her school-related difficulties began long before then.

Around the ninth grade, Kim discovered the Hell's Angels. She ran off for weeks at a time to ride with the gang and then returned home and attended school for brief periods before riding again. She dropped out of school in the eleventh grade. At age 14, she had formed a romantic relationship with one of the Angels. After riding as his partner for eight years, she gave birth to her first child, a son. Her drinking increased, and she abused many other substances as well. She knew she was unable to care for her son properly and gave legal guardianship to his paternal grandparents when he was five.

Four years later she tired of riding with the Angels and for the next seven years she "hopped rigs," hitching rides from truckers who picked her up and allowed her to stay with them until they tired of her. During this time she also began a relationship with her present partner, hopping a truck and leaving him for months before returning to his accepting arms. Early in life, Kim became aware that she needed outside help in order to survive, and she aligned herself with anyone who would accept her presence and run her life for her.

Unfortunately, the men she chose were domineering and usually cruel. Without fail they enabled her addiction. Following a dispute with one boyfriend, she drank a gallon of vodka a day for three consecutive days, and had to be rushed to the emergency room; Kim was seven and a half months pregnant at the time. With the exception of these three days, Kim drank a fifth of vodka a day before and during her pregnancy, living in frequent blackout states.

CREATING AN EXTERNAL BRAIN FOR KIM

Following her emergency room experience, and several weeks of hospital detoxification, Kim entered Step 2, a residential treatment center for women and their children, where I have consulted with the staff for five years. Initially I focused on the children in the house, who had all been exposed to alcohol or drugs in utero. Many of their mothers receiving treatment are children of alcoholic mothers themselves and have difficulty with their recovery programs.

Kim, an adult child of an alcoholic mother, struggled to comply with her suggested program of recovery. When she was referred just a few weeks before delivering her daughter, Hannah, she was sober for the first time since she was five. She assured me she was not sober by choice but because she was being observed closely and did not want to have her baby removed from her at delivery. She had absolutely no intention of staying sober after she delivered the baby.

We discussed her mother's drinking and then helped her deal with her feelings about the possibility that she might have FAS/E as a result of her mother's drinking while pregnant. Her mother had died recently, and Kim didn't want to talk about her. She was, however, open about her own anger, sadness, and relief at knowing that, possibly, the chaos of her life wasn't entirely her fault.

For the most part, she complied with the expectations of her program. These included keeping her living space neat and clean, completing a daily goal plan, and completing written assignments, given by her primary counselor. Written assignments are individualized to address issues specific to recovery from addiction: relapse prevention, getting a job or going back to school, keeping a home, and so on.

Though Kim was not diagnosed with FAS or FAE, she gave every indication of being alcohol affected. For this reason, we began working with her differently right from the beginning of the treatment program. Take the program requirement of keeping her living space neat and clean. Kim's counselor would tell her to clean her room and then get frustrated when Kim wouldn't do it. I knew that, for people with FAS/E, there is a huge difference between *wouldn't* and *couldn't*. I reminded the counselor that Kim had been living on the street since age 14, making two explanations of Kim's actions possible: Kim might not understand what the command meant, or she might not know how to do everything entailed in carrying out the command. The following week, Kim's counselor reported that she had told Kim, "I want to be able to see the floor of your room," so Kim had cheerfully gathered up everything piled on the floor of her room, placed it on the floor of her closet, closed the door, and proudly gone to get her counselor to show her that she had completed the task!

I persuaded the staff that Kim interpreted statements literally and thus really believed she was doing what she had been asked to do. They were willing to give it one more try, but, knowing well the strong, often negative feelings evoked by individuals with this profile, I knew I'd better produce some results soon or else.

What saved us was one of the other women who had arrived at Step 2 at about the same time as Kim. This woman was willing to be Kim's "big sister" and teach her how to clean a room. She took Kim into her room and patiently told her where to put everything.

She did not do anything for Kim; she simply told her, one step at a time, what to do. Then she gave the key instruction that will remain with Kim forever. She said, "Whenever you take anything out of its place, put it back in the exact same place." No problem. From then on, Kim was able to keep her room sparkling clean, the staff was agape in amazement, and I breathed a sigh of relief. A "big sister" had provided an external brain for Kim.

LEARNING TO TAKE CARE OF HANNAH

The young woman who couldn't keep her room clean without definitive instruction was now the mother of a newborn diagnosed with FAE. Kim had great difficulty dealing with the diagnosis. In her guilt-driven denial, she laughed and told me that she knew there was nothing wrong with Hannah: her baby was perfect. But she has been impeccable about reporting to me, her counselor, or anyone else who will listen, the problems that Hannah has with feeding, kinesthetic hypersensitivity, tremulousness, and so on. Hannah was asymmetrical; there was a dissimilarity in corresponding parts of her body, and one of her ears was higher than the other, indicating the possibility of irregular brain growth. As a result, she required physical therapy to assist her development. Kim had trouble accepting this and carrying out the necessary exercises because they made the baby cry. We set up a reward system because it is impossible to convey the long-term benefits to Kim.

We also taught Kim other mothering techniques that can help babies with FAS/E. In order to decrease the child's hypersensitivity to being touched, Kim learned to feed Hannah with Hannah's back against her chest, with Hannah looking away from her mother rather than facing her.* We taught Kim to prepare Hannah for transitions, to bathe her gently and gradually, and to take her to the quiet of her room if the house was too noisy and Hannah showed alarm. We showed her how to read Hannah's cues telling her mother that she was stressed and needed a break. Kim learned well when taught in a manner that she could understand.

---

* For more information, see Jan Hinde, "Early Intervention for Alcohol-Affected Children," in Kleinfeld and Wescott, 136.

Hannah was such a gorgeous baby and so well-behaved that the whole house was involved with her. I worked to help others understand that providing relief is one thing, but forcing Hannah to live in a world with a constantly changing caregiver is unfair and unproductive. Begrudgingly, the staff agreed not to run to get the baby the moment she fussed but to inform Kim instead.

The External Brain in Action

We worked hard to teach Kim to ask for help when she needed it and to be very clear with us when we had asked something of her that she didn't understand. I watched her face and body language closely so I could tell when she appeared confused. I then paused to ask her if she understood me. If she didn't, I tried to be more specific, presenting information in smaller pieces. I praised her for telling me when she didn't understand what I said. She learned quickly and responded well. This is a primary factor in the success or failure of people with FAS/E. If individuals can be taught to ask for help and to say when they do not understand, they have a good chance of getting the help they need. But people with FAS/E need to be taught these skills.

Kim and Hannah required many appointments with service providers. When Kim knew she would be scared, feel guilty, or probably wouldn't understand, she asked one of us to go with her to interpret. I found it interesting to watch the range of reactions of professionals when Kim said candidly that her mother drank when pregnant with her and that a possible result was her difficulty in processing information. She always asked the service providers if they minded if I was present so that I could help her to understand what was happening. Kim explained to the occupational therapist assessing Hannah why I was present, and from that point, the therapist simplified her vocabulary, using concrete examples. When she wanted Kim to do an exercise with Hannah, she demonstrated on Kim first, and then demonstrated on the baby, only then allowing Kim to try it on the baby. I was very impressed with this wise and respectful response to Kim's request for help.

I learned that most professionals speak too quickly, give too many directions at once, use words their clients do not understand, present them with many papers to read, and refer them to other service providers for further assistance. Someone like Kim is unable to process all of this. If no one who understands her special needs accompanies her, she is lost and embarrassed. To save face, she pretends to understand, but she isn't able to follow through after leaving the office and is then judged irresponsible and noncompliant.

Kim progressed well through the academic phase of her recovery program, but emotionally she seemed to prepare for failure. I often reminded her that the best gift she could give Hannah was her sobriety; all would be lost if she drank again. She agreed, halfheartedly. She commented about holding herself back from bonding with Hannah "just in case" and made arrangements with friends to take Hannah if she drank again. Although this frightened me, I understood and was quietly pleased that she was being responsible enough to protect her baby. The ongoing threat of losing Hannah should she drink again was Kim's primary motivation for remaining sober, but it also created stress that, paradoxically, could lead to a relapse.

PREPARING KIM FOR LIFE ON HER OWN

The time came for Kim and Hannah to move from the residence to the halfway house. To maintain the external brain that we'd developed for her, we decided to move her with the other three women with whom she had entered treatment, in the belief that Kim received a lot of love and support from her peers. Kim asked the woman who taught her how to keep her room clean to help her pack, move, and unpack her things, and their new life in the new setting began easily and smoothly.

The ease was short-lived. Kim had applied for subsidized housing when she moved from residential treatment, usually a process of several months to a year. To our surprise, Kim was approved for a two-bedroom apartment three weeks after moving to the halfway house. We tried to be supportive while we worked quickly to find some new way to keep the external brain going. Kim, who wanted to be on her own and to function as a mother, was thrilled.

Her counselor and I met with Kim's romantic partner and discussed how to support her in the way she needed. He wanted to help and made every effort to follow our recommendations. When she went to his apartment he removed all alcohol. He did not drink around her and refused to allow any of his friends to drink or use other drugs when she was present. As an untrained observer, sometimes he told us that we were exaggerating the extent of her problem.

With Kim in an apartment, we had no leverage to maintain support of the external brain. All we could do was continue to be supportive when Kim asked for help—and be patient. Kim was ecstatic and relieved to be free from the limits of in-house treatment. She was pleased to be able to move herself one step closer toward independent living.

The Return to Drinking and Drugs

Within three months after Kim's move to her own apartment, our efforts seemed to unravel. Soon after leaving the halfway house, Kim developed severe abdominal pain. She put off going to the doctor until, doubled over from the severity of the pain, she dragged herself into a hospital emergency room in the middle of the night. She didn't tell the staff that she was an alcoholic in recovery, and they gave her Vicodin (an opiate pain medication) and morphine. It turned out Kim had developed an ovarian cyst. She underwent surgery to remove the cyst, but within three days after leaving the hospital, she was drinking alcohol and shooting heroin with the sister who had introduced her to alcohol 28 years earlier. She placed Hannah with the couple who had agreed to take her. We were heartsick.

My biggest fear was that she would hop a truck and be gone forever. But she didn't. She drank, shot heroin, and called us. She also called the couple, many times each day, to check on Hannah. She called me frequently in the middle of the night, and once when she begged for help I arranged for her to return to the detox center. After 36 hours, she checked herself out of the center and returned to relieving her physical and emotional pain with drugs and alcohol. She wouldn't come home to her apartment in Reno. She wasn't done drinking and using drugs.

Despite my fear and discouragement, I thought that her concern for Hannah might be the leverage we needed to once again establish an external brain for her. To protect themselves from liability, the friends who were caring for Hannah had reported the baby's temporary living situation to Child Protective Services (CPS). When Kim returned—and I never doubted that she would—she would be in the system and would have to go through CPS regarding Hannah. Kim drank and used drugs for another week before going to the couples' house, picking up Hannah, and calling me and her counselor. She said that she was ready to stop using alcohol and drugs.

RE-ESTABLISHING KIM'S EXTERNAL BRAIN

The entire Step 2 staff agreed that Kim should start over again in residential treatment. Kim begged and pleaded otherwise until she talked the staff into an outpatient treatment contract that allowed her to keep her subsidized housing. Among other things, the contract required Kim to stay sober, attend Alcoholics Anonymous (AA) every day for three months, participate in counseling groups, check in daily with her AA sponsor and her counselor, and enter the Step 2 residential program (with Hannah) if the treatment staff thought it necessary. Discouraged by the previous three weeks of drinking alcohol and use of heroin, and determined to keep her daughter, Kim returned to her apartment. (Because I was only a consultant at Step 2, I could only voice my opinion. I would have definitely insisted on her return to residential treatment—and I would have been wrong. She was so grateful to keep her apartment that she was willing to do anything.)

Her commitment was soon tested when a Child Protective Services case worker visited her. Kim received papers in the mail that she didn't understand, so she called me to ask for my help. The county was suing for legal custody of Hannah, allowing Kim to keep physical custody. Much to Kim's consternation, all of her support people favored this move since it wouldn't remove Hannah from her mother but would provide protection should she drink again.

Reno's family courts are understanding, with caring judges who are knowledgeable about the problem of prenatal drug and alcohol exposure. I trained many of them. When the judge saw me there with Kim, she realized that my presence indicated the possibility of fetal alcohol exposure. She then addressed Kim clearly and simply.

The county based its case on two charges: that Kim had failed treatment, and that she had neglected Hannah. She did not deny the first charge—who could?—but balked at the word "neglect" in the second charge because she did not believe she had been negligent. She was hurt and incensed at the charge. She explained repeatedly to the judge that she had been cautious when choosing a place for Hannah to stay. When she was drinking and using drugs, she called the couple taking care of Hannah several times each day to make sure that Hannah was well cared for. When the county social worker fought against dropping the charge of child neglect, Kim wept quietly, along with several others in the courtroom. The judge asked the counselor and me what we thought, and we agreed that Kim had carefully planned protection for her baby and was ignorant of how her behavior would be interpreted legally. After making certain that removal of the charge of neglect would not interfere with the proceedings, the judge agreed to remove that paragraph from the papers. Kim calmed down immediately and seemed at ease, even though she had obtained only physical custody of her daughter and the county had legal custody. She was content because there was no longer a charge against her that she considered unfair.

CONCLUSION

Life with Kim continues its ups and downs. Kim gets frustrated with what she considers our interference in her life. Actually, she only considers it interference when she doesn't like what we are doing; all other times she is grateful and even solicitous. She continually pushes the limits and often calls me to vent her frustration. Each time she calls, I let her talk until she has spent her anger. Then I tell her to go get Hannah. After she has come back to the telephone with Hannah, I remind her that many people love her and that Hannah is the reason for her commitment to recovery. So far, this concrete reminder always helps her calm down.

Hannah, at the time of this writing, is 11 months old. She has ear infections that will require surgery. Her asymmetry still requires occupational therapy, and she sees a speech therapist. Recently, the community health nurse who visits Kim weekly discovered that Hannah's skull is closing prematurely. Kim is frightened about this latest development and has asked for a support person to accompany her to the doctor's office when Hannah is checked. We will recommend testing for Hannah to enter an early childhood special education program when she reaches age three to give her the head start she may need with school.

In spite of everything, Hannah is a beautiful, happy baby. She crawled, sat up, stood, and walked right on schedule. She clearly benefits from early intervention services that have been her good fortune since she was born. I often wonder how different things would be for Kim today if she had the same early interventions that Hannah receives.

Kim's external brain has been thoughtfully, painstakingly built piece by piece by dozens of caring people. Because Kim is an adult who wishes to function like other women her age, she creates a double bind by declaring, "Go away. Let me live my life without your interference," accompanied by, "I'm scared to death. Please help me." Consequently, for us to be able to continue to provide Kim the support she needs, two things must happen. We need to make this external brain more positive and appealing to her than that offered by a drug provider or abusive man. And we need to ensure that the external brain is in place, without a hitch, for the rest of Kim's life.

8
Finding Hope in a Troubled Life
JANEEN BOHMANN

Janeen Bohmann lives in the upper peninsula of Michigan. She is the stay-home parent of a five-year-old boy. Before her son was born, she was a preschool teacher.

MY BROTHER ERIC IS 27 YEARS OLD AND HAS NOT LIVED OUTSIDE AN institutional or supervised setting for more than six months since the age of 14.

To outside observers his life fits the stereotypical worst-case scenario of people with FAS/E. However, from my perspective, many positive and successful developments have ocurred in his life. He has had many successes in his life and has made great progress in controlling the impulsive behavior that continues to get him into trouble. He is less depressed than he was when he was younger, more aware of his limitations, and less eager to blame his behavior on other people. When he does make mistakes, the transgressions are less severe and less dramatic than in the past. He is a much happier and less angry person than he was five years ago. With appropriate support, a functional, sober, law-abiding, and fulfilling life is a realistic possibility for my brother.*

This story is my story, too. As his sister, who loves him so dearly, who has been so angry at what life has dealt him, I, too, have learned how to handle FAS.

---

* Editor's Note: When this book went to press, Eric was receiving this support through living with his aunt. But she is 86 years old, and Eric will need the types of group homes now so difficult to find for adults with FAS/E. See Epilogue, page 136.

BIRTH MOTHER

My parents divorced many years before my brother was born. As a result of my mother's alcoholism and depression, she was unable to care for my three sisters and me. My father was given custody of us, something very uncommon 30 years ago. My mother lived alone, and her alcoholism was chronic and severe by the time she gave birth to my brother. My relatives realized that Eric was not receiving good care, and so my aunt and uncle took him into their home.

When Eric was eight months old, my mother succeeded in one of her suicide attempts. After her death, my aunt and uncle became Eric's legal guardians, and he lived with them until he was 14.

I was 14 years old when my brother was born, and I loved him from the time he was a tiny baby. He was totally endearing as a child, and my bonds of love with him are strong. I have always known that Eric lived a troubled life, but not until he was 20 did I link my mother's drinking during pregnancy with his current problems.

FIRST ATTEMPT AT DIAGNOSIS

In 1975, when Eric was in first grade, his teachers realized he had learning and behavior problems, and they sent him to the Waisman Center, an excellent diagnostic and treatment center in Madison, Wisconsin, for evaluation. He participated in a full day of tests, and a social worker traveled 50 miles to his home to obtain family information. The center concluded that he was hyperactive and should avoid highly processed and sugary foods. Evaluators also noted his small head circumference. This analysis occurred in 1975, when awareness about FAS/E among the best professionals was limited or nonexistent.

Today this diagnostic center is one of the best, most supportive, and sensitive places in our region to evaluate children for FAS/E. A young child with FAS/E now would have many advantages not available to my brother.

SCHOOL YEARS

Eric attended special education classes throughout his public school career. He always lagged academically behind his peers, and some schoolchildren picked on him because he was different. One day I accompanied him to school. The bus ride made the biggest impression on me. Eric tried to attract attention from the other children by doing outrageous things for a laugh. Once he ate a worm. These attempts to seek acceptance only gained him more ridicule and taunting.

I am sure his behavior frustrated my aunt and uncle. They were in their sixties when they welcomed him as a sweet baby into their lives. He was extremely affectionate and fun to be with. On the other hand, he was very active, constantly lost his glasses, and was slow to learn such basic skills as using the toilet and tying his shoes.

Living in the country, Eric had almost no friends to play with. He spent a great deal of time with my uncle, helping him do chores and run errands. A family tragedy worsened Eric's problems in life. As he rested in bed one morning, he heard a gunshot. Since he lived in the country, he thought one of the neighbors was shooting at a stray dog. Later he went outside and found that our uncle, the man he called Dad, had shot himself in the head. Within days, my uncle died.

Before Eric had had a few problems with smoking and drinking. Now he began getting in trouble with the law. He stole cigarettes and used rocks to scratch cars. He became suicidal. More than once he swallowed large doses of my aunt's pills and was placed in the psychiatric unit of the local hospital. My aunt realized she could not keep Eric safe, and he entered a locked juvenile residential treatment facility.

This facility had an excellent staff and programs, but they treated a variety of difficult young people who taught Eric more serious criminal behavior. One day on an outing, a group of teenage residents sneaked away and stole a van. Eric joined them for the thrill of adventure, resulting in serious consequences such as tighter restrictions, being locked in his room, and even being sent to a locked psychiatric ward of this hospital. I believe part of him welcomed the punishment. He didn't believe he deserved a better life.

Between the ages of 14 and 18, Eric lived in several residential treatment centers. He learned a few skills, such as downhill skiing, a sport he loved for the thrills and took pride in. Very depressed, he was treated with many medications (e.g., Navane, Tranzene, Amitriptyline, Tegretol, Triavil), which produced side effects that he didn't like. Through counseling he gained some insight into himself, but he was not ready to benefit significantly. Unfortunately, the troubled teenagers in these centers also taught him more criminal behavior.

Becoming an Adult

My aunt and I felt both optimistic and terrified when Eric turned 18. Because of his age, he could no longer live in a residential treatment facility, so he moved to a group home. We realized that if he got into trouble now, he would go to jail.

One day, some of the residents and the woman who ran the group home held down Eric and forcibly cut his hair. Furious and humiliated, he released rabbits from a barn and set the barn on fire. The fire was quickly extinguished, but Eric, at age 18, had committed a felony—arson.

After many months in jail, he was released on probation. Soon something else angered him, and he decided to run away. He stole a car, and authorities caught him in another state. While on probation for this offense, he stole my aunt's car and demolished it. She didn't press charges, but he had violated probation. For eight years, he was in and out of jail. His criminal behavior, frightening and frustrating as it was, seemed endless.

As he approached 20, Eric tried hard to avoid trouble, but he did not succeed. Why was it so hard for him to stay out of trouble?

As I listened to the news one morning, I heard a story about adults with fetal alcohol syndrome. The reporter could have been describing my brother. I began reading about FAS/E and searching for appropriate placements and treatment centers. There were none. Most of the professionals who worked with him, including the social workers and physicians, didn't believe me when I expressed my concern about FAS contributing to Eric's problems. "He doesn't have the facial features," they would, and still, say.

But the effects of FAS that most significantly influence my brother's life include impulsive behaviors, a poor understanding of cause and effect, a variety of intellectual and physical difficulties like problems in tying his shoes and writing his name, poor money management skills, and difficulty understanding social cues.

Most devastating to Eric are the secondary outcomes related to FAS but not directly caused by it: low self-esteem, anger and acting out, drug and alcohol abuse, suicide attempts, and a dark spiritual outlook. Even after he was treated with medication for depression, his opinion of himself remained dim. Once he told me he felt like an insect.

His self-esteem, however, gradually improved as he experienced some successes. Eric has become less and less attracted to rebellious, live-for-the-moment people and is more willing to listen to his family. He is no longer willing to risk everything for a thrill. Stealing cars and going on drinking binges have lost much of their appeal. He remains impulsive under stress but he is learning to avoid situations and people that hurt him.

SUCCESS AND FAILURE ON HIS OWN TERMS

One of Eric's most significant accomplishments was completing the program at the best treatment facility he ever attended, a center for people with a dual diagnosis of mental illness and drug and alcohol abuse. One reason he did so well was its small size and individual attention.

The program had only six patients. One or two staff people were working, depending on the time of day. Connected to a hospital, the program drew upon physicians, available to provide support to the staff and to monitor medications often. The staff treated the patients with the utmost respect and conveyed a genuine concern for them that Eric responded to quickly. They involved the patients in community activities that were closely monitored, such as Alcoholics Anonymous meetings, work-related occupational therapy, and interesting outings. The security of the routine and the understanding of the limits were reassuring to him.

Highly motivated in this environment, Eric made tremendous progress. He received his first exposure to many ideas connected with sobriety and recovery. Although he did not significantly change his drinking, he learned much about alcohol and drug abuse, and he even made an effort to attend Alcoholic Anonymous meetings after he left the treatment center. He also learned about FAS/E. The counselors and pediatricians here believed my concerns about FAS. This was the only program Eric ever participated in whole-heartedly, and he was amazed and pleased that he had succeeded in a program, that he had chosen to finish something.

The biggest drawback was his short stay; the expensive program meant his source of funding could pay only for one month. Six years later, Eric still speaks of this place as the only really good treatment facility he attended.

As Eric entered his twenties, my aunt and I tried to let go of his life and allow him to make his own mistakes. We found this excruciatingly difficult because we knew the problems to which Eric was vulnerable. Over the next several years, he went to jail many times.

Eventually, he was released from jail and served his parole, and he was free. He found a job at a car wash and proceeded to take people he barely knew out drinking. He blew all of his money on alcohol in one night and had nothing left for food or his apartment. His social worker became the payee for his Supplemental Security Income (SSI) checks, government funds he receives for his diagnosed mental illness, not for FAS. Then he deeply resented a payee controlling his money.

He often blamed other people when he did something wrong. He repeatedly said, "If they would just leave me alone and let me get an apartment, then it would be okay." We wanted to believe this, but some of his old buddies in crime found him, and again he stole a car and went to jail.

Eric believed for a long time he was capable only of learning the hard way, that he needed prison to motivate him to get his life together. Arrested and convicted for auto theft at least four times, he finally got his wish when the judge sentenced him to prison instead of jail.

This may sound odd, but for my aunt and me, having him in prison was an enormous relief. At least we knew where he was, and we didn't have to worry about him. Surprisingly, prison was not his lowest point. Even though he was not taking medication for depression, he still maintained incredibly high spirits. Prison life was predictable and structured. Eric had a safe place to sleep, food to eat, and a manageable routine.

He also did fairly well at a few correctional work camps. He worked in the kitchen or outside in the woods, and took classes. At one, he studied driver's education and earned his license. A driver's license represents an important rite of passage, and receiving his license was the biggest intellectual achievement of his life. He felt fantastic about it.

Often, after spending a few months in a correctional setting, Eric was released and required to wear an electronic bracelet around his ankle. Monitored electronically every day through the telephone, he was restricted to his house unless he had permission from his correctional officer. If he violated this rule, used drugs or alcohol, or removed the bracelet, he would return to jail.

During this time, he attended a treatment facility dealing with substance abuse and mental illness. Here he met his first and current girl friend. Since he had never been involved with a woman before, she was an enormous boost to his self-esteem.

Eric has been living with his girl friend in an apartment for about seven months. His self-esteem has improved considerably over the past five years, even though he is not taking any medication for depression. Although his understanding of himself grows at a painfully slow pace, he engages in destructive behaviors much less frequently than before. He is the one who goes to jail every time he uses drugs or alcohol. He is the one who suffers when he wastes his money on stupid things or destroys property and must pay for it. Someone without FAS/E would likely learn these lessons much faster than Eric has.

Once he wanted to go to prison because he thought that was the only way he could learn. Now he wants to stay out of any penal facility and thinks he deserves to live a good life. As astonishing as it is to me, now he wants to avoid drugs and alcohol.

At times Eric and his girl friend drink heavily, with resulting fights and financial problems. But last New Year's Eve they attended the local Alcoholics Anonymous party. Now he equates alcohol with the worst sort of trouble—jail. Now he is able to say no to people. He recently dropped in unexpectedly on one of our sisters. She wasn't home just then, and some of her friends invited him in. They politely offered him a beer. I sensed his pride when he said to me, "I just told them, 'No.'"

In the past few years, Eric has made more progress managing his money than I ever thought possible. Now he hesitates to ask me for money. I am extremely hopeful that he and his girl friend will be able to manage their collective money and pay their bills in a timely way. His girl friend also receives Supplemental Security Income because of her mental illness. They both have payees who handle their bills and give them a weekly allowance. I am amazed that he is not bitter and angry about having a payee as he was in the past.

Every day that Eric lives outside a correctional setting increases the likelihood that he will not return to it. He once feared he had become institutionalized and would not know how to live outside in the real world. Now I visualize him living in an apartment as a functioning member of society and staying sober. In some ways, that's not much to ask, and in some ways, it is everything.

Eric knows I pray for him. I have suggested he could ask God to help him. That notion used to anger and upset him because he didn't believe anything spiritual could help him. Recently I said, "I pray for you every night." He surprised me when he said, "I do, too."

LEARNING TO DEAL WITH MY OWN GRIEF

Over the past ten years, I have learned to deal with Eric's setbacks more quickly and then to focus on possibilities for the future. I used to be emotionally devastated every time Eric went to jail or every time something bad happened to him. There were years when every time the phone rang at an unusual hour, my heart raced. I was afraid it was the dreaded call from my aunt telling me Eric had committed suicide or had been killed. Frequently, I answered the phone to hear my aunt saying, "Well, Eric's in jail again."

When I first began to deal with the knowledge of how FAS had changed Eric's life, I cried daily for months. I looked at pictures of him as a little child and remembered his loving spirit and exuberance, and I wept uncontrollably. I knew I could never give him back the parts of himself that alcohol had damaged.

One evening as we sat by the fire, he said, "Don't ruin your life just because I am ruining mine." I was speechless. I think I muttered something like, "Okay." That he could sense the depth of my anguish astounded me, although I did my best to conceal it.

That comment touched my heart and jolted me out of my preoccupation with my own sorrow. I began to feel better, and I concentrated more on how I could balance my own life with my concern for Eric.

Fortunately, I soon attended a conference sponsored by the National Organization on Fetal Alcohol Syndrome (NOFAS). I stuffed my pockets full of tissues and listened, learned, and cried. Next I went to the Perinatal Substance Abuse Conference in Madison, Wisconsin. Here I met two birth mothers of children with FAS/E. These women took time to share my sorrow and their stories. I had struggled with anger at my mother, forgiving her for killing herself and for the pain her alcoholic behavior had caused me, but I was stuck when it came to Eric. I wanted to scream at her, "How dare you give birth to Eric and just kill yourself and leave the rest of us to deal with his life! He has to live with the results of your drinking, and we have to witness his struggle."

My anger ebbed when I felt the courage of sober birth mothers sharing their stories, living productive lives, and raising their children with FAS/E. Over the years, attending conferences has sustained me. People need a safe place to talk and to grieve.

Conclusion

Loving my brother has been a journey of tremendous joy and a journey of almost impossible despair. When Eric was a child, he was so innocent and sweet and full of life. As he grew up, it was painful to see how his innocent and trusting nature led him into countless troubles as he so easily followed others.

Now that he is an adult I respect and admire him for the way he has continued struggling for a better life. Whatever his future brings, I will continue to be there for him as best as I can. I know love can't fix him. What matters most is that Eric never doubted my love for him, and I never doubted his love for me. Eric has been courageously picking himself back up and moving forward all of his life. I love him for never giving up.

ᖇ Epilogue ᖇ

Since this was written, Eric became heavily involved with alcohol and drugs. He did not have money for food and drugs so he stole regularly. His use of drugs may have seriously affected his mental health. He began to hear voices and to believe everyone was out to get him.

Eric's relationship with his girl friend ended and he can not get decent references from landlords to get an apartment of his own. He is now staying with my aunt who raised him. She is 86 and needs some help with daily living, so Eric feels useful with her.

My aunt tells me he is no longer using drugs or alcohol. He sounds better than he has in years. "I usually feel lost around people my own age," he recently told me. "They always want me to do irrational things. I do better when I hang around my family."

Part Two

Strategies that Work:

Counseling, Education, Sexuality, Trouble with the Law, Living Skills

9

Working with Adolescents in High School: Techniques That Help

DEBRA EVENSEN

Debra Evensen is an educator with 31 years of experience in working with children with emotional and learning disturbances, including FAS/E. She is project coordinator of a program which provides statewide consultation, education, and training for mental health providers, social service workers, parents, teachers, and people in the judicial system. Ms. Evensen does consultation and training internationally in FAS/E.

TALL, LANKY, AND TALKING TOUGH, BRIAN HAD BEEN SUSPENDED FROM junior high school 15 times since the beginning of the school year. Just after Thanksgiving vacation, his principal called me to discuss the faculty's anxiety about dealing with such an out-of-control student. Thirteen of Brian's suspensions stemmed from his behavior in the school lunchroom. "This kid can't even make it through lunch!" the principal said. When I visited the school, the principal asked me for information about an appropriate residential placement for Brian. "He is not able to handle public school," he said.

Before I could recommend anything, I needed to get to know this student who was causing so much frustration among the staff. I knew he had been taken away from his mother during infancy because of her excessive alcohol use, and that he had moved to this small community in southeast Alaska recently with his grandmother. After meeting Brian in the counselor's office, I said, "Brian, tell me about school." He responded in strong language, but translated, he said, "The teachers hate me. Nobody likes me and they won't give me a chance. I get blamed for everything that goes wrong, especially with the teachers in the lunchroom. They're the meanest."

I replied, "Let's talk about the lunchroom first. Brian, what are the rules for lunch?" He answered by listing them perfectly as they were written in the student handbook. I started to say, "Then why don't you do it?" but I caught myself and thought, "I wonder…" I asked him to come with me to the cafeteria, now empty. "Show me," I said. He couldn't do it! He did not even know where to sit.

Who would have thought this tall eighth-grader, with an IQ in the average range and the ability to out-swear a sailor, truly did not understand the meaning of the rules for the lunch period? I did what any good teacher or parent would do: I showed the now teary-eyed Brian what to do, where to sit, what to do with his tray, and so on. In a short time we were laughing and having fun learning together. We practiced common lunchroom situations, such as what to do if someone else was already sitting where he planned to sit. Then, remembering a Polaroid camera on the counselor's desk, I borrowed it and took pictures of Brian doing these things right. I sent the pictures home with him, knowing he would probably look at them from time to time, visually reinforcing what he had learned. From then until the end of the school year in June, Brian was suspended from school only two more times, and neither incident involved lunchroom behavior.

My experience with Brian contributed to a huge paradigm shift in my understanding of effective methods for assisting teenagers with fetal alcohol syndrome. I have been an educator for 31 years, the first two decades working as a hard-core behaviorist. Usually behavior modification is effective with students with Serious Emotional Disturbance (SED). The misconduct is willful disobedience or deliberate manipulation. With the right rewards, their behavior will usually improve. In the past nine years, as I've traveled throughout Alaska as an education specialist, I've come to understand that adolescents with FAS/E do not respond as expected to standard techniques of behavior modification. They are not deliberately disobeying a rule—they didn't understand the rule in the first place. Rewards and punishments aren't effective for someone who doesn't understand the nature of the behavior that merits the reward or brings forth the punishment. For students with FAS, misbehavior is often a means of communication—they are showing us that they do not know what they are supposed to do.

Several techniques can help us understand how alcohol-affected youths see their world and then help us learn how to change their behavior.

• We need to observe troublesome situations carefully to understand the nature of the problem.

• We need to interpret their responses correctly, to understand that what seems like deliberate misconduct or attention-seeking may actually be neurologically based problems with memory or comprehension. At this point we can then teach habit patterns of appropriate behavior by using role playing or other concrete techniques.

• Finally, we can reduce frustration and misbehavior by using multisensory tools like music, drama, visual symbols, and computers to make learning not only fun but effective for students who might otherwise find it impossible to understand.

FIGURING OUT WHAT'S WRONG WITH BEHAVIOR MODIFICATION AND WHAT WE NEED INSTEAD

When I began traveling as an Alaska state educational specialist, I had 21 years experience working with students with SED. Gaining an understanding of principles that are effective with students with FAS has taken me nine additional years. My first glimpse of understanding developed with a disruptive young child named James, labeled as SED by the school psychologist. I spent a day observing him in class and thinking to myself that this would be an easy situation to change—it would be thrilling, in fact, to see how fast we could turn this classroom and James around. The next morning I took over the class after offering to demonstrate a few techniques for the teacher, who was happy to have a day of rest. I gave the class an instruction. James didn't do it. Calmly, I ignored James, focused my attention on the other students who were doing it right, and then said, "James, you need to _____." He didn't do it. I repeated the direction, again without response. I placed him in time-out for not following directions, where he sobbed his heart out. As soon as he remained quiet for about 30 seconds, I gently helped him return to the classroom and said, "James, you need to _____." And he didn't do it.

Almost nine years later, I can still remember how my body felt, legs rooted to the classroom floor, as I realized that nothing in my vast experience had prepared me for the moment when James did not do what was expected at this stage in the procedure. I was terrified, not to mention just a little embarrassed since the teacher, principal, counselor, and two teacher aides were observing me.

In a flash, I recalled a string of students throughout my career whose behavior and even physical characteristics resembled those of James—adolescents in a program for former street kids in Utah, a student in a psychiatric hospital program who was discharged as untreatable, several pupils in public school classrooms. In that moment, I knew there was an important link between all these former students and James. What was it? I began making the connection after having a heart-to-heart talk with James's mother, who told me she was new in recovery and had done a lot of drinking during her pregnancy with James.

My Journey to Understanding

Later experiences gave me new clues. Fifteen-year-old Diana, diagnosed with FAS and SED, had been in state custody since she was young and had already gone through most of the treatment programs and youth facilities in her community in southcentral Alaska. She had an IQ in the average range and was living in a foster home and attending a special education program recommended for students with behavior disturbance, one I had helped design years previously. This total behavior modification system used a token economy in which the students worked individually on their assignments and received points for completed work and for appropriate behavior. I was proud I had helped create it.

As usual, I spent a great deal of time observing the program in order to make recommendations to the teaching staff. One day I watched Diana's teacher tell the class to get started on their assignments. Most of the students began working but Diana wiggled in her seat and kept glancing out the window, watching others and periodically opening her book. Had I not been observing so closely I would not have noticed her anxiety. Like most others, I would have thought her behavior looked like a lazy adolescent goofing off.

As the period ended, students began taking their work up to the teacher and receiving points on their individual daily record sheets. Diana watched as three students got their points. Then, smiling, she took up her point chart and handed it to the teacher, who looked it over and gave it back to her. Diana said, "I want my points!" The teacher said, "You haven't earned them." Diana replied, "But they got their points!" They repeated this exchange several times, until Diana screamed, "But I just want my points!" and ran crying out of the room and the school building.

I was stunned. Could it be possible that this tall eighth-grade girl really didn't understand the connection between doing what was expected of her and receiving the points as a concrete, positive reward? That's how it looked to me. What I saw was not an angry, noncompliant teenager but a confused little girl. She didn't get it.

Months later I noticed adolescents similar to Brian, Diana, and James in different programs around the state. I began to realize that many students unsuccessful in these traditional behavior modification programs had a prenatal history of exposure to alcohol. A common thread linking them was that teachers and other professionals often described them as "out of control," "stubborn," "willfully disobedient," "not trying," "self-centered," "immature and spoiled," and "deliberately manipulative." Maybe they didn't turn in their work even though it was finished, didn't seem to follow through on what seemed like simple commitments after they had agreed to obey the rules, or did something right one day only to "completely disregard" the rules the next.

When I was able to observe them, a different picture emerged. I saw just how confused these students were, and how similar these teenagers were to children of a much younger chronological age. When I observed a student behaving in a manner that would be typical of a much younger child in a similar situation, I started asking if that teenager had a history of prenatal exposure to alcohol. This behavior was my red flag. Every single time I questioned the parent or guardian of these students about maternal drinking, the answer was "yes."

Replacing Old Models of Behavior

This scenario was repeated time after time in different communities. The problem appeared to be immense, affecting far more students than I ever imagined. My old paradigm about how to control adolescent behavior through behavior modification toppled. The problems of FAS seemed enormous, maybe even hopeless in terms of solutions for our school and mental health systems.

I began to feel retrospective grief as I recalled more students with whom I had previously worked during the past two decades who most likely had FAS, beginning with a girl in my first teaching assignment in 1968. I recalled other students I had worked with:

• Brad, a 16-year-old student in a school program for students who had been living on the streets in 1978. I later worked with Brad again in 1981 in the program for male sex offenders at Utah State prison.

• Jennifer, an eleventh grade student in the adolescent treatment program at Colorado State Hospital in 1982.

• Craig, a boy in my self-contained class for students with behavior disorders, grades five and six, in Utah in 1984.

• Alana, a high school girl in the Kenai Peninsual School District emotionally handicapped program whose behavior in 1986–1987 had reminded me of Craig from Utah.

With the problem unknown and unnamed, I had been unaware of their actual needs. I viewed them from the textbook approaches I had learned in my university training—techniques developed by other professionals unaware of the effects of prenatal exposure to alcohol.

During this time, while on an island in the Arctic Ocean, I was given a ride in an *umiaq*, a traditional Yup'ik boat made of walrus skins. While gliding through the water we saw what looked like a whale in the far distance. I thought to myself that FAS, in its many varieties, is like a whale: huge but not always visible on the surface.

We design and redesign behavior management programs, busying ourselves setting standards for behavior while ignoring what makes our students fail and our programs sink. Exhausted teachers, school administrators, and other professionals try again and again to make the same programs work. When students do not respond as expected, we conclude that they must be choosing to be irresponsible. Assuming that they can link behavior with consequences, making competent decisions that then generalize to other areas of their lives, we decide that they must be punished so that they will learn the consequences of their misbehavior. In effect, we blame the very victims of our misunderstanding and refuse to help them.

Learning the Importance of Concrete Assistance

Then I met Sally, a 17-year-old girl with a history of prenatal exposure to alcohol who lived in an Aleutian community. Raised by relatives due to her parents' ongoing alcoholism and the parent of a small daughter herself, she needed help dealing with life in the here and now. She had been the victim of a sexual attack and with the assistance of the mental health therapists we arranged for her to receive treatment for post-traumatic stress in one of Alaska's psychiatric hospitals and for her daughter to be cared for while she was hospitalized. We felt enormous satisfaction for helping her receive the therapy she deserved.

By 1991 I knew that a history of prenatal exposure to alcohol makes a significant difference in the way a person learns, processes information, and makes sense of the world. Upon Sally's admission to the hospital, I explained to her doctor and therapist that she was possibly undiagnosed FAS/E and would not learn well by talk therapy alone but would need much more concrete assistance.*

They told me not to worry because their program was successful with adolescents with varying abilities, and Sally could be expected to do well within the established guidelines.

Two weeks later, I met with the therapist for follow-up. She said Sally refused to comply with treatment expectations and had been confined to her room after the last group therapy session. Sally had recently told the group that she, like some of the others in the group, was addicted to sniffing leaded gasoline. Since I was quite familiar with Sally and her family and the conditions of the remote community where she lived, I knew this gasoline addiction was simply not true. As we talked it became apparent that Sally, sitting in group therapy listening to the stories of the other participants and trying to fit in, was simply making up stories comprised of a little of those she had just heard. When it all got too confusing, she entered shut down mode, unable to talk at all.

After six weeks of group talk therapy (often very successful with adolescents who do not have FAS/E), Sally was in such a state that her relatives traveled the long distance and signed her out of the program. Upon her discharge the doctor and therapist told me they had been unsuccessful with this patient and felt terrible about it. I explained that I truly believed the missing factor was a lack of information about her prenatal fetal alcohol exposure and what that meant for therapy techniques.

I was beginning to understand that patients with this history need a more concrete method of treatment. Unable to grasp effectively the underlying reasons for responsible behavior and its meaning, and unable to generalize from one situation to another, they constantly live in a world that doesn't make sense. Insight therapy assumes that patients can understand the abstract ideas underlying our society. Without additional help linking what's discussed in therapy with behavior

* See Susan Baxter, chapter 11, for another example of a front-line professional hearing this common wisdom, which proved to be incorrect. Baxter shows how talk therapy can be adapted for individuals with FAS/E.

in real life, teenagers with FAS only grow more confused and anxious.

LEARNING TO INTERPRET BEHAVIOR CORRECTLY

As I continued to work with Sally over the next two years, I realized most of our conflicts with students who experience FAS/E begin with a simple misunderstanding of their behavior. When viewed accurately, we can clearly visualize what might help and figure out practical ways to encourage success. The following chart (see pages 148–149) offers examples of typical misbehavior and the correct interpretation.

WHAT TO DO ABOUT MISBEHAVIOR

As I learned to interpret the behavior of alcohol-affected adolescents, I began to replace behavior modification with a quite different approach for working with them. This approach includes observing students to discover where problems lie, using role-playing to create new habit patterns, and using multisensory teaching methods to reinforce learning.

Observation

Before we make any big decisions about a student who is faltering in school, the child needs to be closely observed. In this critical first step, we often begin to see that the adolescent we thought was so disobedient actually may be trying desperately to meet our expectations.

The following story illustrates the importance of observation. I received a call in the fall of 1994 from the special education director of one of the larger bush Alaska school districts. He described the struggle involved with trying to work with a manipulative eighth-grade girl, Jennifer, who "must be a sociopath." Her parents were willing to label their daughter Seriously Emotionally Disturbed if that would make her eligible to receive more help, but the school psychologist had balked at the SED label as he did not feel Jennifer honestly met the qualifications. Asked if this teenager

COMMON MISINTERPRETATIONS OF NORMAL RESPONSES IN
STUDENTS WITH FAS AND FAE *

Behavior	Misinterpretation
NONCOMPLIANCE	• willful misconduct • seeking attention • stubborn
REPEATS THE SAME MISTAKES	• willful misconduct • manipulative
DOESN'T SIT STILL	• willful misconduct • seeking attention • bothering others
DOESN'T WORK INDEPENDENTLY	• willful misconduct • poor parenting
DOESN'T COMPLETE HOMEWORK	• irresponsible • lazy, slow • unsupportive parent
IS OFTEN LATE	• willful misconduct • lazy, slow • poor parenting
USES POOR SOCIAL JUDGMENT	• willful misconduct • poor parenting • abused child
IS OVERLY PHYSICAL	• willful misconduct • deviancy
STEALS	• deliberate dishonesty • lack of conscience
LIES	• deliberate dishonesty • lack of conscience • sociopathic behavior

* Prepared by Debra Evensen

Accurate Interpretation

- has difficulty translating verbal directions into action
- doesn't understand

- can't link cause to effect
- can't see similarities
- has difficulty generalizing

- has neurologically based need to move while learning
- is experiencing sensory overload

- has chronic memory problems
- can't translate verbal directions into action

- has memory deficits
- is unable to transfer what is learned in class to the homework assignment

- doesn't understand the abstract concept of time
- needs help organizing

- is not able to interpret social cues from peers
- needs help organizing

- is hyper- or hypo-sensitive to touch
- doesn't understand social cues regarding boundaries

- doesn't understand concept of ownership over time and space
- demonstrates immature thinking (finders keepers)

- has problems with memory and/or sequencing
- is unable to accurately recall events
- tries to please by telling you what they think you want to hear

had a history of prenatal exposure to alcohol, the special education director said he did not know but felt that it wasn't relevant information.

The teaching staff regarded as most irritating her "refusal to get to class on time." She was constantly late, no matter what the penalty was for tardiness. Most recently they had been working with Jennifer on a system that awarded her a point for each timely arrival and a zero for each tardy incident. Three zeros in a week meant she had to attend Saturday school. She continued to be late to almost every class with a "complete disregard for the rules." After three and a half months of Saturday school, Jennifer's parents called a meeting with the school counselor and said, "Enough! This just isn't working."

In a teleconference with the parents, teachers, and school psychologist, I discussed the importance of observation for understanding what else might be in the picture. The counselor took my advice and observed Jennifer. What the counselor saw astonished her: Jennifer was one of the first students to enter the building, happy and bubbly, with plenty of time to reach first period. She found her locker and began looking through the mess inside to find her school supplies. As she searched, the hall filled with noisy talkative students who distracted Jennifer repeatedly. Then she would again remember to look for her things. The counselor said she could visually see Jennifer's anxiety level rise.

Most of the other students were sitting down in class when the bell rang. Jennifer grabbed her book, slammed the locker door shut and ran into class—late. The teacher, collecting homework as Jennifer entered, asked if she had her assignment. She whispered, "No," and he pointed to the door: "Go get it!" Jennifer, checks burning and head hanging, returned to her locker, sat on the floor and again attempted to find the completed homework among the stack of loose papers. Jennifer was so quiet that the counselor had to really listen to realize she was crying.

What seemed like disobedience followed by typical teenage disorganization was actually characteristic of a disability. The counselor met with Jennifer and asked her to draw what she needed to get to class on time. Jennifer drew a picture of a girl trying to find her school supplies in a very messy locker. The counselor and Jennifer's mother asked Jennifer what would help. She said, "I can never find my things. Maybe if I had a way I could reach into my locker and get all my things for one class at one time, that would help."

Mother and daughter then figured out a way to design stylish bags colored differently for each class. Then (with permission from the school authorities) they hung enough hooks in her locker for each class bag. Now Jennifer enters school, hangs her parka in her locker, grabs the green English bag and heads for first period. With pencils and paper in each bag and an extra box of sharpened pencils in the locker, she arrives with the necessary supplies. Most important, she is seldom late to class.

Eventually, Jennifer's adoptive parents discovered she had been heavily exposed prenatally to alcohol. She recently received a diagnosis of FAS and receives additional assistance in school under the category of Other Health Impaired (OHI).

Forming Habit Patterns

I like the term commonly used to describe teenagers with FAS—"stretch toddlers"—because the image emphasizes their naivete in many social situations. They need to learn critical social skills, as well as understand how and when to apply them. Take Bill, 14 years old and diagnosed with FAS. His IQ was 95 and he attended a regular junior high ninth-grade classroom. Three neighbor boys invited Bill to accompany them on a toilet-papering spree on another boy's house. Bill followed one of the boys in unwinding a row of toilet paper and decorating the front porch, while the other boys papered the fence and trees. When the resident turned on the yard lights and looked out the window, Bill's three friends ran and hid, unable to get Bill's attention to tell him to leave fast. Oblivious to the fact that he was about to get into trouble, Bill continued intently to decorate the porch (as a much younger child might do). The father stormed down the stairs and confronted Bill: "What do you think you are doing?" Like a toddler who truly didn't realize he was in trouble, Bill answered, "Toilet papering your house." The furious father reported to the police that "this young man just stood there and defied me."

The same week Fred, a 15-year-old boy with FAS, was laughing with fellow ninth-grade boys in school over a dirty joke they had just heard. A teacher walked into the classroom and the other boys immediately quit talking and pretended to be involved in their assignments. Fred, missing the cue, continued talking. The angry teacher assumed Fred was being intentionally insubordinate. She had him suspended from school for noncompliance. It was the fourth time he gotten into trouble for misunderstanding a social situation, reacting with behavior normal in a much younger child.

I began viewing these teenagers as toddlers in adolescent robes. They need more social skills to get through adolescence. Usually we teach critical interaction skills to youths with emotional/behavioral disturbances in group settings. The teacher outlines, through verbal description, a certain situation requiring a response (i.e., what to do when someone teases you, or how to ask for help in class). The participants role play or act out the situation and figure out the best way to respond. We expect these same participants to react similarly to a comparable situation in real life.

For students with FAS, this may be an impossible task. The nature of the disability means they have difficulty making connections and generalizing information from one situation to another. Since they often do not see the underlying meaning or the conceptual foundation of appropriate social expectations, they cannot grasp the similarities between one scenario and another. For example, during a discussion with a group of foster parents of adolescents with FAS, we discussed the concept of "good girl" in American society. To be a good girl may mean adhering to slightly different social expectations depending on the particular generation, community or religious environment in which one lives. Whether a person agrees or disagrees with "being a good girl" is not the point. The point is that we're all expected to understand the basic concept.

A foster mother shared how knowing what it meant to be a good girl during her teenage years made a difference in the behavioral choices she made at that time. She recalled attending a party and deciding whether to participate in the drug of choice. Knowing that if she became intoxicated she might be persuaded to join in sexual activity for which she was not prepared, she chose to stay sober. She wanted to be a good girl and understood the links connecting drugs, sex, and losing this self-concept.

After our discussion this foster mother questioned her 15-year-old daughter with FAS about her understanding of the concept of "good girl." The conversation went something like this:

> Mother: "Honey, what is a good girl?"
> Daughter: "Me."
> Mother: "What do you mean?"
> Daughter: "Me. I am a good girl."
> Mother: "How do you know?"
> Daughter: "Because you and dad tell me I am."
> Mother: "So what does it mean to be a good girl?"
> Daughter: "Be like me."

Obviously, this girl will need additional assistance in figuring out how to deal with certain social situations. Unable to understand the underlying concepts beneath our social structure, she would find it impossible to apply these concepts to her own life decisions.

Rather than attempting to develop understanding of abstract concepts, I have found it far more effective to teach concrete habit patterns through role plays.

Scripting the role play together especially is helpful. The students participate in writing the play and then take turns acting it out.

This script was written to help a teenager learn how to ask for help from the teacher:

After class:

> Teacher: "Class Dismissed."
> Student: "I need to talk with you. Would this be a good time?"
> Teacher: "Not now. Could you come back later?"
> Student: "When should I come back?"
> Teacher: "Come right after school gets out at the end of the
> school day."
> Student: "Thank you. I'll be back."

After school:

> Student: "Hi [teacher's name]. Is this still a good time for you
> to talk with me?"
> Teacher: "Yes."
> Student: "I need extra help with the lesson. Could you go over
> it again with me?"
> Teacher: "Of course."

Later, after the teacher has helped the student understand:

> Student: "Thank you so much for your help."
> Teacher: "You are welcome."

With the appropriate assistance and given enough time, adolescents with FAS can function well in social situations. But they need to learn social scripts through such practice and repetition.

Designing a Multisensory School Curriculum

In the lower elementary grades, we help young children memorize facts by using such multisensory methods as singing songs, memorizing limericks and rhymes, or employing hand signs, dance steps, and body cues. Pictures and reminders help students recall the letters of the alphabet, national holidays, and other information. As children grow older, the system expects them to continue learning without this assistance, usually dispensing with the methods that helped in childhood and relying only on lectures and other auditory methods. For the typical adolescent, such lecture methods may mean that learning is not a lot of fun, but it is possible. For the alcohol-affected student, learning by auditory means alone may be impossible. Since prenatal exposure to alcohol causes functional damage throughout the brain, the best approach to learning may mean stimulating many senses and different areas of the brain through those early childhood methods.

This important point was made clear to me as I worked with Greg, a seventh-grader who was disruptive in class. He refused to finish his work and was so inattentive that he disturbed his peers. His teachers believed he needed to be in a special school and his loving but frustrated parents were tired of lecturing and grounding him in a futile attempt to make him behave in school.

When I observed Greg, I saw the pattern. Greg was not a manipulative, willfully disobedient adolescent but a young boy trying his best to fit in like the other kids and to do what was expected. He didn't know how to do the academic work without additional assistance, didn't know how or whom to ask for help, and was overwhelmed and overstimulated by the activities and pressures of a typical junior high school. When the pressure grew too much, he threw a temper tantrum—normal in a preschool child but unacceptable and even a little scary in a 12 year old.

When I asked Greg to show me about school by drawing me a picture, he sketched a picture of students and teachers and lots of things happening. I noticed the prominence of the teachers' mouths, and he explained they were talking and talking. "Teachers talk too much," he said. He was showing his inability to make sense of the many long explanations and instructions he heard from his teachers and counselors each day. I worked with his parents and one understanding teacher to simplify his schedule, make it consistent from day to day, prepare him for transitions, and provide a more nurturing atmosphere.

In eighth grade, Greg had great difficulty writing fast enough to take notes competently in class. His teachers complained constantly about his poor handwriting. He was always behind, in constant turmoil, and often sent out of history class for being off-task. Greg's mother said the history teacher's lectures were so abstract that they made the material almost meaningless to him. Daily frustration over uncompleted work in their home was becoming unbearable.

It wasn't long before I was in the special education director's office admiring his brand-new computer when I asked if he would mind seeing what Greg could do with this computer. He suggested I retrieve Greg from class immediately. A half-hour later, Greg's mother walked by the special education office, glanced in, and stopped short. She saw her son completely involved with looking at a biography of President John F. Kennedy illustrated with colored pictures and accompanied by the narration of his famous "Ask not what your country can do for you" speech. When Greg looked up "grizzly bears," he could click on the screen to actually hear the sound of a bear growl. Greg's mother watched her son with tears of happiness streaming down her face.

This special education director is one of those compassionate human beings who make us proud. Turning to Greg's mother, he said, "If this computer can make such a difference with Greg, then it belongs with him." By the next morning, the computer was transferred to the resource room, where Greg spent the next several months learning and exploring. This experience transformed him. Doing all of his assignments on the computer allowed Greg to learn, remember, and make better sense of what he was learning. His bad handwriting no longer mattered. This computer, now classified as appropriate assistive technology, helped Greg improve his grades from mostly *Ds* to *As* and *Bs*.

Other things changed for Greg as well. His teachers became encouraged at his success and felt they could make a difference, too, which changed Greg's environment. Staff found it easier to like him and, through their own increased feelings of achievement, supported him much better. This feeling of acceptance spread to Greg's peers, who began including him in their activities. By the end of ninth grade, when Greg decided to run for school office, he flawlessly gave a campaign speech he had written himself, earning a spontaneous standing ovation from the entire student body and faculty. Witnessing this event was one of the most moving moments of my teaching career.

Using multisensory cues can not only teach lessons but also help prevent confusing situations that get students into trouble. We can all remember the happy times in our lives (riding a bike for the first time or enjoying a birthday party). Most of us can also recall being unable to remember important information during stressful events (giving a speech or taking an important test). For the students with prenatal exposure to alcohol, this problem is multiplied. Under extreme stress, they may be unable to think at all or to decide what to do. Overwhelmed and overstimulated by events that seem normal to the casual observer, a student may shut down, be unable to think clearly, react appropriately, or decide what to do next.

Simple cues can prevent this problem. Hank, a seventh-grade boy with FAS, had moved with his family to a community in southcentral Alaska right before school started in September. The first day a peer showed him which bus he was to ride home. Unknown to his parents, he counted to himself which bus it was in line (fourth). Whenever he rode the bus home after that, he simply got on the fourth bus. But during a dark January blizzard, the buses lined up in a different order, and Hank, tired from the day of school, climbed on the fourth bus as usual. The bus driver didn't notice the bundled-up newcomer.

Often when people with FAS are in the greatest distress they show it the least. They retreat into shut down, which to the casual observer may look like everything is fine when in reality they are in crisis. Hank didn't realize he was on the wrong bus until it had driven out of town in the opposite direction from his home. Frustrated and overwhelmed, he was unable to think of what to do next. Finally, approximately six miles out of town, he stood up and told the bus driver to let him off. The driver later said that Hank seemed to be perfectly calm to him, like he knew exactly what he was doing. There were homes nearby, and the driver let him out.

Panic-stricken, Hank walked through the snow the entire six miles back to school, where his frightened parents found him, cold and exhausted, at 10:30 that night. Had the temperature been a little colder, he might not have survived the ordeal.

The next day Hank's parents met with the school administration and some of Hank's teachers to ask for additional supervision to make certain Hank took the correct bus in the future. The principal, unaware of the cognitive difficulties involved with FAS, said firmly, "Seventh-graders need to be responsible for themselves." Only after further events did the school staff realize Hank was already doing his best and needed additional aid to be able to function safely in the school environment.

Using a technique they had followed with the kindergarten children, they mounted a different animal symbol on each bus to distinguish them from each other. They also worked with Hank's parents to design several laminated cards that went in his billfold. Titled "What to Do," these cards included simple instructions to follow when he got lost, became confused, or just needed help.

CONCLUSION

Working with children and adolescents who have a history of prenatal exposure to alcohol has changed my way of thinking and affected my approach to my work. I have learned compassion, accepting not only their errors but also my own. Now when I make a mistake or forget something important, I remind myself that I am just a human being doing the best I can.

Recently, while giving a training session on adolescents with FAS for workers in juvenile correction and mental health, I mentioned that prenatal exposure to alcohol in Alaska schools is an invisible "whale of a problem." I added that only after naming and focusing on the whale can we begin to deal with it. An Iñupiaq woman stood up and said, "My people can tell you how to eat a whale—one bite at a time! After a lot of people have taken a few bites, the whale doesn't seem so big after all."

10
Finding the Right School
For Devorah

DIANE B. MALBIN

Diane V. Malbin, M.S.W., is a cofounder of the FAS/Drug Effects Clinical Programs in Portland, Oregon. Preliminary findings on positive outcomes for people with FAS/E and their families have been presented nationally. In addition, she provides professional training for educators, clinicians, and health care providers on alcoholism and fetal alcohol syndrome across the country. She serves as consultant on FAS/E for various agencies at the local and national levels. She is the mother of a child with FAE.

WHEN MY DAUGHTER DEVORAH COMPLETED THE FIFTH GRADE, SHE was a happy student with good friends and pride in her ability to solve problems.[1] Then she entered middle school and lost her way. A special education teacher and I had worked out an Individualized Education Plan (IEP) that we hoped would be used in sixth grade. The plan emphasized experiential and concrete approaches to learning; information was related to her life. Implementation of the plan and accommodating how Devorah learns best, however, was not possible within the structure of the public school.

When we realized that Devorah was beginning to despise learning and see herself as a failure, we pulled her out of the public

---

[1] See Diane B. Malbin, "Stereotypes and Realities," in J. S. Kleinfeld and S. Wescott 1993, 253–271.

school system and schooled her at home. That produced results. We let go of grades and tests and instead allowed her to follow her own interests. She began to enjoy learning again. Then we discovered a private school with an activity-based curriculum and a philosophy of including students of many different ability levels in projects and respecting what each contributed. Today Devorah is so happy and successful at school that she tapes classes she can't attend so she won't miss anything.

When we tried to change Devorah to fit the school environment, her feelings about herself and about school plummeted. When we tried to change the school environment to fit the child, she made enormous educational and social strides. The alterations in her schooling were relatively simple and yet profound in their effects, a testimony not only to the importance of changing the environment instead of the child, but also to the crucial need to try *differently* rather than harder. Devorah's gains are especially significant because they occurred during adolescence, a time when many children with FAS/E have increasing problems.

Losing Ground in Middle School: A Poor Fit

Shifting from a rural elementary school with 150 students to a large new middle school created many different problems for Devorah. The middle school was located 12 miles from our home, requiring a 45-minute bus ride each way. Some children become overwhelmed by the noise and activity of the bus ride and arrive at school overstimulated, while others get so wound-up with all the noise and confusion that they become overexcited and are sometimes kicked off the bus. Rather than going wild, Devorah becomes quiet when overwhelmed, and the long, noisy ride just tired her out.

For Devorah, the new middle school was like a huge labyrinth. She was terrified she would get lost and be late for her classes, and so she carried all of her books all day to avoid grappling with her locker's combination lock. She worried that she might have to use the bathroom since that might make her late for class.

These anxieties made changing classes even more difficult, and she returned home exhausted from stress, overstimulation, and mental fatigue.

The complex daily schedule of the middle school also changed from day to day, confusing and upsetting Devorah, who depends on a less complex, more predictable schedule. When she was younger, every morning she would ask, "What are we doing today?" At first I didn't understand or appreciate how important this daily question was to her. Then I learned that what she meant was, "What is the schedule for today? When are we doing what?" She has trouble anticipating events and tends to be in the present moment, becoming uncomfortable when sequences of events change. Some days she would ask me many times what was going to happen. Asking about coming events helped her feel more grounded and secure. Once she knew what was happening, she could relax. The ever-changing schedule at middle school made her nervous and tense.

Other pressures and negative judgments at school eroded her confidence—the curriculum, grades, social demands, and such invisible elements as values and expectations. It was not possible for the middle school to implement the IEP that she brought with her from the previous year. Instead, the school depended on the traditional abstract worksheet and textbook teaching style. Devorah spent her days in both the resource room and the mainstream classes, a system that backfired. In the resource center, with a lower student-teacher ratio than in the classroom, teachers encouraged her to raise her hand for help whenever necessary, which she did. However, when she raised her hand in the regular classroom, her classmates ridiculed her ("Oh, Devorah, you don't know THAT?!" or "Not again!"). Often the teachers did not respond. "At that school the teachers gave up on me," Devorah said later. Devorah is a determined person, but her best attempts to meet other's expectations failed. She became increasingly tired, discouraged, and withdrawn.

No one at the school recognized or responded to Devorah's strengths and needs in a useful way. She learns successfully with approaches that use as many senses as possible: sight, sound, touch. She learns when information relates to her life. Sitting in a classroom reading pages of worksheets or answering abstract questions offers little purpose or relevance to her. Moving frequently between classes, compartmentalizing learning, and breaking up the day into fragments caused her even more distress.

This poor fit meant Devorah was chronically unsuccessful despite her best efforts. The message she received most powerfully was that she was not as good as the others—that she was a burden and inadequate. She was embarrassed by the patronizing comments on her report card, such as "Good job—based on effort." She was twelve chronologically but about eight developmentally, with many social and intellectual interests similar to younger children. Children were grouped by chronological age, however, and there were no opportunities for her to close the gap between her classmates and herself. Devorah judged herself harshly on these differences between herself and others. No matter how hard she tried academically or socially, she never felt adequate. Her deficits defined her, not her strengths, a situation too demoralizing and painful to withstand for long. These implicit messages contributed to serious depression.

I wanted Devorah to succeed in the public schools, having been socialized to believe that success in life is measured by successfully completing the public school gauntlet. I was afraid that if she failed in school, her life would be harder. The paradox was that it was the school experience that was contributing to her feelings of failure. Our supportive messages at home could not counterbalance the messages she received during most of her school hours.

Devorah deteriorated intellectually, academically, socially, and personally. I didn't realize how tired and depressed she was becoming. Concerns about her emotional life were treated at school as being outside the range of the school's responsibility. In the spring I noticed she was increasingly defensive and uncooperative at home. Her behavior as a 13 year old reminded me of her behavior in the second grade when she shut down. I worried doubly because she was older and dealing with the physical and emotional changes of adolescence. Clearly her best efforts were no match for the daily assaults to her self-esteem. She started calling herself "stupid" and a "no-brainer." One day she came home and said she didn't want to live. That was the day her survival became more important than my academic expectations.

FINDING AN ALTERNATIVE TO PUBLIC SCHOOL: HOME SCHOOLING

In retrospect, I was amazed at how far afield we had wandered from our original goals for Devorah: we wanted her to love herself and love learning. We looked at other options together. The local private schools seemed like variations on the theme of the public school, which for Devorah meant failure, not success. As we thought about home school, we worried about limiting Devorah's exposure to real world demands. We also considered the belief that home schoolers don't have enough interaction with their peers. On the other hand, we knew that the kinds of social interactions Devorah had in school were actually hurting her. When she started talking about not wanting to live, I realized that home school was the only option.

We discussed this option with Devorah at the end of the school year. She immediately wanted to be home schooled. We were surprised when her older sister also chose home schooling. Since they were close, and companionship was important, we decided to home school both girls.[2] It was an excellent decision.

We home schooled for one year. During that year I was shocked to see how much Devorah had internalized the handicapping belief that she was stupid. My goal for that year was for Devorah to rediscover herself as a competent person and learner. Without that foundation, I believed her to be at tremendous risk, far more handicapped by her beliefs about herself even than by her FAE.

---

[2] Different states have different guidelines for home schooling. Parents interested in this option need to consult their state Department of Education or local school district.

We used the year of home schooling to explore, to do, to make, and to be. Devorah resisted doing anything that resembled school work, and so we borrowed wonderful videos from the library, made art and crafts, read to each other, cooked, and made music. I had trouble letting go of academics and purchased various workbooks for math, science, and language. They only rekindled Devorah's trauma, so I let them go as well.

During this year, each of the girls pursued several projects, spending long stretches of time exploring and working on them one at a time. They needed large blocks of uninterrupted time to investigate their interests. With no grades or tests, the lack of judgment about their work freed their natural curiosity.

At the end of the year I received a letter from the schools requesting that the girls be tested. If they were not making satisfactory progress they would be sent back to public school. I was unwilling to allow Devorah to be retraumatized, to lose the good ground we'd gained, yet I felt threatened. I knew from other parents' experiences, and, as a counseler, from my own clients' experiences, that the public education system is unable or unwilling to provide adaptations to meet individual needs.

Over the summer we considered our options, even identifying a person who could administer the tests the school wanted. Then we heard from good friends that a promising new school was opening in Portland named the Pacific Crest Community School (PCCS). During our first meeting with the staff, one of the school's dynamic founders talked about the philosophy and values of the teachers and the school. This school seemed to fit with Devorah! We felt relieved and hopeful.

How PCCS Works: A Good Fit

Pacific Crest Community School was started by five teachers who were dissatisfied with their experiences in the public schools and began discussing how to create an optimal school environment. They traveled to other schools across the country, compared philosophies, explored curricula, and developed a mission statement and philosophy. They established a new school for children between ages 11 and 18, but they do not separate children into classes based on age. Individual portfolios containing examples of students' work and comments on the work replaced grades. The founders designed the school to become part of the community and responsive to the needs of the students and their families. The school recognizes diversity—cultural, racial, and cognitive.

The fit between Devorah and the school sounded ideal. Pacific Crest offered structure and predictability without tight control; consistent schedules without rigidity; learning experiences that brought together different academic areas; hands-on, concrete techniques regardless of the subject; interaction among children of all ages; a responsive staff; and greater adaptability and flexibility in every area. As a family we decided that Devorah and her sister would enter that fall with the first class.

At first we wondered what effect the numerous field trips to different places would have on Devorah. But she did not find the field trips unsettling; in fact, they offered her excitement, stories, memories, and permanent learning. The field trips are linked with class studies, so learning is reinforced through experience. If the subject is geology, students go to the mountains; if oceanography or biology, they visit the ocean or wetlands. The idea is to learn by doing rather than through relying solely on an abstract explanation. This approach works for other students at PCCS and is essential for Devorah.

A daily schedule provides predictable structure. Some classes meet for an hour, others for three hours, depending on the subject or teacher. Field trips may mean missing a class, but since the school is small and communication among teachers is good, skipped classes do not create the confusion, makeup work, and aggravations they would in a large public school.

At Pacific Crest, structure means options. Some students have more structure than others—*a structure that they have helped to create.* Other students can organize and structure their own time. For those with FAS/E, changes in structure may be less unsettling when they flow from interests and activities rather than from rigid, arbitrary, and complex institutional considerations.

Pacific Crest includes a remarkable range of learning styles and abilities, from other students with alcohol-related neuro-developmental disabilities to brilliant children. Everyone works together on projects and participates on a rotating judicial council to assure compliance with the rules. The school's values, demonstrated at every juncture by staff, parents, and students, create an acceptance of diversity. Once, someone overheard a group of students talking about how important the students with learning problems were for the school, how much a part of life they all were, how much there was to learn from them. This spontaneous discussion, conducted without a sense of superiority, acknowledged the contribution of all community members. Pacific Crest minimizes the pecking order and recognizes different kinds of intelligence, strengths, and personal contributions.

Each child has an advisor who is more like a mentor. For Devorah and other children with FAS/E, this personal relationship is crucial: Learning comes after the social relationship is established. Pacific Crest is fully accredited, and graduating students have no problem being accepted into colleges or pursuing other goals.

HOW THE PACIFIC CREST EXPERIENCE HELPED DEVORAH: THE CHANGES WE SAW

The summer before the doors opened at Pacific Crest, interested parents, students and staff held a planning meeting. The students became so excited they said, "We don't want to wait until school starts. Let's do something now!" They proposed a two-week camping trip. The staff agreed, providing that the students plan the trip, which they did. Devorah decided to go. She met future schoolmates and earned the nickname "Piston Legs" for being one of two students to make it to the top of a mountain—a tremendous boost for her self-esteem and a wonderful introduction to her new group of peers.

Devorah started Pacific Crest tremendously resistant to academics. She refused to read, write, or do anything that would risk punishment, red marks, ridicule, or other painful feedback. Her beliefs about herself limited her more than her disability. We didn't pressure her to spend more time studying or correct or scold her. I believed that as the environment changed and matched her needs better, her behaviors would improve.

That's exactly what happened. During her first few months in school, Devorah tested the waters, remaining on the edge of academic activities. The staff allowed her to take her time, which was exactly what she needed. While attending a school play, I watched Devorah in the midst of a group of friends. That simple act was something that had never happened for her before in school. Somewhere during the first year at Pacific Crest, Devorah began studying at home. No one told her she had to. She wanted to. She had established good relationships with her teachers, felt valued as a person, and her contribution was important *to her.*

Academically, Devorah has enjoyed a growth spurt. At the end of last year her math teacher, Bill, mentioned that she seems to have experienced one of those "clicks" that happens sometimes for children with FAS/E. This year her favorite class is world history. Her teacher, Becky, brings history alive *with* (not *for*) the students. They dramatize events, hold medieval feasts and celebrations, read stories of peoples' lives, and find meaning in an otherwise distant set of events. In fact, a stew she created in the school kitchen for a medieval feast won rave reviews from the students. When a scheduling conflict caused her to miss an hour of the class once a week, she found this so unacceptable that she developed a solution. She remembered a little hand-held recorder I have and asked if she could use it to tape the missed hour. This worked well and reinforced Devorah's sense of competency in problem-solving.

One teacher describes Devorah as being unstoppable: "Every time we post a sign-up sheet for a new class, she signs up for it." This year becoming overextended is her problem. She'll do homework until 11 P.M., and we have to ask her to stop to go to bed. She remains frustrated by her short-term memory, by reading something and then forgetting, but even so, she now sees herself as a learner, excited by the world around her. She is active and competent in many ways: she takes photographs, jogs, and earns money from our neighbors by taking care of their animals.

Through working on a team with eight other students who built sea kayaks in the traditional way, she's discovered that she loves boatbuilding and woodworking. "Mom," she told me, "I have smart hands." As she completes the equivalent of her junior year, she is already starting on her senior dissertation project: building a wooden dinghy. She has had to talk with boat builders, find plans, check measurements. It is incredibly exciting to watch her blossom, glow with excitement, and strengthen her belief in herself as a competent, wonderful young woman.

Conclusion

Many questions about Devorah's future remain unanswered, including living situations, support services, and even college or vocational training after high school. We accept that her timeline will be atypical, that she may not be ready to leave home until she's 25 or so, and that in the meantime she can continue developing skills for independence.

Like everyone else, Devorah needs to be heard, to matter, to make sense to herself. At Pacific Crest, her opinion is valued, her contributions appreciated. Her life is far from perfect; frustrations related to FAE appear periodically, and the disability persists. Her positive experiences have made these more manageable. Her disability no longer defines her—it is simply one part of who she is. At Pacific Crest, she is not a problem. Rather, she has a problem, one she can deal with.

11

Adapting Talk Therapy for Individuals with FAS/E

SUSAN L. BAXTER

Susan Baxter, M.S., a licensed psychological associate, is a private practitioner in Anchorage, Alaska. She was employed from 1991 to March 1996 as the FAS psychologist in the pediatrics department of the Alaska Native Medical Center in Anchorage.

ABOUT THREE YEARS AGO, A WORRIED MOTHER NAMED MAUREEN approached me about providing therapy for her 14-year-old daughter, Sarah, who has FAS.[1] In addition to threatening suicide, Sarah had been flying into unprovoked rages so uncontrollable that she had bruised and bloodied her knuckles as she knocked holes into her bedroom walls. These overwhelming rages and their potential outcomes terrified her family, who didn't want Sarah to harm herself or anyone else but did not know how to intervene. Maureen said it felt "as if family members were being held hostage" by Sarah's behavior. Unlike real hostages, they had no idea what ransom would buy their freedom. Sarah was as much a hostage as anyone else because no one understood or seemed able to help her with her behavior.

I was reluctant to take Sarah's case, although my academic training had included an internship that exposed me to children

---

[1] This case study is based on the course of therapy for one young woman with FAS. However, it incorporates similar experiences described by approximately 15 other teenagers and preteens with alcohol-related disabilities. Details have been changed to protect the confidentiality of each individual, and all names are fictitious.

and adolescents with FAS and I had stayed current in the field.[2] I wasn't sure that therapy would help her. One of the most consistent messages I had encountered was that traditional "talking therapies" were ineffective for individuals with fetal alcohol-related disorders.[3] Some people believed the disability prevented the development of insight. Another message was that clients would be unable to generalize[4] to their real lives what they had learned or discovered in a therapy session. Nevertheless, expecting to be challenged in every skill I possessed, I agreed to see Sarah for four sessions to assess her status.

Those four sessions extended into a long journey of understanding not only for Sarah but for me. After two and one-half years of counseling, *her progress shows that traditional therapy can help alcohol-affected adolescents. The key is to link talk therapy to concrete, physical representations of the issues.*

I used role-playing, practice dialogues, and play therapy to appeal to Sarah's natural sense of adolescent drama and her need for multisensory learning. I helped her understand relationships with her family through the use of a baby book. A friendship map with lines and circles represented her relationships to her friends. Such methods made it possible for her to visualize these abstract concepts. Through these techniques, Sarah overcame her resistance to therapy and explored her identity, learned better ways to communicate with her parents, better managed her moods, and gained control over her sexuality. Her suicidal images and actions gradually disappeared.

Working with Sarah was a delight and a revelation that has irrevocably changed me as a human being and as a professional. In a way, her story is my story, too.

---

[2] While perpetually seeking more information about these problems from the scientific research literature, I also tried to forge links with parents of affected children because they seemed to possess a collective knowledge that, while informal, exceeded the quality and quantity of formal knowledge held by the professional community.

[3] This statement refers to all diagnostic labels such as FAS, FAE, FADE (Fetal Alcohol and other Drug Effected programs), and ARND (Alcohol Related Neurodevelopmental Disabilities).

[4] "Generalize" is a clinical behavioral term that means the ability to both transfer learning from one situation to another and to apply it. It refers to several processes that are delineated in literature regarding social learning and behavior modification theory.

FIRST STEPS

Sarah was a tiny, dark-haired teenager with a charming, gamin face and an early history similar to the stories of other children with FAS/E. Her mother reportedly consumed one or more cases of beer per week throughout the pregnancy, had little or no prenatal care, and was intoxicated at delivery. Sarah weighed less than six pounds at birth, had some facial features of FAS, and had experienced alcohol withdrawal and other problems. Among other abnormal neurological findings, she demonstrated a peculiar relentless "bulldozing" activity in which she pushed herself and her bedding from one end of her crib to the other for 24 hours without relief.

At about three months, Sarah was placed in her first foster home. She began to show signs of hyperactivity and developed the definitive facial features of FAS. A diagnosis of severe FAS was confirmed. Maureen and her husband Dan took in Sarah as a foster child at age two and adopted her when she was three.

Maureen was a certified teacher with training in child development and Dan was a drug and alcohol counselor. Though familiar with the diagnostic descriptions associated with FAS, it was the first time for both parents to be totally reponsible for full-time care of an affected child. When Sarah's rages appeared, they had expected to be able to manage her behavior, and their ineffective efforts eroded their sense of ability as parents. Their feelings of helplessness contributed additional strain to an already stressful situation, and raised feelings of self-doubt relative to their respective professions. Now at a crisis point, the family was seriously considering hospitalizing Sarah in a psychiatric facility or a residential treatment program to help with her behavioral and emotional problems.

I liked Sarah at once. The feeling did not seem mutual. She was very suspicious of the process we were beginning. She admitted there were conflicts at home but denied they had anything to do with her. In fact, the position she took (and would cling to for many months) was that she was just fine while everyone else in her family was "messed up." She felt she had no choice about coming to therapy and perceived it as a way to get her parents "off her back."

I was temporarily on familiar ground. Here was a young woman with a common adolescent resistance to therapy. My first task would be to connect with her. Later we would identify a goal for using the enforced time we had together. I acknowledged how frustrating it must be for her to be in counseling when she believed that other members of her family were responsible for causing conflicts. I noted that, unfortunately, we could not change her parents or anyone else, but I was willing to help Sarah in any other way I could. I also told her we would review progress after four weeks and if she absolutely did not find it useful, I would recommend to her parents that we stop meeting.

The four-week assessment produced several therapeutic goals that could be addressed in a concrete manner:

• Like many parents of alcohol-affected children, Maureen and Dan acknowledged Sarah's difficulties in using words to label and understand her emotions. However, they found it difficult to help her because they could not separate their own feelings from hers. A primary goal of the therapy, then, would be to provide Sarah with opportunities to experience her feelings in a safe environment where they could be contained and she could learn to describe them.

• After acquiring a greater awareness of her feelings, Sarah would need to practice talking about them, identifying the circumstances that evoked them, and asking for help in resolving problems. This would require practice dialogues and role playing.

• Sarah needed to learn to trust herself and her parents to be able to solve problems together. Occasional joint therapy sessions would assist with this objective.

• Sarah and her parents needed to agree on what to do if Sarah felt suicidal or explosive while she was developing her new skills. Because she could not use words after she reached a certain level of agitation, she needed to release physically the escalating tension. Only two activities helped: running and hitting. Sarah's parents provided her with an inexpensive walking machine and a sturdy punching bag, and gave her permission to take walks on a trail near their home. She could take time-outs whenever needed as long as she chose one of these safe options and then returned to work things out.

Sarah agreed to therapy organized in six-week intervals, with an option to quit after each interval. After about a year, during which she made solid progress with school and home relationships, she decided she no longer needed therapy and stopped coming. Three months, later, however, she herself asked to resume her sessions when she feared that her feelings were getting out of control again. After that, she continued meeting without any reluctance.

Exploring Suicidal Ideation, Threats, Gestures, and Rages

When we first met, Sarah said she didn't have any problems and didn't know what to talk about. I told her that thinking about suicide was a problem and that her frequent threats worried me. I wondered if she could tell me more. "Oh, that," she said, and to my surprise, was willing to talk about her threats, though not much else.

Over the next few weeks I learned that not only had Sarah made suicidal threats, she had actually made several suicidal gestures that her parents knew nothing about. Sarah talked about the act of suicide itself and her beliefs about what would happen afterwards. She understood death as an end to discomfort, but not as the end of living. Sarah did not want to die. She made suicidal threats and gestures when she was frustrated or couldn't solve a problem. For example, when Sarah's parents assigned a chore to her without helping her get started, she would procrastinate rather than ask for help. Her parents would then nag her about it, and eventually, Sarah would lose all control, screaming:

> You only care about this house, you don't care about me. I have too much to do and nobody cares. I may as well just die. I might just as well kill myself.

What she really meant was:

I don't know how to do what you asked and I'm really stuck. I need your help.

Sarah's behavior and threats were statements of total helplessness. She could not express her feelings or needs in words. Furthermore, she was terrified of her explosive behavior[5] and the possibility that she might hurt herself or someone else. She expended a great deal of energy holding her feelings in so they would not get out of control (she later called it "stuffing"). This left her with little energy to manage changes or additional stress that might occur in her day-to-day schedule.

Even in the face of small demands, her stored-up anger and frustration escaped her control in a huge expression of rage—the rages that her mother had described. Following each such episode, Sarah would be even more fearful and more determined to harness her emotions. She had reached a point in this self-perpetuating cycle where she experienced and expressed very little emotion except during her rages, which were happening more frequently. Furthermore, her feelings were now related to anger or masked by it. Anger was the only emotion she acknowledged.

Handling Anger

Sarah would shut down whenever she began to feel anger. I had to teach myself to wait quietly until she was ready to continue. Once she was calm, I made positive comments about her ability to know when her feelings were becoming too strong and to take time out from them. Because I was tolerant, she developed the capacity to work with intense feelings for longer and longer intervals before taking time out. As Sarah's moods and activity levels shifted, which they frequently did, I pointed out the shifts and asked her to pay attention to what she felt and thought. We considered the changes in her posture, her energy level, and her willingness to talk to me.

---

[5] "Explosive behavior" is a term used by psychologists and psychiatrists to describe behavior that is the result of a lack of skill in managing emotions through verbal communication and problem solving.

Sometimes I asked her to draw a picture. At other times I asked her to describe what she wanted to do at the moment. Her response to this question varied. Sometimes she wanted to run away or to hit something. Once when she looked away from me, she said, "I want to go to sleep." We wrote down reasons why someone might want to go to sleep, and Sarah decided which reason matched hers the best. She tried to remember another time when she felt the same way (when her mother nagged her). Then we talked about what I had said or done that made her feel the same as being nagged (too many questions). We decided what she could say or do to help me understand how she felt. Later, we talked about whether this approach would work with her mother. To encourage Sarah to discuss her feelings at home, we role-played several situations in which Sarah felt nagged by her mother. I sometimes took Sarah's part and she coached me on what to say while she played her mother's part.

Through these activities Sarah learned to label her full range of emotions. She also learned how to establish safe boundaries for herself, often telling me that she did not feel comfortable with her feelings and would like to talk about something else for awhile. I soon discovered that this was not avoidance. Sarah would bring distressing issues up again and again.

Sarah felt most upset when she felt helpless. Often, her helplessness resulted from a change, a stress, or a fear of failing. We worked on ways to change her unrealistic expectations and set concrete goals. For example, a chronic joint problem hindered her participation in sports, but she insisted that if she just worked hard enough she could accomplish as much as the others. We explored ways she could enjoy the rewards of these activities without being perfect, and she began to set more realistic goals, such as making it through the entire season without being benched for an injury rather than trying to be first on the team. She paced herself better, played more strongly, and began feeling more competent and successful.

Sarah and I also formed a suicide prevention contract. She agreed that if she felt seriously suicidal, she would contact me or one of several emergency agencies before taking any action. She carried a small card with her at all times that listed several emergency telephone numbers in case she couldn't reach me. We role-played calling the numbers and how she would describe her condition.

USING PLAY THERAPY TO ENCOURAGE TALKING

In the beginning, Sarah often entered the therapy room to sit, stiff and sullen, on the couch. She rarely made eye contact, refused to answer most personal questions, and did not initiate conversation. I grasped at the rare moments when she became animated (usually while discussing a friend or acquaintance), examining and re-examining them for keys that might unlock her silences. Most of my efforts resulted in shutting her down even further, especially whenever I urged her to try to understand a friend's thoughts and feelings by asking, "What is that like when that happens to you?" She'd say, "It doesn't happen to me," or "I don't want to talk about it anymore," then turn her head away.

Trained as a play therapist, I wondered if similar techniques and strategies would reach Sarah. In play therapy, a child often establishes a metaphor in their play, a story through which they are able to confront an anxiety-provoking issue while maintaining some emotional distance. After doing this for some time, they may move to a reality-based theme and confront their issues more directly.

I decided to approach Sarah's discussions about her friend's problems by assuming they were her metaphors and that they revealed something about her. I listened more and stopped pushing her to reveal her feelings. This improved strategy taught me a lot about her beliefs and values. One day, for example, we had the following brief conversation:

> Sarah: "My friend Joanie is adopted. She's mad at her adopted mother, Mary. She wants to go live with her real mom. Is she dumb or what?"

Me: "So when Joanie is upset with Mary, she'd like to get away. She wonders if things might be better than with her real mom."

Sarah: "Yeah. Do you think it would work? Her real mom drinks a lot. What do you think she should do?"

At this point I was certain that Sarah was asking these questions for herself because she wondered what it would be like to live with her biological mother and she wondered what I thought. I wanted to understand how important this issue was to Sarah and to help her explore it so that she could make her own decision. Staying within the context of her story, I said:

"I'm not sure. You know Joanie better than I do. What's your guess?"

Sarah: "I think it won't work...."

With prompting, Sarah listed the reasons why the relationship between Joanie and her mother would not work out. Her explanations revealed a great deal about her own belief system and her feelings about her own biological mother.

Despite these moments, we continued to confront lots of impasses. Furthermore, Sarah began picking at her cuticles during sessions until they bled, though she brushed off my attempts to talk about it. I was uncomfortable with this turn of events. Had Sarah not continued to be suicidal at this time, I might have recommended discontinuing the therapy.

Moving even closer to a play therapy model, I decided to introduce activities to keep Sarah's hands busy so she would not harm herself. The next time she started picking her cuticles, I tossed her a textured toy. She tossed it back—I thought she was rejecting it. I tossed it to her again and she kept it, squeezing it, turning it, and tossing it from hand to hand. We were both quiet for awhile. As she concentrated on the toy, she stopped holding her body in her usual rigid posture. After a few minutes of this, she said quietly and unexpectedly, "Have I ever told you I was born drunk?"

The next week, I was at the children's play table kneading play dough when Sarah came in. She bypassed her usual spot on the couch and came to the table. She watched at first, then gradually joined. We spent a wonderful hour squeezing, shaping, and talking—about Sarah.

After that, I always had materials available for her session. We colored, painted, used play dough, cut paper snowflakes, folded paper boxes, drew maps and diagrams, and wrote lists. Occasionally she worked on classroom assignments, something I would never have permitted before working with Sarah. As long as her hands were busy, Sarah talked. In the beginning she spoke mainly about her friend, but gradually she talked more and more about herself.

Sarah taught me that activity helped calm her, and that when she was calm, she could think and she could more easily put her thoughts into words. Most important, Sarah taught me that she was just like any other teenager looking for help in coping with the pressures of her daily life. She brought problems to therapy and together we explored options and possible outcomes.

Changing Sarah's Catastrophizing and Negative Self-Talk

Sarah tended to catastrophize about the future. For example, she was convinced she was failing in school, and I believed her. When her report cards showed her grades actually were better than average, she rejected them, saying they were mistakes and she had not earned them. In fact, she rejected all positive feedback. Though I pointed this pattern out to her, it was only after several report card cycles that Sarah could see it for herself. Eventually, she described her incredibly predictable pattern in her own words. She said her grades often were better than she expected, but she told herself she was failing so she would work harder. Her fear of failing discouraged her, though, and sometimes she gave up and didn't do anything. Her teacher's warnings about missing assignments and possible failure reinforced her beliefs, causing anger, disappointment, and frustration that would send her closer and closer to the brink of explosive behavior. We worked on changing her self-talk from "I'll fail if I don't do this" to "I can do it if I do this much today."

Sarah also said she had been paying attention to her reactions when people said nice things to her at school. She thought she rejected compliments because she didn't feel that they fit with who she really was and they often came from people who didn't really know her. Unless her parents said these things, she did not feel worthy of the compliments of others. This disclosure opened up avenues for improving Sarah's relationship with her parents and her school work habits. Her disclosures were especially exciting because they indicated Sarah was learning from therapy and transferring it into the real world.

By this time we had been working together long enough that I could identify other cyclical patterns of emotional upheaval and behavior that corresponded to quarterly changes in Sarah's school schedule and to seasonal changes in family life, such as vacations, summer visitors, family trips, and holidays. I made a calendar of these events and matched them with notes showing Sarah's mood changes. We talked about FAS and its impact on the brain and central nervous system. I explained to Sarah that these changes were uncomfortable for her because it took her body and her nervous system longer to adjust. I did not expect her to learn to anticipate these changes, only to learn that change was difficult and if she felt sad, frustrated, or angry, it might help to look for something new or different in her life. To my surprise she did learn to identify, anticipate, and plan for the anxiety that she experienced with many changes. Once when her family was planning a vacation with a variety of activities, Sarah told her mother that she would try hard to manage but pointed out that change was very hard for her because of her FAS.

About this same time, Maureen reported that Sarah had not made a suicide threat for some time. Further, her rages were no longer happening daily or even weekly. Maureen also said that Sarah was talking more about daily events and spending slightly less time isolated in her room.

180 / Susan L. Baxter

Moving from Therapy to Real Life

Since I had been warned that children with FAS do not generalize from therapy to real life, I was surprised to see that Sarah did
transfer concrete ideas from therapy to her own life. I had to be
quite careful about what I said, because she took my words very
literally. Once we were discussing smoking, a habit Sarah had
taken up and now wished to stop, we shared all of the methods
we knew that people had tried. I mentioned someone who had
tried to stop by allowing herself one cigarette per day, relighting it
each time she wanted to smoke a few puffs. The next week, Sarah
announced that smoking used cigarettes was disgusting and tasted
so bad that you would have to quit if that was all you had.

Moderating Morals, Values, and Judgments

I had been taught that children with FAS could not be counted
on to develop a moral code or a sense of social judgment. I found
just the opposite to be true. Sarah's sense of values and moral
judgment was firmly in place and basically drawn from her parent's
teachings. She considered herself extremely honest and expected
the same from others (in fact she was sometimes brutal in her
self-evaluations). She tested me from time to time, and I found it
important to keep her honestly and openly informed, especially
about all contacts with her parents, either planned or incidental.
The problem was that she had an all-or-none system, which
resembled the black-and-white thinking of children at a much
earlier stage of cognitive development. She applied her values
rigidly and could not tolerate behavior that fell into the gray area
between. For her, the gray area did not exist. Anyone who violated
her rigid code was not worthy of her trust.

Sarah described her parents as "two-faced" when they ven-
tured into the gray areas of her value system: They made and
expected her to follow rules that they didn't follow themselves. A
particular issue for her was their behavior with regard to privacy.
She was not allowed to enter their bedroom without permission,

yet they went into her room for a variety of reasons that would seem legitimate to most parents. But not to Sarah, who believed that all bedrooms should be either open or closed to others, regardless of the reasoning.

Probably the most difficult gray area revolved around the consistent performance of chores. Sarah and her parents had daily chores, and occasionally Dan or Maureen missed or postponed a chore because of other demands or allowed Sarah to do the same. Sarah did not grasp the differences in the circumstances and sometimes asked for an inappropriate suspension of her chores. She became extremely upset when the request was denied because she felt the rules were always changing.

We talked about the fact that everyone, even parents, found making decisions difficult in these areas and that we all make mistakes. We tried to identify the gray areas in her own life, which were usually situations that had several negative outcomes but involved highly appealing activities. For example, Sarah had several neighborhood friends with whom she could play without parental permission. Another group of friends required parent approval because they had influenced Sarah to make unsafe choices such as riding her bicycle on thin ice. Sarah had no difficulty informing these friends about her rules when she was approached by them individually. But when an approved friend and a permission-only friend approached her together, it was hard for Sarah to apply her rules. Our goal was to help her consistently recognize these areas and to talk her decisions over with someone who could help her be sure she had considered all of the consequences and how the rules should be applied.

Sarah could understand her own mistakes, but she wanted her parents to be perfect. Because of her own uncertainty, she needed consistency from them. Later, as she gained strength in her own sense of identity and drew on a broader support network, she depended less on Dan and Maureen for all of her structure and validation. This resulted in fewer conflicts about changing rules. However, Sarah's increasing independence led her into more complex social situations that Dan and Maureen monitored more closely. Sarah regarded the monitoring as a lack of trust which escalated their conflicts in another direction. Helping Sarah reframe her parents' behavior as positive and caring has been a major thrust of her current therapy.

Exploring Identity Issues and Isolation

Obviously, values and beliefs were important to Sarah. But one day when I asked her what she thought about a specific issue, she lashed out at me, complaining that I shouldn't ask her questions like that. She said:

> If you really want to know what my problems are, you would listen to me. You would understand that I don't know who I am. I don't know what to think or believe. I am only a burden to my parents. I have no real friends. I have no one to talk to except you, and I don't belong anywhere.

She further complained that she had neither a past nor a future, and that she really had no purpose in being.

I took out a paper and wrote her name at the top of it. I divided it into three sections. In one, I wrote, "Who am I?" In another I wrote, "What do I believe?" And in the last one, I wrote, "Who are my friends?" I was determined to make these abstract concepts concrete for her. I told her that we could work together to find answers to each question; we would begin working on one of them today, and the next week I would have a plan for looking at the others.

I asked her to draw a small circle in the middle of a piece of paper and put her name in it. Next, I asked her to start making other circles around her on the paper. She was to write the name of a person she knew in each circle. The more circles she drew, the more names she thought of. After awhile I asked her to stop and told her we could add circles any time she wanted. Then I asked her to tell me about some of the people she had named, including how she knew them, whether she saw them often or not, and how much she liked them. I asked her to draw lines between herself and others, adding three lines if she liked them a lot and they liked her back, and a dotted line if they were only acquaintances. She used a zigzag line to connect herself to people she didn't get along with. Finally, I asked Sarah to connect other people to each other in the same way.

Sarah didn't need any interpretation to realize that she was not isolated—the drawing mapped this out for her in a very concrete way. She was connected to a rather large network of friends, and she was the key person in several sub-groups where everyone talked to her but not necessarily to each other. While constructing her map, Sarah realized that one of the girls she knew was very much like her and was a potential friend. Although the girl had confided in Sarah from time to time, it had never occurred to Sarah that she might confide in the girl or that they could become friends. Now, she was convinced that she had a friend who could understand her in nearly every way.

I kept Sarah's friendship map in my office. She would ask for it and make changes in it as her typically fluid adolescent relationships shifted. The map became an important tool as she explored her own identity and how she fit with various social groups.

For her next visit, I prepared a notebook for her to use in my office. One section would list the things that Sarah thought were important—answering the "What do I believe?" question. The other section would be for her to write memories about her childhood (the "Who am I?" question). Just for practice, I asked her to describe the very first memory she could recall. This turned out to be a very dramatic event in which her village home was flooded and nearly destroyed. She recalled losing a cherished toy in the flood. I encouraged her to write in her journal everything she could remember about the incident.

For several weeks, Sarah wrote in her journal, entering mostly statements I prompted her to write whenever she described something as "good" or "bad." These statements became the basis for describing her beliefs and her values.

Then one day she came to therapy with a package she could hardly wait to unwrap. Inside was a scrapbook about Sarah that she had never seen before. One day after we started her journal, she had asked her mother why there was no baby book for her. Her mother showed her the scrapbook, and they took some time to go through it together. Maureen had shared stories about each of the pictures and items in the book, and Sarah and I also went through the book together. I listened as she recounted each story; this was a perfect opportunity to reinforce how important she had always been to her family and to each of her foster families for them to have preserved these things for her. The book also presented an opportunity for Sarah to talk about her feelings about her biological family.

After that, Sarah referred to the scrapbook as her baby book and asked if she could leave it in the file drawer where I kept her chart and the journal we had started. We only looked at it once or twice more, and I sometimes asked her if she wanted to take it back home with her. She never wrote in the journal again. She didn't need it. The scapbook had given her part of the identity she had been seeking. And at least for the time being, she kept it where it was safe, along with the other parts of herself that she had revealed to me, and which we were gradually piecing together.

ADDRESSING FEELINGS ABOUT HAVING FAS

Sarah's was an open adoption. Recapturing her past also brought her face to face with her relationship with her birth mother. Occasionally she talked about her anger that her mother had chosen to drink, causing FAS in her daughter. She was even more concerned that her birth mother continued to drink, contributing to a dysfunctional lifestyle. But she was most worried that she would be like her mother. I was surprised, then, when she began to talk about visiting her birth mother. She also discussed the two paths she could follow: She could be like her birth mother, or she could be like her adoptive parents.

Eventually Sarah arranged a visit with her birth mother. This was a difficult time for Dan and Maureen, who worried that Sarah was flirting with her birth mother's lifestyle. However, after a few visits, Sarah concluded on her own that her birth mother could make her own choices and that she (Sarah) could also make hers, and they didn't have to be the same. Her anger gave way to sadness and a sense of loss, which she talked about.

Sarah also began to ask questions about her diagnosis and her particular deficits related to FAS. I answered them as honestly as I could, although it was difficult, as it always is when you must tell someone about their limitations. However, Sarah did not always focus on the limitations. For her, each answer seemed to be a key that helped her release another little bit of anxiety. One day when we discussed how FAS often impaired memory functions, Sarah looked at me with wide eyes and said, "That explains it. I'm not just lazy." The more she learned, the more she accepted herself and her disabilities. She also developed a genuine compassion for others with disabilities, and she adamantly opposed discrimination based on individual and cultural differences.

IMPROVING INTERPERSONAL COMMUNICATION

At times when Dan and Maureen worried about Sarah, their fears resulted in heated discussions with her and with each other that left hurt feelings and unresolved issues. Early in the therapy when Sarah complained about family members, I told her the therapy room was a good place to work on her own frustrations, but we probably weren't going to change her parents or siblings. One thing we could do was to help her find ways to talk to them so that they would listen.

A particularly troublesome problem for the family was Sarah's bedroom and how clean she kept it. Sarah was reluctant to invite her parents to talk about this problem, but I assured her everyone would have a chance to talk, and talking certainly couldn't make things worse, and she agreed to try it in a session following her regular time.

I asked Sarah's parents to come prepared to discuss their concerns about bedroom cleaning and outlined for them the rules that we would follow. Sarah and I role-played several ways the discussion might go. Everyone was apprehensive when we started the family meeting. I explained the rules again. Only two people would talk to each other at a time and the conversation would follow a fixed format. The speakers would describe the problem as they saw it using "I" statements. Then they would make a request about how they would like things to change. The listener would express what he or she thought the speaker was trying to say. The speaker would confirm or clarify. This would go on until the family agreed on the nature of the problem and the speaker's proposed solution. Then the listener could respond with his or her own perspective.

At first I worried that Sarah might not be able to use this communication format effectively. To help her understanding, I encouraged the family to focus on concrete behavior rather than on attitudes, arguments, or issues of respect. Interestingly enough, Sarah seemed more comfortable than her parents. She readily understood what her parents said and easily translated it into her own words. She had the most trouble talking about her own feelings. By the end of the session we had started to identify specific tasks that needed to be addressed and to establish guidelines to which every-one could agree. In one more family meeting we completed a basic contract. The contract outlined Sarah's specific chores with the steps required to do each one, and it clearly stated rules and guidelines for requesting and giving help. Dan and Maureen also committed to reteaching Sarah when she made mistakes rather than punishing her.

Much more than a negotiated contract resulted from these two sessions. The family found that in this format, they could safely discuss their problems without fighting because it avoided blaming and name calling. Occasionally, they used the same strategy to solve problems at home. Other times they decided their feelings were too strong and they needed the safety of the therapy room and an objective third person to help them stay on track. In these joint communication sessions, they addressed curfews, psychiatric evaluation, depression, medication, driving privileges, tobacco and alcohol use, whether Sarah should change schools or get a job, and finally, birth control and sexuality. Eventually, they discussed some family dynamics, a process as helpful to Dan and Maureen as it was to Sarah.

SEXUALITY ISSUES

On several occasions, Maureen had expressed concern about Sarah's vulnerability if she began to date. She wanted Sarah to have access to birth control. Then, when Sarah, who had firmly expressed distaste for boys all along, suddenly blurted out that she had a boyfriend and they had been kissing, Maureen confronted a fear she could not manage. Dan took over. He and Sarah discussed the issue in their next family meeting while Maureen looked on anxiously.

Dan: "Sarah, your mother and I sometimes worry about how often we make choices without thinking ahead to what might happen. One of the discussions that comes up for people your age is whether to date or not. The next decision is about kissing. After that is the decision to have sex or not. We know you've already made decisions about dating and kissing."

Sarah: "I've already made decisions about all of them. I have a boyfriend, I might kiss him, but I'm never having sex until I'm married."

Dan: "I appreciate that you are making that decision for yourself right now. I believe with all my heart that you do not intend, at this moment, to ever have sex. But I'm still worried. Two months ago you said you would never kiss a boy. You changed your mind. You didn't know you would meet someone you would like so much. You might change your mind about sex, too. If you decide to have sex, there are other choices you will be making at the same time, whether you think about them or not. Can you tell me what can happen when you have sex?"

Sarah: "Parents get really mad at you."

Dan: "Your parents may be disappointed, but not mad. What else?"

Sarah: "Dad, we had a class in school. I know what can happen. You can cause babies and you can get AIDS."

Dan: "Exactly. Now, your mother and I prefer that you wait to have sex until you are much older. We think it is a mistake for teenagers. But becoming pregnant or getting AIDS is an even bigger mistake. We can't be there to help you decide what to do if a boy asks you to have sex. You will make your own decision. But we can provide you with birth control to protect you from becoming pregnant. There are several different kinds of birth control and we can decide together what is best for you."

Dan and Sarah listened respectfully to each other's views. I did very little to facilitate their discussion. Dan and Maureen had carefully worked out his approach in advance, and they had tried to anticipate all of Sarah's possible responses. Sarah resisted the idea of birth control at first because she still did not believe she would ever need it. To avoid being daily reminded of this conflict, they decided against birth control pills or an implant and selected an injection administered once every three months.

Dan and Maureen also strongly encouraged group activities rather than individual dating, and they decided to open their home to groups of Sarah's friends for supervised activities. Dan and Maureen realized they could not guarantee their plan would protect Sarah from unwanted pregnancies or from sexually transmitted diseases, but for their family circumstances, they had offered her the choices that they believed were the best for everyone.

MOODS, DEPRESSION, AND ILLUSIONS

In one of the family meetings, Sarah complained of feeling very tired and often sad. This opened the door to the issue of her depression. We noticed that her moods rose and fell in a cyclical pattern that fit with a form of depression called dysthymia. I thought medication might also help reduce Sarah's suicide risk, which she acknowledged was still present (she always denied being suicidal, but couldn't deny it as an option she might consider "if things got bad"). After an evaluation by a child psychiatrist, Sarah began taking an antidepressant medication that helped her mood swings, though finding the correct balance took time.

During this stabilization period, Sarah entered a particularly stressful phase. A devoted grandparent became seriously ill and the possibility arose for emergency travel on short notice. This created unpredictability for Sarah. A few weeks later Sarah's married sister came home for an extended stay, bringing her husband, children, and pets. Sarah's daily routine was drastically changed and also became more unpredictable. In the midst of this situation, Sarah reported that someone was walking through her bedroom at night. She could clearly see the figure, but she could not identify who it was. She insisted she had not misinterpreted shadows and objects in the darkness of her room—she could even feel a slight stir in the air from the person walking by. However, no one in the family had been in Sarah's room, and there was no evidence that an intruder had been in the house. The episodes occurred at approximately the same time in the evening. Sarah's psychiatrist said her experience was not a hallucination but an illusion, most likely created by a combination of the stress she was experiencing, environmental circumstances, and possibly disrupted sleep patterns or a nutritional deficit.

Sarah was the first adolescent I knew with FAS who had such an experience. I contacted a few other practitioners who regularly worked with FAS-affected children and adolescents and had observed similar events. Under unusual circumstances and high stress levels, some form of transient reality distortion or disconnect seemed to occur very briefly in a few youngsters with FAS. The most useful response that parents and clinicians could take seemed to be a calm, reassuring stance. We assured Sarah that this phenomenon was not unheard of, was most likely related to her stress and fatigue, and was not likely to continue (it didn't). For further reassurance, I asked her to schedule another appointment with the child psychiatrist to confirm that her medication did not need adjusting and to eliminate other related medical conditions.

SARAH'S ACHIEVEMENTS

At age 17, after two and one-half years of therapy, Sarah came to her session one day and drew a picture as she told me about a recent death and a separation in her life. The drawing's subject was a boat, a moon, and a land mass. More than a year previously, during an equally disruptive crisis, Sarah had also drawn a picture of a boat, a moon, and a land mass.

The two drawings were very different in feeling. The first drawing depicted a helpless, frazzled figure facing formidable mountains with no safe approachable shore. The figure had no hands and no connection to the oars. Red and orange colors dominated, and the mood depicted angry, frightened helplessness.

The second picture used pale colors and restful lines. An accessible, safe shore appeared, and a sail on the boat suggested more control. This picture was strongly bordered, corresponding to Sarah's developing abilities to contain and express her feelings more normally, as well as her emerging ability to set firm boundaries for herself. The new picture made a statement about Sarah's progress that words could never express, speaking eloquently of Sarah's greater capacity to tolerate stress and cope with problems.

Through therapy, Sarah has learned to ask for help. She has learned to trust her parents more than before. Even more important, she has learned to trust herself and her skills. And finally, she can identify sources of help for a range of situations and knows how to access them. Sarah still becomes overwhelmed and has difficulty acting on her knowledge. She continues to struggle with change, with new environments, and with the absence of structure. That may never change. What has changed is her understanding of her responses and how often she manages to solve problems on her own.

Implications for Therapy

Clinical work with adolescents with FAS requires more than therapy. Counselors must be aware of available resources in the community and be able to make referrals confidently to psychiatrists, physicians, and social services. In addition, counselors must be acquainted with the school system, its certification processes, and the personnel who administer special education programs. They need to understand the legal system and how to work with public advocacy agencies. For some adolescents, immediate needs create a stronger emphasis on case management than on therapy. However, I believe therapy forms an essential component of a comprehensive services program and that it should not be minimized or overlooked.

Working with Sarah taught me that insight is possible for young people with FAS/E, but it must be done through more than talk alone. Concrete, visual strategies work best, along with a simultaneous emphasis on the development of expressive language. From Sarah I also learned that a latency period often occurs between the achievement of insight and its application to daily activities. Expect the repetition of mistakes before understanding is achieved.

My years with Sarah also taught me that teenagers with FAS have the same needs that other teenagers have. They need friends, a sense of identity, a clear system of values, and the ability to set boundaries for themselves and for others. Their sexuality and the increasing intensity of their emotions confuses them. They differ most in that they rarely have adequate language to convey the intensity of these feelings, which can then overflow into acting-out behavior.

If Maureen were to ask me today to do therapy with Sarah, I would respond with confidence and hopefulness. I would trust my clinical perceptions and the therapeutic process. I would trust Sarah to accept her diagnosis of FAS and to understand its effect on her skills, confident that she could use her resources and knowledge to shape realistic expectations for herself and ultimately to chart a successful path through life. Valid therapeutic methods exist that can teach coping skills, allay strong feelings, and build self-esteem. For young people with FAS, the value and power of such therapy should not be overlooked.

12
Trouble with the Law

MARIE JONES[1]

This chapter describes our family's experience with the criminal justice system and what we learned. Though this will not be a blueprint for others, it is our hope that the knowledge we gained might help someone else. Details of our son's case have been changed or omitted to protect the family's privacy, and he has been given a pseudonym, "Dave." Dave has given his permission to discuss his story, and he has contributed to this narrative.

BEFORE DAVE WAS 21, HE HAD BEEN SUCCESSFUL AT WORK AND IN school. This does not mean there were not difficulties, but as a family we had managed to cope quite well. We knew Dave had FAS when we adopted him at 11 months of age, so he had the advantage of an early diagnosis. This gave us an opportunity to respond to his behavioral and learning differences in a manner that best suited him from the start. Throughout his school years we became advocates for him, sharing with teachers, neighbors, and relatives anything we had learned about FAS. Dave was not considered a discipline problem—he had never gotten into any serious trouble. We had always managed to find schools and a job where he would do well.

By the end of his first semester in seventh grade, it had become clear that Dave had problems handling six different teachers, classrooms, and six groups of classmates each day. He needed consistency, predictability, and structure not possible in

---

[1] Marie Jones is a pseudonym.

the traditional junior high or middle school program. We enrolled him in a private school for the learning disabled. Here he blossomed, winning an award for his science fair experiment. The dress code of a blue or yellow dress shirt and navy blue slacks simplified getting dressed in the morning and provided additional structure and predictability to his life. He continued at this school until tenth grade, when he returned to a public school with a smaller population, higher staff-to-student ratio, and closer attention to individual needs than his former public school. With support and concrete suggestions from a school counselor and a vocational counselor, our son obtained his first real job in a local grocery store, where he worked for four years.

As a junior in high school, Dave settled on a trade in food services that he pursued through high school. Always an enthusiastic and conscientious worker, he received a "Student of the Year" award in his occupational field when he was a senior. The next year he began taking one or two courses a semester at the community college while working part-time in his field. We rejoiced at how well he was doing.

Despite all this, when he was 21 and attempting to negotiate the adult world, his world and ours came tumbling down. When we returned from vacation, a card placed in our door asked our son to call a policeman. Here we made our first and very crucial mistake. Wanting our son to know he must take responsibility for his own actions, my husband took him to talk with the detective. Before they left, we discussed the importance of my · husband's presence during the interview. However, when my husband asked to sit in on the interview, the authorities told him they understood learning disabilities and his presence would not be necessary. The next thing my husband knew, they were fingerprinting our son.

When they returned, I asked my son, "Did they tell you your rights?" He said, "They told me I could leave at any time, but Mom, he had a gun." This was not an adult who understood his rights. This was an adult who had the social skills of a nine year old, a young man who sees all people as his friends even if he can't remember their names, a person who is friendly, outgoing, talkative, and unable to sense danger. This is a young man who can use properly inflected words in context whose meaning he does not understand. These were extremely black days in our lives. As parents, we felt that we had betrayed our son.

Our son was charged with a serious offense, and we did not know what, if anything, had occurred. We contacted an attorney with experience working with the developmentally disabled. Two days later, we returned home from work to find the house strangely quiet. Our son was nowhere to be found. Our greatest fear was that he had become frightened and run away.

Soon the phone rang with a collect call from the county jail. Nearly hysterical, I asked, "Are you all right?" He answered calmly, "It's O.K., Mom, they gave me an apple and a sandwich." The trusting, naive 9 year old in the 21-year-old body could not comprehend the panic and disbelief I felt.

The criminal justice system moves slowly with many delays and cancellations, which we attempted to use to our advantage. We reached out for assistance from any and all with expertise in this area. Initially we were determined to discover the complete truth; in reality, memory and cognitive defects make this impossible. Two psychologists in two different towns 50 miles apart concluded individually that no criminal act had occurred. Another expert more knowledgeable in the field of criminal justice and FAS advised that our son plead "no contest" and focus on a more favorable sentencing outcome. This approach would involve educating our attorney and the judge, which seemed more hopeful than attempting to educate an entire jury. However, we failed miserably at both these goals. Our own attorney—let alone the judge—did not quite seem to believe that FAS existed or that it should have any relevance to or effect on this case.

As we sat in the courtroom, the tone became more and more negative, and the words were unintelligible to our son, who turned around and said, "What's going on?" I said, "They are talking about sending you to prison." He turned white, his body rigid and shaking. Just that quickly Dave was sentenced to 2 to 15 years in prison and led away to the county jail awaiting transfer to the state prison. We were terrified.

Protecting Dave in Jail and Protecting What He Had Learned

Our main concern was Dave's safety in a correctional facility. His childlike nature, his desire for friends, his willingness to please, and his difficulty in distinguishing friend from foe and safety from danger made him extremely vulnerable. Our second major concern was that our son would lose all the good behavior and productive habits we had worked for so carefully these past 21 years.

Experience and the literature show that a person with FAS needs consistent structure and a routine to manage his life, as well as continual reinforcement. We also knew that young people with FAS are especially apt to solve social problems by imitating others. In a correctional facility he might take on the behaviors of those around him. Prison presented life-threatening dangers for a person with limited social and living skills. If he survived, the young man who returned to us would be far less able to function in society and far different from the person we released to the authorities.

We needed a plan to support our son in specific ways from a distance. Through the efforts of our pastor, officials acknowledged the threat posed by other inmates and assigned Dave a single cell. In a display of his nature and his social skills, he wrote a note to the person who had assigned him his cell and thanked her, telling her that he was happy that it had a window where he could look out on a shopping mall and see a clock that told him the time of day. He told her how the sun came in the window and helped him stay warmer. Soon it became clear to nearly everyone that something was different, and some employees at the facility began referring to Dave as "our little Forrest Gump."

He called us daily so we could continually reinforce important information and concepts. We reassured him constantly that we would do whatever it took to keep him safe. His therapist continued his weekly appointments inside the facility, offering Dave support,

GETTING IT TOGETHER
by Dave Jones*

Dave is alive to the details of the world and to its beauty. He lives with his parents and attends classes, making a C grade average. He studies Food Service Sanitation in a certified program that includes hands-on cooking classes. He pays rent, does much of his own laundry, and cooks occasionally (his specialty is Cranberry Chicken Casserole).

This is what he offers others.

WHAT MAKES ME HAPPY—HELPING OTHERS SEE THE ROSES

I try and find things that get overlooked by everybody else: the details. If I was driving down the street and if I saw wildflowers around the road, I would stop and look at those and not someone's garden. I am more alert to different details.

Last summer me and my Dad dug up a bunch of rose bushes and he was going to throw them away. Why throw them away? I took them and planted them somewhere else, way out in the backyard, so people driving along the road could see them. A lot of weeds in the garden have nice flowers. I will keep them. I don't care if they are weeds; they look nice.

JUGGLING WORK, SCHOOL, AND HOME

I have a big glass jar that I put everything in where I can see it: keys, watch, wallet. And I have a little green metal box I also use. I keep important papers like receipts or paperwork for the car in a bright red envelope.

In class, if the teacher writes it down, I know it's important. I take a tape recorder to class and play the tape at home if I missed something. The other kids want to borrow the tape.

At school, everything is focused around the computer. I have trouble writing. I do a lot of my homework on the computer, notes and stuff, because it's hard to write by hand. Also, I don't have the problem of losing my homework. If I lose it, I can print it out again.

My mother knows an old Chinese proverb: Tell me, I forget. Show me, I remember. Involve me, I understand. This describes me the best.

---

* Judith Kleinfeld interviewed Dave for this story, then edited the transcript. The story was checked by Dave and Marie Jones.

contact we could not provide, and consistency and predictability with his previous routine. The minister and the attorney would also visit.

Folks in the community called to see what they could do. We asked them to write him a note or send cards and postcards. His mail came from all over the United States, giving him something to look forward to and helping him feel that people cared. Our church set up a legal defense fund for him, which gave us hope as well as financial assistance. Twenty-five years of living and working in the community, as well as our professional credibility, provided a network of support for all of us and sustained us through the stress caused by this experience.

MOUNTING AN APPEAL AND GETTING BACK ON TRACK

As soon as we felt certain that Dave was safe, we turned our attention to mounting an appeal. Our attorney told us we could not appeal so we went before the judge ourselves. The judge indicated that, in fact, we could file an appeal through a criminal appeals attorney. We did this immediately. Our new attorney was eager to learn about FAS and agreed that the judge did not have all the information he needed to render a just decision.[2]

In the end, this bright, articulate and dedicated attorney obtained a resentencing. The new sentence called for 90 days in jail, five months on an electronic tether, ongoing therapy, and five years' probation. This was not the end, because the prosecutor appealed the judge's right to resentence. He later dropped the appeal.

Our son spent a total of 90 days in jail. We brought him home shortly after midnight, stopping by our church on the way home to spend a few moments giving thanks for his safe return. This was a concrete way to help our son remember the many people in the church and the community who had helped us. He recognized that support; he says that when he was most afraid, his

---

[2] Parents who need to advocate for young people with FAS/E in the legal system may find useful the judicial opinion of Judge C. Cunliffe Barnett (see Appendix 1). Judge Barnett discusses FAS and its legal implications.

parents and friends helped him through it. At home, he was so happy for the little things: getting a glass of milk from the refrigerator, sleeping on a softer bed, being able to shower without fear.

The next week Dave called his counselor at vocational rehabilitation, who in turn contacted the boss where he had worked. His employer was eager for Dave to return to work and was willing to work around curfew restrictions, therapy appointments, and meetings with the probation officer. In September, Dave enrolled in a vocational class at the community college and received a *B* for his final grade. He began volunteering at several agencies one or two days a week, helping with landscaping and other yard work at our church, and doing odd jobs at a family practice medical clinic. These efforts did much to restore his self-esteem, as he was helping others and received many kind words of thanks for his efforts. He also continued with therapy and began to put his life back together.

Although we survived this crisis with family and spirit intact, our experience should serve as a critical lesson for everyone with family members with FAS. People with such neurological deficits should not talk to officers of the law without an attorney. Our son now knows that he does not have to talk to policemen because he has the right to remain silent. He knows he has the right to call his attorney. He knows if that call is not completed, it does not count as a telephone call.

People with FAS/E should carry a card to remind them and others of their rights.[3] It could say something like this:

> To all law enforcement officers: I know that it is my right not to talk to you. I know it is my right to call my attorney.

The reverse side should include:

> • Name of an attorney knowledgeable and experienced in representing cognitively challenged clients

---

[3] For sample cards and brochures about the rights of disabled people when arrested, contact The Arc of the United States, 500 E. Border Street, Suite 300, Arlington, Texas 76010, phone: (817) 261-6003, e-mail: thearc@metronet.com; or contact: Project II/ GOARC, 3610 Dodge Street, Suite 101, Omaha, Nebraska, phone: (402) 346-5220.

SUCCEEDING ON THE JOB
by Dave Jones*

Dave has worked at the same job in a local restaurant for three years, an exceptional achievement for a person with FAS. With his pay based on his performance, he has received several raises since he started. His success stems from his own hard work and a good attitude, as well as from teamwork among his therapist, a vocational counselor, and his employer and coworkers.

The thing that makes me happiest right now is work. I have a few close friends at work. I try to help them out as much as I can and they help me out as much as they can. It makes work easier for me in terms of stress. If I need something and the person has time, they can go get it for me.

I wash dishes and do food preparation. I wash shellfish and I work in the pantry making salads. I set up for Sunday brunch, arranging the salmon on the platter, getting different salads ready, and making the dressing. I set up the dining room area, get the tongs and spoons out, and carry the food from the kitchen to the dining area. I enjoy it. It's fun. Most of the time it's pretty steady and easy work. The best part of the job is working with the other people in the kitchen and dining room. I like the people.

When one of our managers quit, my vocational counselor talked to my new boss and told him a little bit about me and some of the learning difficulties I might have. She worked with me and the new manager and made sure that things went smoothly so I didn't have any problems.

My psychologist also helps me work out problems. One of the problems is that there are a lot of different kitchen supervisors. Who do you need to listen to? One person or both of them? Whose job gets done first? My vocational counselor talked to the manager, and the psychologist helped me figure out an approach. I did some listening as well as talking, and I talked to the managers to get it resolved.

Sometimes it gets too busy and I can't keep up. Then I have to ask someone for help to get back on track. Most of the time I work by myself, but I need someone else to help me get everything done.

---

* Judith Kleinfeld interviewed Dave for this story, then edited the transcript. The story was checked by Dave and Marie Jones.

- *Telephone number*

- *Name and telephone of the person's rights representative*

When stopped by the police, people with FAS/E should do three things:

- *Be respectful*

- *Show a driver's license*

- *Say, "I need a lawyer."*

Dave, supported by my husband, is now part of a national advisory group examining the manner in which the justice system deals with individuals with disabilities. Although Dave is trying desperately to reap something good from an otherwise devastating experience, he doesn't dwell on it because he knows that dwelling on it won't help him. I tell him that other people are working on the problem and he should have faith that they will resolve it. The traits that the prison officials noted about Dave—his naivete and his ability to live in the moment—have protected him emotionally. As Dave puts it, "I have a very positive life right now. It's filled with energy and happiness."

13

Sexuality and Young Adults with FAS/E

SARA MIRANDA AND KAREN LEVINE

Sara Miranda, LICSW, is a social worker who has been active in the area of developmental disabilities for the last 21 years. Her work has included counseling teens and young adults with developmental disabilities and providing support to their families. She is currently an assistant division director for family support at the North Shore Arc in Danvers, Massachusetts.

Karen Levine, Ph.D., is a developmental psychologist with extensive experience working with children and teens who have learning, behavior, and communication issues. She is the co-director of the Neurodevelopmental Evaluation and Service Team at Spaulding Hospital in Boston, Massachusetts, and also is the clinical director of Autism Services for the North Shore Arc in Danvers, Massachusetts.

PARENTS OF CHILDREN WITH FAS MAY WONDER HOW THEY WILL HELP their son or daughter successfully negotiate a time that typical teenagers find so difficult. Most adolescents express a new or heightened interest in the opposite sex, confusion over a flood of unfamiliar feelings, and a desire for increased independence and privacy. Teenagers face many new situations that require them to use their own judgment. Adolescents with FAS share the same physical and emotional changes as their peers. However, their journey through this stage has some real differences (see chart, next page), and they need an extra level of support.

SEXUALLY RELATED CHANGES IN ADOLESCENCE FOR THOSE WITH DEVELOPMENTAL DISABILITIES*

TYPICAL DEVELOPMENT IN ADOLESCENCE	DIFFERENCES FOR ADOLESCENTS WITH FAS
Physical and emotional (hormonal) changes	Same—may be more confusing to interpret
Wishes, hopes, dreams, fantasies	Same—*may* be more difficult to distinguish between likely and unlikely (e.g., dating a movie star) scenarios
Cognitive changes; increase in abstract reasoning and judgment	Abstract reasoning and hence judgment *may* be impaired or develop later
Interest in teenage activites: dating, dances, etc.	May desire same activities but may not have access to a peer group for these activities, or may not have interest
Increasing independence	*May* need the supervision that a younger child needs, yet have a teenager's desire for independence

* Prepared by Karen Levine.

One mother describes a typical pattern:

> *Our 17-year-old daughter with FAS sometimes seems like "an accident waiting to happen" She is very pretty, physically affectionate, flirtatious, and too friendly with strangers. Last week she broke her curfew, but informed us it was "All right, because I'm so much in love."*

Using case experiences, we discuss why teenagers with FAS need additional guidance about sexuality, explore specific challenges, and provide teaching strategies.[1]

COPING WITH DREAMS AND FANTASIES

• *Sixteen-year-old Mike has fallen in love with his attractive, married, 35-year old piano teacher. She is kind to him, but Mike thinks she has a crush on him! He wants to ask her out.*

• *Fifteen-year-old Alison has fallen for the president of the senior class. She writes out his name over and over on her notebook and talks of wanting to marry him.*

For young teens to fantasize about inaccessible heroes and heroines is perfectly normal. This is the age of falling in love with the lead cheerleader, the movie star, the science teacher. Teenagers with learning difficulties can find it difficult to understand the different categories of relationships and appropriate behaviors. What is the difference between a friend and an acquaintance, between a friend and a boy friend? What does it mean if I wink at someone, if I hold their hand or hug them? If a coworker smiles at me or pats me on the back, does he want to be romantically involved?

We live in a world of social cues where dress, appearance, and gestures give us important information. Understanding these signals will mean that the teenager can avoid embarrassing or risky situations that have negative consequences. One young woman

---

[1] Many of these strategies have come from our work with teenagers with FAS/E, but some approaches are useful generally for adolescents with similar disabilities. See especially "Life Facts" and "Life Horizons" in Resources at the end of this chapter.

placed in a restaurant for vocational training almost lost her position because she could not correctly interpret social cues. Fortunately she was able to learn that it was not okay to wink at customers and that friendly smiles from the waiter did not mean he wanted to be her boy friend.

Learning and following the rules of social and sexual behavior is complex. Using a curriculum such as "Circles" can provide concrete, visual images about different types of relationships and the specific behaviors that accompany each category.[2] Each circle is a different color, presenting a quick and easy visual picture of both intimacy and social distance. Acting out the behavior that goes with each type of circle helps youths remember the rules.

Open discussion gives teenagers the opportunity to express their thoughts about boy friends, girl friends, love, and marriage. Many misconceptions can be cleared up this way. When asked what love is, one teenager informed her teacher that "love is roses." The teacher was then able to explore with the whole class what else might be involved with love, including a range of emotions and responsibilities. Videotapes and books that portray relationships can also highlight these concepts for adolescents with learning problems.

When your child focuses on someone who may not be appropriate, you can support your child in his dream ("Wouldn't that be nice if you went out with Michael?"), while at the same time helping them find a more realistic vision ("Maybe you will meet another boy just as nice as Michael"). When a child is unclear whether an unrealistic dream partner, such as the piano teacher, is interested, teach the cues that would determine if the person of their dreams is a realistic candidate ("Does she have a husband/ boyfriend? Has she ever called you? Does she know your name?" etc.). This must be done gently to teach information, never to ridicule the child for misreading cues, as it can be quite embarrassing for the children once they become aware that they may have misunderstood.

---

[2] See "Learning Kits" in Resources, at the end of this chapter.

LEARNING ABOUT LOVE AND DATING

• *Our 17-year-old daughter with FAS has been on only two dates with a young man, but talks of nothing but marriage and "getting a ring." She is completely naive about the dangers of sex. We are very worried about her safety, but we don't want to forbid her from dating or having a boy friend.*

• *Robert is an 18-year-old boy with FAS. Since his sixteenth birthday, he has expressed interest in girls. Initially his parents allowed him to engage in social activities involving small groups of friends, where Robert had to make decisions about relationships but the risks were relatively small. After a year of successful social experiences, Robert then told his parents he wanted to DATE! How should Robert proceed, and how do his parents help him understand the potential consequences of sex?*

Understanding and remembering all of the information about puberty, conception, and birth is difficult for anybody. Teenagers with FAS may have even more trouble identifying and remembering what they need to know. What do you want your child to learn? How can you break it down into simple concrete bits of information? How can you help them remember what to do?

Since young people with FAS need a lot of repetition, using different methods of presentation can avoid boredom. Also, varying the teaching methods can reach those who have difficulty with a particular format.

Excellent beginning books with clear pictures are available.[3] You may want to focus on one or two pages at a time, perhaps even photocopying a single page and putting the book away. In addition to using books with pictures and simple text, consider using the blackboard, plastic models, slides, and videos.

Discussion and role play are essential in helping teenagers consolidate what they've learned as well as highlighting areas that need more work. These formats can also seem like more fun than reading a book or listening to an adult talk. Teenagers often enjoy watching two or more individuals act out a scenario during role play because of the dramatic aspects.

---

[3] See Resources at the end of this chapter.

Through role play, teachers or parents can present situations that require both judgment and decision-making skills. One productive scenario, for example, features a teenage girl who is waiting at a bus stop in the rain when a stranger pulls up in his automobile. The girl does not have an umbrella. A student in the role of the driver asks the girl if she wants a ride home. The teacher can guide the way the scenario develops. If the driver is persistent and argumentative, supply a specific routine phrase for the girl such as "I'd rather ride the bus" that the girl can use in real life. Afterwards, the teacher can ask the class to analyze the situation and think about the girl's feelings, the decision she made, and other choices open to her. New twists (such as the girl knows the driver but her parents dislike him) can be added to stimulate more discussion.

While some parents may prefer doing most of this teaching at home, most families find that working with a teacher is helpful. Parents and teacher should meet before the introduction of any new material to make sure it is covered adequately. Parents can discuss family values, share thoughts on the curriculum, and give feedback on their child's progress. Teachers can suggest appropriate homework and resource materials that can be borrowed from the school.

Many individuals have also benefited from attending a support group that covers this material. This group might meet after school and be run by a counselor from a family service agency. This is a particularly effective way of teaching sex education, with emphasis on safety issues and appropriate behavior. The group can offer a neutral, safe place to explore questions and rehearse scenarios.

Parents also can gradually increase the level of responsibility in independent decision-making by using rehearsal and role play to prepare for difficult situations. Scenarios can include such safety issues as saying no to unwanted advances. Remember that risk-taking does foster development of skills. Allowing teenagers to make some safe bad choices helps prepare them for the future.

Underlying all decision-making is the need to stop, think, and act. Using these words while rehearsing and role playing social situations can be helpful. To help Robert prepare for dating girls, Robert's parents encouraged him to double date with his cousin, a responsible peer. His father rehearsed possible scenarios in response to Robert's questions "When can I hold her hand? When do I get to kiss her?" His father encouraged him to stop to think and consider how the girl was feeling before acting. When Robert asked how he could know what she was feeling, his father suggested asking her directly.

Because it's hard for some of us to understand what we can't see, explanations of conception, birth control, and sexually transmitted disease are made more difficult. Individuals with FAS/E may have a harder time believing in a process they cannot see—such as a sperm fertilizing an egg. Added to this difficulty is the reality that pregnancy does not always follow sexual intercourse, and the baby does not immediately follow conception. Now we have to explain the concepts of time delay and risk. These same learning challenges apply when we explain how disease is passed from one partner to another. Perhaps the most puzzling piece to understand is the notion of chance. Unprotected sex, for example, might or might not result in pregnancy or disease. People sometimes cope with risk by using "magical thinking," sometimes related to such superstitions as knocking on wood or throwing salt over your shoulder. Young people with FAS/E may use magical thinking that sounds like this: "Nothing will happen if we do it just once."

Sex is a place where using the "always-never" rule can help sexually active teenagers with FAS make the right choice to minimize the possibility of pregnancy and reduce the risk of a sexually transmitted disease. The teenager needs to learn that unprotected sex is *always* unsafe sex, and that condom use is *never* optional. Of course, many other basic ideas regarding safety, appropriate choices, and values must be taught.

• *Our 14-year-old daughter Melissa talks frequently about wanting to get married and have babies. She has significant learning problems and poor attention and I wonder if she will ever be capable of marriage and children. What do I tell her?*

The wish to have a child seems almost universal in young people, regardless of disability. Supporting your child in this wish is important, as it is a healthy, normal desire. People with significant learning disabilities can become capable parents, depending on the areas the individual has trouble with. However, if you are quite sure your young teen will not become capable of independent parenting, it will be beneficial to point out other important and recognized roles that adults have with children, like godparent, aunt, and teacher's aide. Point out capable adult role models who do not have children, so parenting isn't the only adult role your child notices.

We all need hopes and goals that may be beyond what we will actually achieve. Children can be encouraged to conquer steps towards fulfillment of their dreams. Melissa may be encouraged to develop her love of being with children by working in a nursery as she gets older. Through this experience she may find a job path for herself, whether or not she is able to achieve her dream of becoming a mother. People with significant learning disabilities or mental retardation can fall in love and marry. They may need help for certain aspects of independent living. They may even need others to live with them. Raising children, however, clearly requires an important set of skills, persistence, and problem-solving abilities.

Exploitation/Vulnerability

• *My 20-year-old son was alone in our apartment and apparently saw an ad for an "escort service" in the paper. He invited two women over. They fortunately did not approach him sexually but instead robbed our house! I was horrified he would call an escort service, but it turned out he misunderstood and thought it was a "dating service" and thought it would be a good way to meet girls.*

• *Our 18-year-old daughter has been involved with a 30-year-old man. Our daughter is a lovely girl, very sweet, pretty, and bright, but she has no street smarts. This older man doesn't work and we are afraid that he is somehow using her to get money. We are very concerned that he is exploiting her.*

Sometimes it is clear when a youngster is being exploited. This 18-year-old girl involved with an older man who doesn't work, for example, is at very high risk. Clues that someone may be exploiting your child in a relationship include: the child is often unhappy about the relationship; there is a big difference on some important characteristic such as age or ability that places your child in a potential position of being very dependent on the other person; your child becomes depressed, listless, or irritable with the relationship. When you suspect that your child is being harmed, of course you need to protect her. Often it will be necessary and helpful to involve an outside professional such as a psychologist or social worker. This person can provide advice and guidance for all of you and also evaluate the effect of the relationship on your child.

Sometimes you are not sure whether your teenager's boy friend or girl friend may be exploitative. The best approach is often a direct one. You may be able to have an open talk where you express your concerns and discuss guidelines that must be followed if the relationship is to continue. Include both individuals in the discussion, or inform your own teen before having a one-to-one talk with the significant other.

TOUCHING OTHERS

• *My 14-year-old son is a big boy and likes to come up behind people and hug them as a way to show affection. His teacher had him dismissed from school and called a meeting, accusing him of sexually approaching her and trying to grab her breasts, but I've seen him do what she was describing to his father. It's just his way of playfully showing affection.*

• *When my 8-year-old daughter is with adults she likes, even if she has never met them before, she will go over and sit on their laps.*

• *My 19-year-old son has always played well with younger children. He has been especially close to my neighbor's 9-year-old boy. I was shocked when the neighbor stormed into my house with full intention of making a police report about my son. She angrily told me she had discovered the boys in her garage, and that my son was touching her son under his underpants.*

Some children with FAS may have difficulty discriminating with whom it is appropriate to be physically affectionate and with whom it is not. Once a child approaches school age, begin teaching socially appropriate behavior with strangers, teachers, and acquaintances. Role playing and curriculum such as Circles are ideal for teaching the unwritten social rules about touching. Social skills teaching should be written into the child's Individualized Education Plan (IEP).

The more consistent and rigid that social rules are, the easier they will be to remember. Rules such as "Don't sit on anyone's lap unless they are family" would be helpful for the eight year old who routinely sits on people's laps. For the boy who hugged the teacher, appropriate rules would be "Don't hug anyone outside of family and ____ and ____ (name some best friends)" and "Only hug facing someone so they know you are there." Teachers and parents can help each other by teaching consistent rules. For children of all ages, however, lots of physical affection at home with family is great.

Of special concern is inappropriate sexual behavior that may harm those involved and result in legal action against the person with FAS/E. In the case of the 19-year-old boy, the age of the younger child—nine years old—is especially distressing. The younger child is clearly a victim, even though the older boy may have little understanding of the emotional or legal consequences and may not have intended harm.

In this serious situation, the most effective way to teach is to use rules that are concrete and absolute. Simple and consistent rules simplify decision making: "Always do x—never do y." As young people with FAS/E thrive on structure and routine, the use of always-never rules fits well with their natural learning style. As Barbara Morse points out, "Children with FAS do best with a highly consistent routine because such structure reduces demands on the brain to process new information.... A familiar routine acts as an external structure for children who have difficulty internalizing behavior."[4]

Parents should be alert to the possibility of sexual contact between friends of very different ages. At times even the best teaching efforts will not prevent a crisis. The 19 year old and his family (and of course the younger child) would benefit from seeing a professional counselor. These parents may want to consult a lawyer who has knowledge regarding FAS/E and individuals with developmental disabilities.

MASTURBATION

• *I was shocked to see my two year old rubbing against his teddy bear like he was masturbating as he was going to sleep. Is this part of FAS?*

• *My teenage son seems to masturbate anytime he thinks he might be alone, like watching TV, or in the car in the back seat. He seems to have some sense of privacy about it and never does it in really public situations, but I'm worried he'll do it when there is someone there who will be offended.*

Children are sexual beings from infancy. It is not uncommon to see toddlers and two- and three-year-olds (any child, not necessarily children with FAS) masturbating as they fall asleep. There is only cause for concern if a child is doing this frequently during the day, instead of other play activities. This could be a sign of some sort of stress or unhappiness, and, of most concern, could indicate sexual molestation. If a young (preadolescent) child masturbates frequently during the day, a medical evaluation is important to rule out any kind of abuse. However, occasional masturbation, especially just before sleep, in children at all ages, is not cause for concern.

For all ages, a consistent easy rule is: masturbation should be done only in private in a child's bedroom. This rule can eliminate

---

[4] Barbara Morse, "Information Processing," in J. Kleinfeld and S. Wescott 1993, 34.

gray areas—figuring out what is private and what could become public. The child can be reminded in a matter of fact, not shameful way ("That's a private thing to do—remember where you go to do private things?").

Choices

• *My 20-year-old daughter Jessica has had a few brief relationships with boys but nothing serious. Two months ago she came home saying she had "met the man of her dreams." She told us he was 21, worked at McDonald's, and lived with his parents. Each day she brought home little things he had given her, one day a rose, the next day a cheap ring. Finally we got to meet him at a cookout his family was having. We were shocked when we met him. His clothes were dirty, his hair was greasy, his family was definitely living on the edge in a rundown house, and he smelled bad. When I saw him with his arm around my Jessica it was all I could do to be polite. I swallowed my pride and stayed for the meal. Everyone was pleasant and I do have to say the young man was very attentive to Jessica. Do I support this relationship? He wouldn't have been my choice for my little girl, but he seems nice to her. How do I know if this is right for her?*

• *My son Andy, 18, has never had a girl friend. Lately he has been saying he thinks he might be gay. He went to the movies with another boy who seemed to me to be gay. Help!*

Teenagers and adults with FAS/E typically have all the same emotional desires for love relationships that others do. But they often lack the skills to choose an appropriate partner because of learning difficulties, faulty information processing, impulsivity, and poor decision-making skills.

Most important: keep the lines of communication open between you and your child. With any teenager or young adult, parents may not approve of the youngster's choice of date or partner. Try to figure out whether your disapproval is due to your general fears for your child's well-being, or whether you may be sensing a truly unhealthy situation. Figuring out when to let go and when to intervene is probably one of the most difficult aspects of parenting teens, and it becomes more difficult when the teenager has a developmental or learning issue such as FAS/E.

Get to know your child's dates and partners personally, as Jessica's parents did. This is the best way to determine whether the situation is healthy. Invite the date for dinner. Offer to take them both to a movie and dinner. You can also show your interest by asking about what your child likes or does not like about this person. Talk about how exciting it is to find someone. If you have specific concerns, it is best to tell your child exactly what worries you ("She seems like a likable person, but she doesn't call you when she says she's going to and then that makes you sad" or "You seem to really like him but he stole some money from us so I don't trust him again yet"). You can show enthusiasm about the concept of your child dating while expressing concern about a particular partner's behavior. Watching your child together with the date is the best time to get clues. For us, the bottom line is that the partner should treat your child well, and that your child is happy with the relationship most of the time.

Some teens go thorough a period of experimenting to figure out their sexual identity. Sometimes teens who haven't had dates with the opposite sex assume this might mean they are gay, by a sort of process of elimination ("I haven't had a date with a girl so I just belong with guys"). Clearly some adults with FAS will be gay or lesbian, just as some adults without FAS are. Having FAS does not affect one's sexual orientation.

AND THEY LIVED HAPPILY EVER AFTER...?

• *Sometimes it seems my child has so much to overcome. He is 17 and has severe learning disabilities, but he is a very sweet boy and he has a best friend. There are several girls he likes, and he has asked two out but they said no. Tell me, can it EVER work out? Can people with FAS have successful happy love relationships?*

Yes! Yes! It can work out! While we don't have a lot of data on adults with FAS who are more mildly affected, since they often are not diagnosed, we do know that people with significant learning disabilities, with mild mental retardation, can have successful, happy love relationships. When it works out, as it is for the rest of us, this is one of the most wonderful things that can happen to a young person! That your son has friends is good as this indicates he has many of the building blocks of a love relationship. Make sure your teen has opportunities to meet other teens who would be realistic partners. Finding a pool of potential candidates is obviously key.

While parents want their child to be in a successful relationship, it is also important to remember that partnership is not the only measure of a good life. Having friends, family, exploring interests, and having a sense of control are all dimensions of happiness.

Some useful resources for dealing with sexuality issues are listed below:

Books

The following books are all available in paperback.

J. Cole. *How You Were Born.* New York: William Morrow and Co., 1998.

> This is a good book on reproduction complete with photographs and diagrams. Sexual intercourse is not mentioned specifically. The author's note is a helpful guide to parents.

Lydia Fegan and Anne Rauch. *Sexuality and People with Intellectual Disability.* Baltimore: Paul H. Brookes Publishing Co., 1993.

> This is a guide for parents, teachers and counselors that covers topics such as menstruation, masturbation, help with growing up, sex and marriage.

Susan Meredith. *Where Do Babies Come From?* London: Usbourne Publishing Ltd., 1991.

> This is an excellent book with many colorful diagrams. Parents may wish to copy one page at a time. The book includes a simple discussion of intercourse as well as conception, pregnancy, childbirth, and newborn care.

Peggy Siegel, *Changes In You*. Richmond,Virginia: Family Life Education Associates.

> This paperback comes in two editions, one for boys and one for girls. Both have useful parent guides. These are wonderful books, beautifully illustrated, with gentle explanations of puberty. This book also comes accompanied by slides.

Learning Kits

J. E. Lindemann, *SAFE: Stopping AIDS Through Functional Education*. 1991.

> This is a set of useful teaching tools developed for individuals with developmental disabilities. Each unit is made up of study points, role play and vignettes, with illustrations and slides. The kit also includes a video on condom use.

The following kits are available from James Stanfield and Co., P.O. Box 41058-B, Santa Barbara, CA 93140; 1-900-421-6534; Fax 805-897-6534:

Circles Curriculum: "Intimacy and Relationships," "Stop Abuse," "Safer Ways."

> This is a good teaching tool that illustrates categories of relationships and appropriate behavior for each one.

Life Facts: "Sexuality," "Sexual Abuse Prevention," "Trust and Personal Safety," "AIDS."

> This excellent kit contains slides and illustrated sheets as well as a teacher's guide with key points, exercises, worksheets and role plays. Material includes both simple and explicit illustrations, allowing the teacher or counselor to adapt the lessons to the individual learner.

Life Horizons I and II.

> This would be best for the advanced learner who would not be overstimulated by the material. The slides are photographs rather drawings.

14
Growing Up with FAS/E
PAMELA GROUPE GROVES

Pamela Groupe Groves and her husband Stan have adopted six children, including four with FAS. The have also been foster parents to many children with disabilities. In 1989, Ms. Groves founded a newsletter, Growing with FAS,[1] *to provide parents with a way to exchange ideas and to relieve the isolation of caring for children with FAS/E.*

ONE OF THE JOYS OF LIVING WITH CHILDREN WITH FETAL ALCOHOL syndrome is that they live more in the moment than the rest of us. They can show us how to savor a moment, how to revel in an experience. Many of us rush around and allow the beauty and delights of life to pass us by.

Alcohol-affected children can also teach us to enlarge our own definitions of success—and not only for them. We, too, need not be so bound by conventional measures of what counts in life.

My 15-year-old daughter, Elisabeth, has the developmental skills of a much younger child, but seeing the world through her eyes is a privilege. She appreciates butterflies, shapes in the clouds, breezes ruffling the trees, the expanse of the ocean—and she shares her exuberance. As the adoptive parents of four children with FAS, my husband and I have learned that youngsters with alcohol-related birth defects do not let life just pass by. They fully embrace it, presenting parents with a delightful invitation to savor sweet

---

[1] For a sample copy of *Growing with FAS*, send a self-addressed, stamped envelope (SASE) and $2.00, checks payable to Pamela Groves at 7802 SE Taylor, Portland, Oregon 97215. For specific questions or requests for referrals to others in your area, send a SASE to the same address.

surprises. While visiting grandparents who live in a rural setting, it was not enough for us to watch deer walk through the yard—we had to track them, find out where they sleep, and try to move close enough to touch them. We did not casually stroll through the Shasta Caves; we carefully observed and wondered aloud what, where, when, why and how. For these children, living in the moment is the flip side of not living in the future.

Another wonderful quality of my children is their sense of humor. They show it with joyous smiles, contagious laughter, and wit. Our 13-year-old son knows how to seek the humor in mundane or serious situations. We have held our stomachs in gales of laughter more times than we can count. Often, we have tapped into that humor to help him through frustrating, painful, or difficult moments. While not a cure for all of life's stresses, it does help both of us to be able to look at circumstances with an edge of humor.

These endearing qualities can bring out the best in others. When two close friends of Elisabeth's died tragically, she was devastated, as we all were. Elisabeth asked if we could leave flowers at her friends' house, which we did. Others began to add more flowers, and Elisabeth made sure they had water and were tended to. Her example throughout her grieving process was a guide and inspiration for every one.

Appreciating this positive outlook and spontaneity requires expanding our definitions of success. Most people don't get excited about a ten year old learning to tie shoes or a seven year old going on a shopping trip without one tantrum. Yet, relishing these surprises rewards our parenting children with FAS/E. Rather than focusing on expectations, we should recognize and nurture our children's actual, and often special, abilities—whether a good sense of humor, joy in life, or an ability to bring out the best in others.

As the editor of the newsletter *Growing with FAS*, I often hear from parents concerned about how to help their children live up to their potential in ways both small and large. This chapter addresses questions about the practical problems parents face as they ready their youngsters for the responsibilities and demands of daily life.

GETTING LOST: HOW TO AVOID IT

Sharon Hanes wrote to me about her 12-year-old daughter's problem getting lost, even in the most familiar settings. Her daughter also has a poor concept of risks in the street, she said. "People look at me like I'm nuts when I tell them I cannot let my daughter, with a 70 to 75 IQ, go out in the street to retrieve a ball or walk a couple of blocks to a friend's house by herself. She may find her way to her friend's house one day, but on the next, she gets lost doing the same thing."

> I tell Susan, over and over again, that if for any reason, she does not know where she is or where to go, Do Not Leave the Building! I tell her to go to a nearby classroom or office and just explain to an adult that she is lost or doesn't know what to do, and that an adult will help her. Also, at the beginning of each school year, or whenever there has been a big change in routine, I insist that there be an aide to help her until the new route becomes routine.
>
> This has been stated on her Individualized Education Plan, but I have still had to follow up to be sure it was being carried through. In grade school and now middle school, this has worked. However, once she gets to ninth grade her schedule will be more confusing and so will the atmosphere.
>
> How should I handle mounting confusion in high school?

My Response

Getting lost is a common problem for those with FAS/E. For older children, losing their way is even more difficult because others expect them to navigate by themselves.

Your description of your daughter's experiences are so familiar to us! Our 17-year-old daughter, a junior in high school, has had many problems orienting herself. She seems so normal in appearance that people find it hard to accept she processes information differently. Each year I have found myself, just as you describe, having to remind teachers and even education specialists who should know better but don't seem to understand the way FAS affects a person's learning process and behavior. They seem to think, "Time has gone by, she must be better now."

In her grade school, a building with a simple floor plan, she could not find the library or cafeteria alone. During middle school, she never did master her combination locker. She could not find her way alone to a friend's house if it was off our block. In her first year of high school, the staff expected too much of her, and she came home in tears every afternoon.

The staff also wanted her to switch from the special education bus to public transportation at the start of high school. We insisted on a planned transition to public transportation. Slowly, over two years, we took on the task of helping her to ride the bus alone. She took the bus with family members, friends and "travel trainers" supplied by special education. Learning to use public transportation increased her ability to find her way and, more important, find confidence in herself. Our daughter can now walk to the mall with a friend and can ride the public bus to school, to a friend's house, and to her job as a cafeteria aide in a nursing home.

Here are some suggestions for helping to orient young people with FAS or FAE, especially as they enter the confusing world of high school:

• *Cluster classes and lockers.* Request that your child's classes and locker be grouped as close together as possible, even if it means selecting different classes. For my oldest daughter, this meant dropping physical education in favor of a class easier to find.

• *Map your child's routes.* Request a map of the school and a copy of the class schedule before school starts. With your child, develop a simple map showing the route to each class and highlight the office, bathrooms, stairways, cafeteria, and so on. Then practice, practice, practice. Make certain your child has at least one copy of the map and schedule before leaving for school, and always keep an extra set at school. Make sure your child knows how to find the office from all areas of the school.

• *Find a "travel trainer."* If the school cannot provide someone to help your child learn his or her way around the school, find someone who can. Possible sources include: a college student who is studying to be a teacher, whose assignments may include working one-on-one with a school-age student, or someone from a special needs support group in a church or local community. Perhaps some young person outside the immediate family will help foster independence and yet not draw attention to your child. Work out a plan for changing from assisted movement to moving around alone.

• *Find a class where your child has strength to provide relief from stress.* Make sure that your child takes at least one class in an area of personal strength to relieve some stress during the day. For our daughter, it was an art class.

PUBERTY

Puberty is a life marker for entering a new stage in life, a new maturity, a growing up and a growing away from dependence on parents. All of us understand the physical and emotional changes of adolescence, having survived it ourselves. People with FAS/E undergo all of these difficult changes, but their developmental and behavioral disabilities can cause even more complications. Parents often express concern over the onset of puberty, helping adolescents understand the puberty process, hygiene, and sex education.[2]

When our daughter Elisabeth was eight years old (and age four developmentally), her breasts began to develop and a few stray pubic hairs began to appear. A pediatric endocrinologist said she was experiencing precocious or early onset of puberty.[3] These signs of early puberty alarmed my husband and me. We were

---

[2] For information about sex education, see chapter 13 by Sara Miranda and Karen Levine.

[3] It is not fully undersood why, how, and when puberty begins, but brain damage, including that caused by FAS/E, can alter the onset of puberty and can result in early or late onset.

concerned about her ability to understand what she was experiencing, as well as the social implications of her development. She was in the first grade, and I worried about her being teased by classmates, even victimized by boys at higher grade levels. Her doctor agreed that early puberty would be very traumatic for her. He prescribed oral provara to slow the symptoms.

Whether puberty occurs early or not, talk to your child about body changes casually, incorporating discussions into everyday life. When puberty approaches, talk about the changes before they occur. If you see signs of early puberty, seek information and medical advice.[4]

Menstruation
A mother writes:

How do I get my daughter to understand puberty, menstruation and taking care of menstruation needs?

My Response

At age 13, Elisabeth began to menstruate. This surprised my husband and me because she had been taking oral provara for four years and had six months remaining before she would stop taking the medication; it usually inhibits menstruation. I had not yet begun to teach her about her period. I recommend beginning preparation to teach your daughter about menstruation much earlier than I did.

Fortunately, my daughter's period started on a weekend, and she was at home. I gave her a quick version of what was happening to her. I said, "women have a little room inside, and each month it

---

[4] These are some resources I have found useful:

- "Precocious Puberty: Information for Families," from the Department of Pediatrics, Division of Endocrinology, University of Iowa Hospitals and Clinics, Iowa City, Iowa 52242. This booklet is informative and easy to read. It includes medical terms and treatment issues.

- The MAGIC Foundation (Major Aspects of Growth in Children) provides information on endocrine disorders affecting childrens' growth and development, including precocious puberty. The phone number is 1-800-362-4423.

gets ready to grow a baby. The room has a special lining, and when there isn't a baby growing, the lining comes out because it isn't needed." My daughter accepted this information matter-of-factly and without concern. It has been two years since we had this discussion, and she has adapted well. She becomes more independent in her hygiene and self-care each month.

Here are a few suggestions:

• Get materials on puberty for young people with mental retardation.[5]

• Mothers or older sisters may be able to talk about their own menstruation cycle and care in a natural way before the daughter's cycle begins.

• Establish a schedule for changing pads if remembering is a problem. Maintain this schedule whether or not a change is needed.

Hygiene
A mother writes:

> *At four years old our now nine-year-old son had strong body odors associated with puberty. At eight, he had pubic hair. At nine, underarm hair. He is concerned about dressing with peers in the locker room. Body odor is a problem, because he is not bothered by it.*

My Response
Parents often describe their children with FAS/E as being hypersensitive to body sensations but oblivious to the need for body hygiene. Listed below are techniques suggested by parents. Not all the strategies will work with all people and it will take trial and error to determine what works for your family. What is crucial is routine, repetition, organizational structure, and being willing to try new ways of handling hygiene training. Be creative!

---

[5] Contact your local chapter or write: The Arc, P.O. Box 1047, Arlington, TX, 76004. Phone: (817) 261-6003.

Hygiene Supplies:

• Keep supplies like shampoo, body wash, combs, and tooth-paste in a storage container. Place the container in a specific location.

• Let the child help choose the supplies. This increases enjoyment of using one's own items.

• Color code items such as towels, toothbrush, comb, and the storage container for quick identification.

Hygiene Routine:

• At an early age, begin a routine of daily bathing and shampoo. By establishing a routine, the individual does not have to remember when the last shampoo occurred or determine if a bath is needed.

• Keep a daily task checklist. It can be in the form of a chart, card file, or whatever works best for the individual. The checklist can combine pictures and words and include the specific time for each task.

• Begin the routine of using deodorant at an early age. My daughter began using deodorant at age six, and it paid off when she reached puberty, because she was used to it by then.

• Role model shaving, with an electric razor, long before it is time for the individual to shave. When it is time to learn to shave, pick an electric razor that best suits the individual and encourage the use of a preshave lotion. As with bathing, encourage daily shaving to establish a routine.

Grooming:

• When individuals are old enough, begin teaching combing and styling their own hair.

• Have family members role model taking care of grooming needs in view of the individual and talk about how important and enjoyable grooming is.

• While at school, include activities related to hygiene on your child's Individualized Educational Plan, such as learning to check one's hair and face in the mirror when in the bathroom and washing hands at each visit.

Clothing:

• Role model checking for spills and taking notice of clothing wear and tear. If a spill occurs, teach individuals how to tend to it with spotting solution or dabbing with water. Encourage individuals to monitor the condition of their clothing.

• Devise organizational techniques for hanging and storing clothing. Place picture codes on dresser drawers or use under-the-bed storage drawers or colored boxes for keeping like items together. Hang coordinated outfits together on combination hangers.

• Role model and teach sorting laundry and using the laundry machines.

Nudity

A frustrated father shares a common concern:

My 16-year-old daughter gets caught up in her evening shower routine and walks undressed from the bathroom to her bedroom. It's as if she is oblivious to the fact that her teenage brothers may have friends upstairs, dad might be in the living room . . . I would like her to have more modesty!

My Response

People with FAS/E often do become engrossed in what they are doing and do not think about consequences, such as someone seeing them unclothed. Though it is difficult to instill a sense of modesty, we can teach skills that will protect their modesty.

Here are some helpful thoughts others have shared:

• From an early age, make it an after-shower routine that people in the family dress in the bathroom into street clothes or night clothes. When not taking a shower, the routine is to dress in the bedroom. Establishing this routine from toddlerhood may help. If the toddler years are far behind you, try to encourage this routine now.

• Make it a habit to keep the bathroom door closed while in use.

• Post a homemade STOP sign on the bathroom door that lists the crucial items that must be done before leaving the room. Try to establish a routine of checking that list (flush the toilet, turn off the water, get dressed, and so on).

• Develop a concise, easy-to-understand explanation of modesty and discuss it as needed, starting with every shower. You will need it less often over time.

Becoming Independent: Teaching Self-advocacy

Parents write with a common concern: How can they make sure others will understand that their child needs help?

• *My child's teacher is well-trained in FAS but at times it seems she forgets that special adaptations are needed.*

• *I worry that people in the community won't understand why my child has problems listening.*

• *I worry that someone will take advantage of my child.*

• *I am very concerned about how my child's needs will be made known when I am not around.*

My Response

The harsh reality is that we cannot be with our child at all times, nor can we accompany our growing adolescent or adult with FAS/E into the world. Also, most parents pass away long before their child does.

All parents unconsciously begin to prepare their children to stand up for themselves. We encourage them to raise their hands in class when they have a question. We teach them how to hold their place in line. We train them to count their change at the grocery store. For people who have FAS/E, however, we need to take special efforts to help them advocate for themselves.

We began teaching our daughter her advocacy skills by making sure she understood her diagnosis and helping her develop scripts she could use to request help. When situations arose when she needed assistance, she would say:

- "Please repeat that. I have trouble remembering directions."

- "I have problems forgetting things. Which page are we supposed to be on?"

- "I have trouble finding my way. Please show me which direction the office is."

- "It helps me when the directions are written down."

- "I can do a better job when I have a little extra time."

- "It helps me if I can use a chart to remind myself."

Our daughter Elisabeth has an expressive language level of a five year old. Despite her developmental and language delays, she has learned to advocate for herself. From kindergarten on, we encouraged her to try on her own first, then to ask for help if she needed it. Since she was quite young, she has carried a "speech wallet," which holds pictures, phrases, and basic information about herself that she can show when she cannot communicate something. She also wears an identification bracelet with her address and emergency numbers. Role playing helped her learn to use the bracelet in emergencies.

Though it's better to start teaching self-advocacy to children with FAS/E from infancy on using age appropriate techniques, you can start at any point and still see success. These suggestions have helped others:

- *Name both their problems and their strengths.* Give specific names and descriptions to a particular quality, such as slow cognitive pace or perseveration. After one teenager read an article about perseveration, for example, he said to his mother in a relieved yet matter-of-fact tone, "So that's what it's called. I always wondered."

• *Help children learn how to identify sources of help.* Help them identify who would be a good source of information in certain settings, such as at school or a store. Practice in real-world situations, such as asking a grocery clerk where an item is in the store, is the best way to teach this skill.

• *Let children speak for themselves and take the risk of doing things on their own.* When possible, include children in the meetings, evaluations, and conferences that concern them. Include children in conversations and let them know their comments are valuable and desired. Let children answer for themselves if others ask them questions. This requires an effort but pays off in the long run.

• *Help build social confidence and skills throughout life by providing a variety of opportunities for children to interact with people of different ages and backgrounds, and to act independently.* This means allowing them to do things for themselves, and thus find success or failure on their own. I was afraid to let my oldest daughter ride the bus alone, but she developed a greater sense of self-reliance by doing so.

Betty Penler in *Access Ability* describes her own struggle to let go of her daughter's life:

> I came to realize I was not giving my 35-year-old daughter living in a community residence enough credit for knowing what she wants in her own limited way, and I still wanted to subtly take over. I was almost afraid to see her become her own self-advocate.
>
> The truth is we parents have mixed feelings about letting our sons and daughters take risks and become empowered. We tend to be of divided heart as we prepare them for a future without us. Many of us who are active parental advocates fight like tigers for our cubs to have the right to education, the proper program, group home, ... but as individual mom and dad, we act like the kangaroo who keeps its young ones in a protective body pouch. To empower our sons and daughters we must first let them out.

Parents have expected too little for too long and need to become risk takers and recognize most of our fears are exaggerated. Yet we persist in holding onto those fears, even in the face of demonstrated ability by our sons and daughters. We are so busy doing things for them, we never stop to realize what we are doing to them. We have to learn to listen to our sons and daughters more and identify their needs, not as we see them, but as they express them.

As our children with FAS/E enter adolescence and adulthood, we need to help them stand up for themselves. Many will need some outside structure and support from advocacy groups, support groups, or state and national agencies. Our lifelong efforts at guiding them toward self-advocacy includes helping them connect with these resources.

REDEFINING SUCCESS

Many parents are concerned about the long-term potential of their child. Will they experience the pleasure other parents enjoy in standing back and watching successful, contributing, happy adult children? Will there be a place for their child in the world? How will the family handle the onset of adolescence and the transition into adulthood? As Sharon Hanes wrote:

> *Wendy can be a very loving child and we have many good times together. I do notice, though, that as she becomes older, I am more likely to lose patience with her and have to frequently remind myself, "She is not the average teenager and is not, and may never be, capable of doing certain things."*

My Response

Certainly some individuals with FAS/E will fit into the traditional framework of success. Others may not go on to college, advance beyond a minimum wage job, or develop a wide circle of friends. Does this mean they are not a success?

As parents of children with alcohol-related birth defects, we have gone through the grief cycle in adjusting to the consequences of FAS/E. Yet many of us harbor the dream of the child we expected, the child who would meet the traditional version of success.

Rather than dwell on past expectations, our goal should be to help our children develop the best they can.

Here are *real* examples of people whose accomplishments live up to traditional measures of success:

• An adult graduated from college, with some effort and modifications, and is working in her chosen field.

• A stand-up comic also has bit parts in television situation comedies.

• A man is working his way up from busboy to manager in a major restaurant chain.

• An individual is running a home business based on computer services.

• A man leads a support group for those with FAS/E.

Others will achieve accomplishments better measured by their own progress rather than traditional measures. These people are successes in their own ways:

• A man working at a minimum-wage job for several years lives in his own small apartment, and, with assistance, pays his bills and stays on a budget.

• A young adult is living in a supervised apartment, working in a shelter workshop, and enjoying weekend outings to the park and movies.

• A graduate from long-term residential care is living and working in a half-way house as a full-time janitor.

A key to fostering success in teenagers with FAS/E is to encourage them in a special skill or interest, whether it's oil painting, playing the guitar, swimming, or gardening. Starting from infancy, be aware of your child's strengths and interests. Build on these interests through encouragement, praise, and opportunities to pursue the interest. Keep in the back of your mind how to help your child enjoy those interests over a lifetime, not just in childhood. Remind yourself that for your child, developing leisure interests are just as important as learning multiplication tables or balancing a checkbook.

CONCLUSION

When my husband and I adopted our first child with FAS fifteen years ago, we felt as if we traveled on an isolated trail filled with overgrown branches and vines. We have been amazed and inspired to witness others converging onto the path so that we are no longer alone. The trail is still overgrown in many places, but together we are clearing the way and mapping our routes.

The most valuable contributors to this map will be those with FAS/E. They can tell us what has helped and what has not. They can show us through their unique lives and versions of success that every life is of value and every life has its own path to follow. I feel privileged to know so many dedicated mapmakers.

15
Reaching Independence Day: Managing the Behavior of Teenagers

Jim Slinn

Jim Slinn works at Parents Resources Network in Anchorage, Alaska, helping parents of children with disabilities and providing training throughout the state on parenting, disability, special education, and fetal alcohol issues. He has three adopted sons with FAS/E.

ADOLESCENTS WITH FAS/E, LIKE OTHER TEENAGERS, DESIRE independence. Many lack the judgment, however, to assume greater responsibilities or handle the complexities of living on their own. As one parent of a son with FAS put it:

> I don't know what to do about Daniel any more. When he was younger, I was able to keep him under control most of the time. He was doing pretty well in school and seemed to have plenty of friends. But now that he's a teenager, he seems to be in some sort of trouble all the time, and I just can't seem to get him under control anymore. Not only is his behavior worse most of the time, but it's so different now. What can I do?

I hear similar remarks almost daily when I work with parents on disability and parenting issues. As an adoptive single parent of three sons with FAS/E, ages 24, 13, and 9, I also have a lot of experience with the behavioral changes that parents confront as their children reach out for independence.

What were temper tantrums in youngsters may intensify or become violent and uncontrollable outbursts in teenagers. The need for physical closeness that seemed so appealing in young children may become sexually inappropriate and troublesome in teens. The growing strength and stature of adolescents with FAS/E change the magnitude of their responses, so what seemed manageable in the child becomes unacceptable, even dangerous, in a teenager.

Parents who fall into the trap of trying to *control* the behavior of teenagers with FAS/E find that they experience one crisis after another. The entire concept of controlling behavior is not really applicable to those with FAS/E. Instead, it is more constructive to *manage* their behavior by establishing and maintaining well-structured environments and by repeating and rehearsing appropriate behaviors in various situations.

Moving from the parental home to community living involves slowly creating structured levels of increasing independence while continuing to practice and rehearse proper behavior in as many realistic situations as possible. The suggestions below are based on real-life situations from my work with parents and from my own family's experience.

THE NEED FOR PEER APPROVAL

Bill obtained funding for decent housing and soon discovered he had something that other young people wanted. He hung around the local shelter for runaway or homeless teens and offered others a place to stay as they were about to enter the shelter. Because he had something desirable, he felt important, needed, and powerful. Those who came home with him reinforced his behavior and brought him a constant flow of apparent friends, helping to ease his feelings of isolation and separation. He felt accepted.

His apartment quickly turned into a flophouse as those he invited to stay brought other friends and then held disruptive parties that created unhappy neighbors and an angry landlord. In Bill's mind, he was not participating in the disturbance. He even had enough sense to call the police when the noise level became unbearable or people damaged the apartment. However, he couldn't tell the partygoers to leave for fear of losing all the acceptance he thought he had gained. Eventually he was evicted, labeled as "trouble" or a "gang member."

The need to belong motivates teenagers more than anything else. With guidance and structured learning at home and in school, children with FAS/E generally appear to fit in with their peer groups. But as these children mature into teenagers, they tend to grow more isolated as their peer group advances intellectually and socially, and as schoolwork becomes more abstract and less rote. Rather than competing with others and risking rejection and failure, these youth become loners. All the while, however, they want to belong in a group again.

This separation may occur so gradually that it's almost unnoticeable, especially at first. For example, a youth with FAS/E may seem like part of a group hanging out at the video arcade, but upon looking closer, you find he is playing a game alone in a corner while the others play elsewhere. Being near the group provides a sense of belonging without the stress of having to meet their standards and expectations.

Since those with FAS/E are great mimics, they will copy the behaviors of whatever group they feel they belong to. This trait can be a blessing if they mimic appropriate behaviors, *so the trick is to help them form relationships within a positive peer group*—which can be more difficult as they grow older. I helped one of my sons choose friends and associates by supporting some of his positive behaviors. He likes to earn money and is skilled with cars, so by emphasizing these interests I found him a job at a small local gas station. There people recognized and accepted him for his abilities, improving his self-esteem and making his teenage years happier.

Another way to supervise and guide youths in their social life is to talk with them. Ask them open-ended questions about what's happening in their lives and read between the lines while listening. Since those with FAS/E see the world in concrete, literal terms, they may not see some situations as a problem and may not tell anyone before it is too late to intervene. Ask such questions as: "What would you want to do in this situation?"; "What would happen if you do that?"; "Do you really want to do that?"; and "Do you think that is appropriate?" This type of discussion encourages the adolescent to think about how to behave and respond. The answers also give parents some idea about what their child is doing and suggest how much guidance is needed in various situations.

Bill's situation was difficult because he had already chosen the wrong kind of friends to approach. A parent would find it difficult to walk in and kick the friends out because then the situation would escalate into a conflict between a parent's desire to protect a child and the child's desire to grow up. Here a third party—a community agency that supervises such housing assignments or a payee—could intervene as a neutral force.

GAINING INDEPENDENCE: DRIVING AND SHOPPING

Children with FAS/E have a hard time transferring behaviors from one situation to another. Any change becomes an entirely new scenario without guideposts. Sometimes this inability can lead to serious problems. For one teenager with FAS/E, driving a car to run an errand for Mom was the same behavior as driving a car for someone to commit a robbery. To him, he was simply doing his friend a favor by driving to the store so the friend could pick up a few things; it was not robbing anyone. Getting in trouble for this made him think driving someone—anyone—to the store is wrong.

My son loves to do the shopping and does quite well as long as he does not have to worry about the money. The problem surfaced when I sent him into a different store for bread and he returned without it, saying the store didn't have any. Back at the store, he showed me where the bread aisle should be according to the layout of our familiar store. Since not all stores, even in the same chain, are laid out in the same manner, the bread would not always be on aisle 15 or just after the packaged desserts. In his mind, because aisle 15 did not contain the bread as it was supposed to, the store did not have any bread.

Teaching my son to shop successfully did not happen overnight but took many months of training and practice. After he had trouble finding bread in the new store, I simply sent him to the same store all the time. The next step was to send him for more than one item. I found that if he went for milk and bread, I would get what I asked for within a reasonable time, but that if I asked for bread and milk, I got what I asked for but it took twice as long. Why? I sent him in again and watched. He would always move through the store the same way, so if I asked for the items in order according to the store layout, one aisle after the other in the same direction, he found them very quickly. If I asked for them out of order, he would go through the entire store looking for the second item and then have to start over until he found it.

Consistent structure works best in these situations, since any changes seem completely different to teenagers with FAS/E. To make shopping easier, I learned to ask for items in order of the store's layout and worked with him so he now knows where 25 common items are located anywhere in the store. Any interchange of colors can completely confuse teenagers with FAS/E, so it's best to write notes about household chores on one color of paper and notes about what's needed at the store on another color.

The thought of teenagers driving brings the most trusting parents to their knees, but parents of youths with FAS/E may need life support systems! To make matters worse, many teens with FAS/E have little trouble getting their driver's licenses. Most written tests are given on computers, devices that many teens with FAS/E can handle well, and the multiple-choice questions are far easier for them than essay exams or other tests that require abstract thinking. The road test is also easy to pass; after all, the examiner asks them to do one thing at a time, and as long as all drivers do what they are supposed to, driving by teens with FAS/E can be peaceful. Fortunately, most drivers do what they are supposed to most of the time.

However, on their own in the real world, teens quickly discover that other drivers do dumb things and don't always follow the rules. These deviations upset youths with FAS/E, who are usually concrete and structured. Keeping them focused on what they are doing can help alleviate their frustrations. Once on their own, though, no one can direct them. Peers can also create distractions that result in driving problems.

Parents can rehearse many situations while talking at home and then later while driving with the teenager: "You saw a ball go down the street. What are you going to do for that?" "I'm going to take my foot off the gas." "Then what will you look around for?" "I'll look for any children running into the street." (This kind of rehearsal also works while teaching youngsters to ride bikes safely.) Another way to encourage success is to enroll teenagers with FAS/E in a driving school where they can practice their skills and rehearse potential traffic situations with an adult other than their parents.

DEALING WITH ANGER

Children with FAS/E tend to be physically assertive. At age seven, a temper tantrum with hitting and kicking is manageable. The same behavior at age 15 is dangerous; the possibility of physical injury becomes much more real. To the teenager, his behavior hasn't changed. To everyone else, the child is bigger and stronger, and so the behavior seems different.

Confrontation by parents only escalates the situation. Teens notice if their parents respond differently to what the teens know to be the same behavior, especially if parents become angry or upset. Teenagers learn how to get their parents to lose their cool, and to any teen this is power over the parent—power they will use.

Instead of reacting differently to temper tantrums, parents need to manage these outbursts much the way they did when their child was younger: "That behavior was unacceptable. You made this mess so you must clean it up. Take time out to think about your behavior and to get back under control." The problem is that if we want youths to learn age-appropriate behaviors, they need age-appropriate consequences. Sending a 13 year old to stand in a corner doesn't seem right, but a misbehaving teenager might not understand that being sent to her room is disciplinary. How do we substitute age-appropriate consequences?

The solution is to gradually stage these new responses to alleviate the child's perception of change. The misbehaving teenager will understand a time-out if she has been given time-outs in the past. Gradually change the locations and lengths of time: five minutes in this corner, then five minutes in her room, for example.

No gray areas can exist. All inappropriate behaviors must be addressed as soon as possible by applying consistent and predictable consequences. Relaxing for even a weekend will result in chaos for many days. Any changes you introduce will require a long learning period.

THE DESIRE FOR RELATIONSHIPS WITH THE OPPOSITE SEX

Dating is particularly challenging for youths with FAS/E since they don't understand well the concept of personal space. A young man may sit next to his date on the couch and innocently put his arm around her, which can seem like uninvited intimacy. A teenage girl with FAS/E does not see anything wrong with petting and necking; after all, she likes it and it fulfills her need for closeness. Young men and women both feel the need to be close to someone and to belong, and yet they don't really understand the complex world of sexual relationships, which can sometimes lead to charges of sexual attacks, harrassment, or promiscuity. Not only do they not have the skills to stop things before they go too far, they may not even be able to see where things are going.

We must remember that:

• Youths with FAS/E feel the same drives as any other youths their age.

• Their ability to think through a situation is not at the same level as their peers.

• They have a hard time interpreting and understanding the complex social cues so important to romantic success.

While teenagers with FAS/E may not have all the coping skills they need for sexual relationships, their natural drives propel them to that part of society where they are accepted and their needs are met. Once they arrive there, it can become almost impossible to turn them around.

Again, rehearsing and discussing how to interact with members of the opposite sex can help parents and children prepare for romantic relationships. Beginning at an early age, introduce proper and appropriate behavior and then constantly rehearse situations as the child matures into adolescence. During a long period of chaperoned dating, discuss and practice over and over the way to behave appropriately with the opposite sex, including how to use condoms.

One parent approached dating like everything else—systematically. She started with practice dates between her son and his sister. During these practice dates, the mother walked him, step by step, from how to ask for a date to how to say good night. The mother then allowed her son to ask a girl he liked to go with the family for ice cream or a hamburger. She talked openly and honestly with the girl's parents, and then she walked him through the outing. As time passed, she changed from walking between the young couple to walking beside them to walking behind them, gradually increasing their space and freedom.

She used the same approach at home. At first she would almost plan what would happen while the girl visited. Then she retreated to merely taking an active part in what they did. From there she moved to just being around, slowly fading into the background while still being available if needed. She emphasized candid discussions after each date to work out the best responses. Many parents and professionals regard this technique as a good training tool for any social skills a child needs to learn.

PREPARING YOURSELF AS A PARENT

Parents know best where their children are weakest or where they have had problems in the past. That knowledge is key to preparing for potential problems. A child who had difficulty understanding personal space and boundaries can face sexual harrassment charges. Someone with trouble understanding ownership might well be caught shoplifting. A child with anger management problems may damage property.

Parents need to be prepared to pick up the pieces if their teenager breaks some rule or law. First, realize the trouble is not always a reflection on you, the parent. There is no way to rehearse and practice appropriate behaviors for the many situations that can arise or to anticipate what can happen. Parents of children without special needs can't do this, either. Be gentle with yourself, and don't wallow in guilt should your child run afoul of society's laws and rules.

The following strategies can help parents cope with legal problems and other difficulties:

• *Don't try to do it alone.* Find someone who will provide support and friendship and act as an advocate should you need to appear in court, talk to a probation officer, discuss the situation with an attorney, and so on. Find someone who will listen to you talk out a problem or check your perceptions of the situation. Parents need a shoulder to cry on sometimes, so establish a trusted support system for yourself with the same energy and dedication you would use finding one for your child.

• *Be ready to educate those in the legal system.* When teenagers with FAS/E become involved in the legal system, their parents must be prepared to educate the players about the problems and organic behaviors of FAS/E.[1] This is probably the most important action parents can undertake, not only to help their child but also to advocate for all children with FAS/E. With information and education, those in the system will have an opportunity to change their perceptions of the youth from being bad to having an affliction. When they understand that FAS/E is not an excuse but a reason for the young person's behavior, they will be more likely to focus on ways to prevent the behavior in the future rather than on punishment.

To prepare for meetings about your child's behavior, parents should take these steps:

• *Keep notes, reports, professional observations, and other materials that identify the problem as ongoing, as something that*

---

[1] See Judge Barnett's decision, Appendix 1, as a way of educating those in the legal system.

has been addressed by many people, including the parents, over a long period. Emphasizing that the behavior is not new can help parents deal with guilt as well as establish a creative, positive treatment plan. For example, if what appears to be stealing has been a problem throughout childhood, being picked up for shoplifting as a teenager is predictable and not necessarily criminal in a moral sense. Proper documentation demonstrates that the behavior is not spontaneous or due to peer pressure, and that the parents have not denied or ignored this challenge but have sought help and guidance while facing the issue.

• *Familiarize yourself with the literature and other materials that address the constellation of problems associated with FAS/E, as well as any research on the subject.*[2] The teenager's problem may then be viewed as part of a larger and more defined collection of behaviors linked to a birth defect. This will foster understanding of the reasons for what seems like antisocial behavior, and it can spur finding professional help to avoid or alleviate a recurrence.

Once a family finds itself dealing with the justice system, bring together the players to discuss the problem collectively. Each player focuses on a specific angle that sometimes precludes the ability to see the other side. In group meetings, everyone receives the same information at the same time, regardless of differing perspectives, and they are more likely to approach the issue together rather than from a single viewpoint. Although everyone may resist meeting together, parents should be persistent and forceful, perhaps even enlisting help from the judge or magistrate. Those involved may include:

• the defense attorney, who is responsible for protecting the client's legal rights while obtaining the best possible outcome

• the prosecuting attorney, who represents the government in pursuing a legal remedy to an infraction or crime

---

[2] In order to convince service agencies that FAS means organic brain damage, concrete photographs are useful. Such photographs are provided for this purpose in Barbara Morse's chapter 21, "Diagnosis and Thereafter: What We Know Now and Where We Are Going."

• the probation officer, who supervises and monitors the offender after the legal determination

• the child protection worker, who emphasizes family and individual safety

• the judge or magistrate, who listens to all concerned, then decides and passes judgment

• a guardian *ad litem*, who attends to the best interests of the youth with FAS/E with court approval

At the meeting, present the information and documentation, and use this forum as an opportunity to educate everyone on the behaviors associated with FAS/E. Written information presented to each person individually might not be read, whereas everyone has a vested interest in knowing what all the others in the room do— dramatically increasing the probability that the material will be read.

A group gathering also increases the possibility that the outcome will be helpful rather than punitive. The focus can switch from punishment to structure coupled with rehabilitation. Parents may obtain help and guidance that might not otherwise be available.

It's important to recognize that even the most knowledgeable and loving parents often are not the best choice for providing a structured living environment and consistent guidance once the youth reaches 19 or 20 years of age. A modified group home may be more effective than a mother-in-law apartment. Teenagers with FAS/E still view their parents as having control, and guidance from someone not as close to the situation can be more effective. Teenagers will regard a professional more as a teacher/mentor/guide than as a controlling force. Removing parents from the day-to-day conflicts can allow parents and children to enjoy their time together more.

CONCLUSION

Rearing any child can be stressful and frustrating at times; this is even more true for parents of children with FAS/E. When we parents start looking for help, we sometimes hear people say that we need better parenting skills, that if we were better parents we would not be having all these problems. If only they knew. I think it's important to remember the saying: *Rather than try harder, try differently and try smarter.*

One of the basic but forgotten requirements is to take care of ourselves. We cannot become so wrapped up in trying to meet the needs of our children that we ignore, deny, or forget about our own needs. We must take time for ourselves. We are not superparents, nor should we feel we need or have to be. We need places in the house where we can be alone. We need adult friends and interests that have nothing to do with FAS/E without feeling guilty. Parents of children with FAS/E are under great pressure to maintain consistency and vigilance, but we are of little help if we are burned out.

We must also remember that success stories exist. Yes, it takes hard work. Sometimes it can be frustrating. But when we ask,"Why?" we see the answer in our children's eyes.

16
Adolescents with Disabilities: Insights for Individuals with FAS/E

CLAIRE D. COLES AND MARY ELLEN LYNCH

Claire Coles, Ph.D., and Mary Ellen Lynch, Ph.D., are associated with the Maternal Substance Abuse and Child Development Project at the Emory University School of Medicine in Atlanta, Georgia. Dr. Coles also is the director of Psychological Services, Marcus Institute, an affiliate of the Kennedy-Kriegen Institute, at Emory University.

JOAN LEARNED THAT HER DAUGHTER MELISSA, WHO HAS FAS, WAS accused of sexually harassing a male student in her classroom by blowing in his ear. She fights with other girls over boys and likes to aggravate her male classmates. "There is always some hell breaking loose" in Melissa's classroom, her mother says. "Melissa blurts out whatever she wants to say. The thoughts in her brain are not always very nice."

Melissa, now 19, has had trouble at home, at school, and with the law since she entered her teenage years. At night, she roamed the neighborhood kicking mail boxes, swearing, and threatening children. People frightened by her behavior called police more than a dozen times, and she has been arrested twice, for physical aggression toward a teacher and toward a police officer. Following these episodes, she was hospitalized for several months and now sees a therapist.

Diagnosed at the age of 14 months with FAS in 1979, Melissa shows the characteristic physical features as well as borderline intellectual functioning and these social difficulties. Her mother drank heavily during pregnancy, and at birth Melissa weighed less than five pounds although she was a full-term baby. Because of severe neglect, she entered foster care at nine months and came into Joan's care before she was two. She had problems with intellectual tasks, attention, and impulse control during elementary school, but she did not show serious behavioral or conduct problems. She has received medical and special educational services all her life.

Her mother, frustrated by Melissa's behavior and concerned about her future, is widowed and knows she cannot care for her daughter forever. Although Melissa is now a young adult, she herself seems only mildly concerned about the future and says she will live in Joan's house even after her mother is gone. Recently, Joan has been talking with her daughter about the possibility of a group home.

The Difficulty of Adolescence for People with FAS/E

Melissa's problems are unfortunately common among adolescents with FAS/E. For every person, adolescence is a time of both difficulty and opportunity. For those with FAS or other alcohol-related disabilities and their families, this stage of life can be particularly stressful. While the research literature dealing with this period of development is very limited, the clinical descriptions of adolescents and young adults with FAS often present a bleak picture.[1] As with Melissa, young people suffer from many social and academic problems and have difficulty achieving expected developmental goals, including independence from parents, self-esteem and identity, appropriate sexual behavior, academic and vocational functioning, and other necessary life skills.

The difficulty of adolescence for young people with FAS has only recently been recognized as a central problem. Little scientific work has been done on this issue. To understand what is going on,

---

[1] Dorris 1989; LaDue, Streissguth, and Randels 1992; Lemoine and Lemoine 1992; Streissguth et al. 1991.

we need to consider the typical developmental process during adolescence and to examine how a disability such as FAS may affect it. We can also learn a great deal from the experiences of adolescents and adults with other types of learning problems and neurobehavioral disorders.

LONG-TERM DEVELOPMENT IN ALCOHOL-AFFECTED INDIVIDUALS: THE RESEARCH FINDINGS

While more research needs to be done, long-term follow-ups of adolescents and adults report significant problems. Deficits in intellectual functioning continue to affect development and limit opportunities. During adolescence, the problems with behavior and the more general life skills that are called "adaptive functioning" may be even more significant than academic and intellectual deficits. In one study of clinically-referred children who were followed into adolescence and adulthood, these individuals had many personal and social difficulties, including hyperactivity, memory and attention problems, inappropriate sexual behavior, drug and alcohol use, lying, stealing, and troubles with school, the law, and authority. As children, many had been victims of abuse and neglect.[2]

In a pioneering study, Streissguth and her colleagues provided a description of "secondary disabilities" that often accompany the primary neurological damage in alcohol-affected individuals. The study identified very high rates of legal, emotional/behavioral and vocational problems in a group of 473 patients, adults who had been referred as children for clinical services.[3]

The quality of the caregiving environment has been linked to the severity of problems during adolescence. In Germany, Spohr, Wilms, and Steinhausen (1993) predicted a gloomy future for alcohol-affected young people, particularly for those with the greatest physical effects and those who had the most highly disorganized caregiving environments. In their sample, many of

---

[2] LaDue et al. 1992; Lemoine and Lemoine 1992.
[3] Streissguth et al. 1996.

those diagnosed with FAS had a history of physical and sexual abuse and had suffered neglect. Many had lived in numerous foster homes. Similarly, Lemoine and Lemoine (1992) reported on a 20-year follow-up of their original group of French children. They found that most were institutionalized as adults. Those who showed the most severe physical effects were also the most likely to have lower IQs (most in the mentally retarded range, which is lower than 70), neurological problems, and other medical conditions. But those showing milder effects, ironically, were at greater risk in other areas. Among individuals who were more mildly affected, for example, there were more serious adaptive and psychiatric problems, with some having attempted or completed suicide. As children, they had experienced very negative family lives (unstable environments, significant substance use, poor care-giving), and the severity of outcome was associated, in part, with such experiences.

These findings are certainly disturbing. Faced with such information, it would be easy to give up hope for these alcohol-affected individuals and to assume their prenatal brain damage was so significant that it is impossible to change or improve outcomes. However, it may be more useful to take a different approach, to look at the questions these reports raise and use them as a basis for future investigations and intervention, and for thinking about just why adolescence is such a difficult period for young people with FAS/E.

THE TASKS OF ADOLESCENCE

Adolescence is a period of many changes and transitions. The rapid physical growth of puberty, development of more abstract thought capabilities, and increase in social expectations all occur as the child makes the transition to adulthood. Every adolescent must deal with vital developmental tasks during these years:

1) increasing levels of independence in both functional and emotional areas of life

2) developing skills for more complex social relationships

3) dealing with sexual maturity

4) developing a sense of self and identity

5) eventually assuming adult work and family roles.[4]

Usually, as adolescents move toward adulthood and become more independent, they can make more choices and bear more responsibility for the outcomes of their decisions and behaviors. They make decisions about school courses and activities, have closer relationships with other teens, and begin dating. They think about the future and their opportunities in work, school, and life. As adolescents mature, they become able to assume responsibilities in the adult world, ranging from working at part-time or even full-time jobs to driving automobiles to becoming parents themselves. Decisions made during adolescence, not only about education and work plans but also about risk-taking behavior (sexual activity, use of alcohol or drugs, delinquent behavior), are significant and can have long-term effects on opportunities later in life.[5]

It should not be surprising that individuals with FAS, like other disabled persons, often fail to deal effectively with these issues.

IMPORTANT QUESTIONS TO CONSIDER

Why do problems become so pronounced during adolescence and adulthood when, earlier in life, many children with FAS/E seem to respond to treatments and to a structured environment?

Demands and social expectations escalate for all adolescents and those with disabilities have a far harder time meeting them. They require considerable support from their families and from educational and social services. Sometimes such supports do not exist or are not structured in a way that works for a particular young person or family. In addition, families and society have great

---

[4] See Leffert and Petersen 1995, Crockett and Crouter 1995, and Elliott and Feldman 1990.
[5] See Crockett and Crouter 1995.

difficulty with some areas of life, such as sexuality and substance abuse, and often do not handle them well. It is not that alcohol damage becomes worse at adolescence but that society's expectations escalate!

Are problems identified in persons with FAS unique and the result of specific brain damage associated with alcohol exposure or do similar problems occur in others with developmental disabilities?

Yes, and no!

At the present time, we do not know to what extent the problems often found among adolescents with FAS are unique. It may be true that certain kinds of neurological damage occur only as a result of alcohol exposure, although this has never been demonstrated. For the most part, the reports of adolescents and adults with FAS are very similar to the reports describing problems seen in adolescents with other disabilities. For example, in the recent Seattle study,[6] 79 percent of adults with FAS reported having employment problems. While this number is startling, a British study that sampled a population of adults with disabilities of all kinds showed that 89 percent were unemployed, suggesting a similar level of dysfunction.[7] In addition, while many young people with FAS are reported to show sexually inappropriate behavior, this was also a high-frequency problem in other disabled groups. The problems with sexuality, however, may not be exactly the same. Adolescents with FAS, for example, may be able to attract sexual partners easily but may not have an understanding of the subtleties of sexual rules. For instance, adolescents with FAS may be likely to make sexually inappropriate comments on impulse or assume that feelings of attraction are reciprocated when, in fact, this may not be the case. The average adolescent has better social judgment skills and would be less likely to make these impulsive errors. Future study on FAS in this age group may make it easier to answer this question in ways that suggest effective prevention and intervention activities. Meanwhile, research and practical experience

---

[6] Streissguth et al. 1996.
[7] Wacker et al. 1983.

concerning adolescents with other types of disabilities can be useful as a source of ideas.

Do all individuals with FAS/E have the same problems, or do certain situations help or hinder their development, for instance, certain caregiving histories?

In all groups of individuals, whatever their characteristics, there is a range of developmental outcomes. Some will function better than others; some have greater problems in adapting to life's challenges than others. This is as true for alcohol-affected individuals as it is for those with Down syndrome, autism, and those developing typically. Those aspects of life that hinder development are called "risk" factors and those that help promote more positive outcomes are called "protective" factors. Risk factors are conditions in a person's life that may worsen a problem or introduce another problem, known as a "secondary disability" and a number have been identified in individuals with disabilities.[8] Risk factors related to more serious outcomes in FAS also have been investigated[9] and are similar to those which are important in other groups. These include:

- Experiencing a highly disorganized caregiving environment early in life and then being placed in multiple foster homes

- Negative caregiving environments, particularly living in conditions of poverty with dysfunctional, substance abusing families

- Being the victim of child abuse and witnessing violence.

A number of protective factors have been identified in studies of risk and resilience among disabled individuals that appear to be associated with more positive outcomes. Individual differences include better social skills, response flexibility, physical attractiveness,

---

[8] Patterson and Blum 1996.
[9] Stratton, Howe, and Battaglia 1996; Streissguth et al. 1996. See also Spohr, Wilms, and Steinhausen 1993, Streissguth et al. 1991, and Lemoine and Lemoine 1992.

and certain personality traits (e.g., "easy" temperament). Other factors identified include family characteristics such as more structure, appropriate parenting style, stress-coping strategies, and a positive outlook.[10] The Seattle study of secondary disabilities associated with FAS identified a number of protective factors which are more often present when there is a more positive outcome for this disorder. These factors include:

- Living in a nurturing and stable home during the majority of childhood

- Having basic physical and emotional needs reliably met

- Diagnosis of FAS before six years.[11]

These studies show that the caregiving environment can influence the outcome for children with FAS/E. It is clear that, like other disabled adolescents, those who have been alcohol-affected have the potential to respond positively to interventions. In short, the range of possible outcomes for alcohol-affected individuals is very wide.[12] Intervention and treatments to improve educational and vocational problems can be designed to improve the future for alcohol-affected adolescents significantly.

Are there specific interventions or treatments that would prevent or improve the social problems and other secondary disabilities that are seen in individuals with FAS/E?

Undoubtedly. However, for a number of practical reasons, we are still at an early stage in our understanding of what these will be. To some extent, this situation exists because little attention and few resources have been directed at finding such solutions. FAS has not been a priority for funding by mental health, education, or social systems. Even those who work with other kinds of disabilities have been reluctant to include alcohol-affected individuals unless they met criteria for inclusion under other categories.[13] The result

---

[10] Patterson and Blum 1996.
[11] Streissguth et al. 1996.
[12] Stratton et al. 1996.
[13] Coles and Platzman 1992.

has been a complete lack of systematic information about treatment methods.

In addition, our knowledge on the needs of affected individuals is limited. In the past, the adolescents with FAS who have been studied have been the most seriously affected both in terms of their prenatal exposure to alcohol and their negative life experiences. In coming to understand a disability, science and clinical practice usually begin with the most serious cases since it is those with the greatest needs who are referred for treatment or who come to the attention of the educational, social, and justice systems. However, the most affected provide only a partial understanding of the needs and capabilities of those exposed to alcohol and it is likely that their life circumstances make it difficult to sort out the effects of alcohol from those resulting from other risk factors. There are surely many other alcohol-affected adolescents whose behavior and/or life circumstances have not brought them frequently to the attention of physicians and psychologists. Those adolescents may be living much more successful lives and experiencing fewer secondary disabilities. When we can examine systematically the lives of those young people who are doing well, we will begin to understand how they have been protected from the most damaging aspects of FAS. The chapters that parents and front-line professionals have written in this volume are excellent sources for such ideas and may prompt more investigation in this area.

Nevertheless, at the present time, little systematic research has been done on the ways to treat FAS/E to produce the best outcomes for individuals and families. Knowing that adolescence is a particularly stressful time for young people with all kinds of disabilities, it may be time to examine methods for intervention with this group and treatment for those with identified disorders.

Ideally, such research would begin with a survey of alcohol-affected youth and their families, nationwide, to identify the most common issues as well as risk and protective factors. When both population and problems have been identified, specific treatment protocols can be developed and implemented to identify those that are most effective. For instance, because many individuals with

FAS are treated for attention deficit/hyperactivity disorder, it would be appropriate to evaluate the degree to which the commonly prescribed stimulant medications alleviate behavior problems and make learning more effective. Specific educational interventions could be developed to address common academic deficiencies (e.g., math disability) and then tested among those with FAS and with IQ-matched students without FAS. Social deficits may be remedied by the types of social skills training suggested by parents and teachers in many of the chapters in this book. There are more possibilities.

Conclusion

Despite the difficulties that may be encountered in carrying out research on intervention and treatment of alcohol-affected individuals, it is clearly time to begin such efforts. The reports of parents and professionals in this volume, and the evidence available from studies of other adolescents and their families coping with disabilities strongly argue that it is possible to support individuals with FAS/E and other alcohol-related disabilities in achieving satisfactory lives.

References

M. C. Borjenson and J. Lagergren, "Life conditions of adolescence with myelomenin gocele." *Developmental Medicine and Child Neurology* 32 (1990): 689–706.

L. Crockett and A. Crouter, "Pathways through adolescence: An overview." In L. Crockett and A. Crouter, eds. *Pathways through adolescence: Individual development in relation to social context.* Mahwah, N.J.: Lawrence Erlbaum Ass., 1995, 1–12.

"People with work disability in the U.S," *Disability Statistics Abstract*, Vol 4. Disablity Statistics Program, University of California, San Francisco: U.S. Department of Education, NIDRR, May 1992.

M. Dorris, *The Broken Cord* (New York: Harper and Row, 1989).

G. R. Elliott and S. S. Feldman, "Capturing the adolescent experience." In S.S. Feldman and G.R. Elliott, eds., *At the threshold: The developing adolescent* (Cambridge: Harvard University Press, 1990), 1-13.

A. Hallum, "Disability and the transition to adulthood: Issues for the disabled child, the family and the pediatrician," *Current Problems in Pediatrics* (January 1995): 12–50.

R. LaDue, A. Streissguth, and S. P. Randels, "Clinical consideration pertaining to adolescents and adults with fetal alcohol syndrome," in T. Sonderigger, ed. *Perinatal substance abuse: Recent findings and clinical implications* (Baltimore, Md.: Johns Hopkins Press, 1992).

N. Leffert and A. Petersen, "Patterns of development during adolescence: An overview," in M. Rutter and D. Smith, eds. *Psychosocial Disorders in Young People* (Chichester, England: John Wylie & Sons, Ltd., 1995), 67–103.

P. Lemoine and P. Lemoine, "Avenir des enfants de mere alcooliques (etude de 105 cas retrouvés a l'age adulte) et quelques constatations d'interet prophylactique [Follow-up of children of alcoholic mothers (study of 105 cases seen in adulthood) and some recommendations about prevention]," *Annales le Pediatric* (Paris) 39 (1992): 226–235.

J. Patterson and R. W. Blum, "Risk and resilience among children and youth with disabilities," *Archives of Pediatric and Adolescent Medicine* 150 (1996): 692–698.

E. Schopler and G. Mesibov, *Autism in adolescents and adults* (New York: Plenum Press, 1983).

H. L. Spohr, J. Wilms, and J. C. Steinhausen, "Prenatal alcohol exposure and long term developmental consequences," *Lancet* 341 (1993): 907–910.

A. P. Streissguth, J. M. Aase, S. K. Clarren, S. P. Randels, R. A. LaDue, and D. F. Smith, "Fetal alcohol syndrome in adolescents and adults," *Journal of the American Medical Association* 256 (1991): 1961–1967.

A. P. Streissguth, H. M. Barr, J. Kogan, and F. L. Bookstein, "Understanding the occurrence of secondary disabilities in clients with fetal alcohol syndrome (FAS) and fetal alcohol effects (FAE)," *Final Report* (Seattle, Wash.: University of Washington Publication Services, 1996).

D. P. Wacker et al., "Life outcomes and satisfaction ratings of multihandicapped adults," *Developmental Medicine and Child Neurology* 25 (1983): 625-631.

A. G. Zetlin and J. L. Turner, "Transition from adolescence to adulthood: Perspectives of mentally retarded individuals and their families," *American Journal of Mental Deficiency* 6 (1985): 570–579.

Part Three

What
Families
Need
from the
Community

17

Using Community Mentors to Help Teenagers with FAS/E Develop Social Skills

JANET ADAMS*

Janet Adams and her husband Tom have eight children, seven of them adopted. The family keeps busy playing T-ball, basketball, swimming, and track while adding on to their house in Minnesota.

WHEN TONY JOINED OUR FAMILY NINE YEARS AGO, HE WAS A BLOND, blue-eyed six year old who seldom smiled. We knew that he had epilepsy and what his adoption agency file noted as a "minor temper problem," that his birth mother had been in several alcohol treatment programs, and that her parental rights had been terminated because of her severe abuse and neglect of her son. The social worker told us our adopted son showed no signs of FAS, attributing his problems to his past abuse. We knew only enough about FAS to question our ability to parent a child with those problems. We did not know enough to ask about FAE.

TRYING TO HANDLE TONY'S PROBLEMS

Although we knew about Tony's difficult early life when we adopted him, other serious problems emerged during his first three years with us. He experienced almost continuous trouble at school and was diagnosed with reactive attachment disorder and

---

* Janet Adams is a pseudonym.

other emotional disabilities. He refused to speak when asked to make a choice or answer a question. He had difficulties with visual perception and fine motor skills and felt such extreme sensory defensiveness that he could not tolerate any touch and found it hard even to walk down the hall if other students were around.

For a time, Tony needed less help in school and it seemed that he had overcome his problems. But in the fourth grade, he began to get into trouble again, to the point of destroying his surroundings. The only thing that could stop him was physical restraint. Tony responded to unfamiliar situations and inconsistency by acting out this way, and my husband and I quickly sought to find out what was wrong.

We learned that the student aide who had worked with Tony at the school and was his friend had left to take another position. The person who took his place didn't have the training to respond to Tony's special needs. Tony thought that acting out would help bring his friend back to the school.

After we explained to Tony that his friend was working some-place else, the situation at school got a little better, but it was an unsettling time for several months while he got used to the new person. His destructive behavior occurred at home and got so bad sometimes that we even called the police to come and remove him until he was calm. But the officer accused us of abusing Tony based on his self-inflicted scars and scratches. In tears, I explained the wounds to the officer, who left us with Tony and a fear of asking for outside help.

We knew something needed to be done, but we didn't know where to find answers. My husband and I would sit and stare at the clock, dreading the time the kids would come home and we would have to face Tony.

Then, during a routine follow-up for Tony's epilepsy, the neurologist described him as a "a slender boy with FAS." I was shocked. After several phone calls seeking explanations, we ended up at the University of Minnesota, where Tony was diagnosed with FAE.

Although this clarified many things that hadn't made sense before, the more we learned, the more concerned we became about the long-term outlook. We weren't sure if the lack of early intervention could be overcome. School slowly improved, but Tony was becoming more self-abusive at home and even threatening suicide. We placed locks on the knives, scissors, can openers, and anything else he could stab himself with. We slept fitfully, listening for him moving around in the kitchen. We were burning out. If life at home was so difficult, how would Tony ever make friends, play sports, learn social skills, or do any of the things that mark a normal adolescence?

FINDING HELP FROM THE PERSONAL CARE ASSISTANT PROGRAM

One day we heard about a Minnesota Department of Human Services program called Personal Care Assistant, or PCA. A trained PCA comes into the home and helps the client perform and learn basic skills of daily life, such as dressing, bathing, taking medication, doing chores, preparing for school, and so on, relieving some of the strain on the family. In Minnesota, this service is available through Medical Assistance and paid by Tony's subsidy. A physician writes an order for a PCA assessment, which is done by a county health nurse using a form from the state. The nurse then tailors a plan for each person's needs. Parents participate in selecting the PCA.

Because Tony physically can do many things, his plan called for many reminders and cues to help him remember to do them during his daily routines. The PCA supervised Tony from the time he got off the bus until he went to bed. The PCA also was available six hours a day on weekends if we requested it. He made sure Tony cleaned his place after eating, took his medications, and cleaned his bedroom and bathroom. He supervised Tony when he was playing outside with other children and helped him choose weather-appropriate clothing, which parents don't always have time, energy, or patience to do. Because the PCA was paid to help Tony learn these skills, he didn't have the emotional ties that frustrated us.

Having such a buffer at stressful times helped, but Tony needed another type of helper who could work with him outside our home. In 1995, the Minnesota Department of Human Services added Community Integration Specialist, or CIS, to the PCA program. A CIS can accompany clients to community events, such as movies or school sports events. A Habilitation Counselor, whom we haven't used, can also enter the workplace to help adolescents move out of the school system and into the adult world.

FINDING THE RIGHT SOCIAL ROLE MODEL FOR TONY

In the PCA program, two or three staff people would rotate coming to our home. Some got along better with Tony than others, and it was clear he got along best with male PCAs. If Tony didn't get along with one of the PCAs, then we would ask for a new person. Some were not present long enough to form a bond with Tony. Despite these drawbacks, he benefited from the program. The most striking benefit occurred with a PCA named Nick.

Nick was a high school senior who had worked in nursing homes before becoming a mentor for Tony, then in seventh grade. Having a senior like Nick talk to him in the school halls gave Tony status he had never had before. When they ran into Nick's friends during the course of their activities, these other high school students accepted our son as well. Nick and his friends were close enough in age to provide a natural environment for learning social behavior. Tony, who was electively mute for much of his life, learned social skills he had never used before.

Tony talked to Nick when he wouldn't or chose not to talk to us, and he received more individual attention from Nick than we could give him. In many ways, Nick filled the gap left in our son's life when his older brother went to college. When Tony wanted to join the diving team, I found it much easier to let go, knowing he would be supervised by someone who understood his needs and could keep him safe. Nick also volunteered at our church youth league, again giving me the confidence to allow Tony to participate without my direct supervision.

Nick's mentoring proved much more effective in teaching Tony social skills than any school program designed for this purpose. He took Tony to basketball and hockey games at the school, setting up more peer contact and allowing Tony to observe good social interactions in an informal atmosphere. They went to the beach, the library, and the grocery store. When Nick was coaching an elementary football team, he took Tony along as an informal assistant coach. One parent called me to say what a nice young man Tony had developed into. She told me that he walked along the sidelines talking to team parents about the practice and how well their children were doing. Four years of social skills training in school couldn't get him to say hello when somebody greeted him, but with less than a year of Nick's help, he was initiating appropriate conversations.

MOVING TOWARD INDEPENDENCE

The PCA/CIS program also helped Tony become more independent. A few years ago, Tony needed an aide to ride with him between school and home. Now Tony was on a swim team and participated in out-of-town meets, traveling on the bus without special supervision. This was possible only because a staff person first accompanied Tony to practice and to meets, giving us and the coach enough confidence and experience to allow Tony to attend events unaccompanied.

Tony rarely needed extra oversight at swimming. He became part of a group, and other teammates and the supervisors knew and accepted him. These gains in social skills and maturity would not have occurred without the interaction with peers and the community made possible by the PCAs.

FINDING MENTORS IN THE COMMUNITY

In addition to the mentors provided by agency programs, community groups can offer informal or volunteer support for mentoring teenagers. Church youth leaders and scout leaders are often too busy with the entire group to offer a child individual attention, but they may be able to refer you to another group member willing to volunteer. Sometimes you can borrow volunteers from the local hospital or nursing home. A nearby college with a nursing or education program may be able to recommend someone or to arrange an agreement with professors to provide extra credit for students who volunteer with your child. Some high schools offer mentor programs, or special education aides may be willing to spend extra time with your teenager.

Arranging this kind of support requires some forethought (see "Tips," opposite) because volunteer or unpaid staff may not provide the consistency needed for the best results. Finding people willing to take time to learn specific techniques can be hard. They must commit to learning the warning signs of overstimulation and how to calm the child, and they must have the emotional maturity not to become embarrassed or angry at the public attention that can arise from difficult behaviors. They must also be able to safely restrain the youngster physically, if necessary.

To establish continuity between mentors, we keep a notebook to help pinpoint patterns and trouble spots. Often the various professionals working with our children aren't fully aware of what's going on in the rest of a child's life, and some services are duplicated while others are left undone. The biggest benefit of this log is being able to look back and see just how far we've come when we have one of those really bad days.

Sometimes having an extra person around can invade our privacy, limit spontaneity, and make us feel our house isn't our own. Occasionally a PCA has a personal style that doesn't fit that of our family. However, the benefits for Tony have made it all worthwhile. Those mentors who worked out best learned Tony's routine and kept things moving with a minimum of supervision.

One of the hardest things for me was developing enough trust in the staff to let them do their job. One day Tony lost control at home, and the staff person froze. I instinctively told the PCA to leave the room, treating him like an innocent bystander, so I could handle Tony myself. A couple of minutes later I realized this was

Tips for Using a Personal Care Assistant or Community Mentor*

⟿ Make sure you have the right to interview a potential mentor provided by agencies and retain the right to decline a placement without having to provide a specific reason that would appear on a personnel record.

⟿ Develop a clear list of expectations, review it with the agency and the mentor, and post it where it is easily visible.

⟿ Mark a calendar with appointments, activities, or changes in schedule so the staff person can review it each day.

⟿ Have an emergency plan in place.

⟿ Try to schedule staff when you need them most. For example, if bedtime is especially stressful for your child, having a buffer available then can make life easier.

⟿ Clarify how staffing will be handled if the PCA/CIS is ill or otherwise unavailable; sometimes it is easier to do without than to rely on someone unfamiliar with your child's problems, and other times an extra pair of hands or eyes can really help.

⟿ Keep a daily log of your child's behaviors to familiarize potential or current mentors with the frequency and types of incidents that arise.

⟿ Organize important papers in a three-ring binder, including:
• weekday and weekend schedules that are easily updated
• a copy of the current care plan
• a list of expectations for the mentor
• school and medical records
• the daily log or blank sheets to note trouble spots and needs.

---

* Prepared by Janet Adams.

the staff person's job, so I called him back and instructed him step-by-step on how to take over the hold from me, what to say, and when to release Tony. Then I went into the kitchen, started supper, and watched to see how things went.

That incident liberated me in many ways. My mind had believed the staff could care for Tony, but my heart didn't. Once I saw someone else caring skillfully for Tony, I found it easier to allow him out of my line of vision. Trusting someone else to handle my child was hard, and yet it was such a relief, too.

Conclusion

Community mentors have done wonders in helping Tony become more comfortable with people. One day, the school nurse called to say Tony had approached her in the hall and asked if she could "do something about his thumb" (he had a hangnail). Then he chattered all the way to her office. She kept looking at him because she couldn't believe she was talking to our normally silent son. He was also assigned detention for being tardy seven times in a two-week period—because he was talking to others in the cafeteria and lost track of time. Although Tony still doesn't answer questions readily, this semester a teacher wrote his name on the board for talking in class. When he looked up and saw his name he said, "Cool!"

ᕭ Epilogue ᕬ

Tony had to be placed in long-term foster care a year ago, because he began to direct his physical violence toward his family, especially me. Sadly, his doctors believe that he suffers from apparent flashbacks of abuse inflicted by his biological mother, and Tony confused me with her. After several incidents, it became unsafe for him to remain in our home. Without a mother-figure in his foster home, he is doing well. His flashbacks have diminished significantly, and he continues to receive counseling. Tony is also participating in a high school work-study program. He has goals and values, and recognizes the importance of education, family, and getting a good job. I hope one day that we can reestablish our relationship.

18
Community Involvement: Lessons from Native Americans

Rodger Hornby

For more than two decades, Rodger Hornby worked with Native Americans as a psychologist, primarily with the Northern Cheyenne and Lakota tribes of the Plains Indian people. Now deceased, this chapter honors his commitment to young people with FAS/E.

IN MAINSTREAM SOCIETY, MANY PEOPLE OFTEN JUDGE AND EVEN condemn the child or adolescent with FAS/E who cannot meet their social expectations. I have found that Native American cultures are much more accepting of those with alcohol-related birth defects, using gentle guidance with family and tribal members who have FAS/E.

THE DYNAMICS OF DIAGNOSIS

Early diagnosis is essential for the optimal development of alcohol-affected children. Too often, the parents are not informed at birth or later that their child has FAS/E, but they may sense something is wrong or even fear that FAS/E is the problem. Unsure about what to do, they provide only sporadic stimulation or inconsistent attention during the child's early developmental years. Their frustration increases as their efforts to correct problems weaken or cease. Guilt intensifies when the child doesn't progress, and frequently parents deal with their feelings by ignoring the child.

Once the child enters school, the problems worsen. Parents may feel incapable of dealing effectively with their child's problems and then project their own frustration and anger onto the teachers. When a school alerts them that their child may have significant learning or developmental problems, parents may feel their youngster is being singled out. Often they blame teachers for being ineffective, or some assume that racist thinking is at fault.

The case of Matilda illustrates these complicated reactions. Matilda, a 28-year old single mother of five children, contacted me because the school reported that her 13-year-old son had behavior problems and was not doing well. Someone at school told Matilda that her son might have fetal alcohol syndrome. Matilda felt angry with the school, yet obligated to allow her son to be evaluated, as the school insisted. Because I did not work for the school and she knew me from a different family situation, Matilda asked me for help.

Matilda had been married twice and had a history of alcohol abuse. Initially she was cautious about discussing her drinking when pregnant. I asked her to summarize the developmental experiences of each of her children, her general behaviors and reactions during her pregnancies, and her parenting responses following their births. Eventually she said that she drank heavily during the 14 weeks after her son's conception because she did not know she was pregnant. Had she known, she would have quit drinking, she said. She began to cry and express how guilty and angry she felt, and how she believed everyone was critical of her for bearing a child who possibly had FAS/E.

Her response to these feelings was to deny vehemently any alcohol use or the possibility that her son has FAS/E to others, to her family, and sometimes even to herself. Her physician actually knew of alcohol abuse early in the pregnancy but never informed Matilda that it might affect her baby. The physician's lapse provided an easy target for Matilda's anger and frustration.

Assessing her son's condition was the first step toward resolving her guilt and anger. I encouraged her to contact the Indian Health Service hospital and schedule a medical evaluation for her son. Matilda resisted telling the doctor about the school's concerns, the possibility of FAS/E, and her drinking patterns during the first trimester of pregnancy. Together we decided that I would provide the doctor with her social and drinking history and express her concerns as a parent. Matilda essentially needed and requested advocacy services for herself in dealing with the doctor. With this accomplished, she took her son to the doctor, he received a psychological evaluation, and he was diagnosed as having fetal alcohol effects.

Service providers, such as this doctor, can be unfamiliar with Lakota expectations for the conduct of professional business. In mainstream society, such an assessment usually starts out primarily with business followed by socializing. The Lakota establish a relationship through socializing, and then they turn to business. If the service provider does not understand this sequence, problems can mar the assessment process. Additionally, Native Americans view assessments and interaction with professionals as a participatory relationship, not one of expert to subordinate. This requires professionals to feel comfortable sharing a little information about themselves, their beliefs, and their concerns. This exchange does not have to be highly personal, but it should be genuine and authentic.*

Once a good relationship is established, the therapist can focus on gathering the client's developmental history and the parents' history of substance abuse. The substance abuse background must be approached in a nonjudgmental, nonthreatening manner. Too often, non-Indian providers question in a rather intrusive and seemingly accusatory manner that results in a distorted or inaccurate history. The key is to establish a collaborative relationship that allows clients to be candid, open, and honest. If a client seems to resist or denies facts, it is probably necessary to back up and form a cooperative relationship before gathering the history.

---

* See Hornby 1993 in "Works Cited" at the end of the book for a more extensive discussion of providing services to culturally different individuals.

Working Beyond Guilt to Build Parent Advocates

Discovering that their child has FAS or FAE is painful and difficult for parents, who must struggle to resolve their guilt and overcome the despair of daily confronting their child's condition. I have found the most effective approach is to teach parents to become advocates for their children. Therapists can help parents accept and improve their child's situation by offering:

• Nonjudgmental acceptance

• Information about FAS/E

• Readily available educational strategies and intervention techniques

• Advice about improving their own behavioral skills

• Encouragement to act as advocates.

Matilda's case provides a good example of how this approach can work. The diagnosis of her son's FAE understandably distressed her. As counseling helped her address her feelings of despair, anger, and guilt, she became more motivated to work with her son. I suggested that her son needed her advocacy rather than a punitive or corrective response.

Initially, Matilda was unclear about an advocate's role. I reminded her how we had contacted the doctor, and I pointed out that she could encourage her son's development just as I had helped her see the doctor, obtain a diagnosis, and resolve much of her feelings. She became very interested in helping her son. She read a variety of materials, including the book *Fantastic Antone Succeeds*, research articles on fetal alcohol effects, parental information published by the Indian Health Service on fetal alcohol effects, and specific remedial materials available from both the school and other resources. As Matilda read and discussed these materials with me, she began developing a systematic way to work with her son. Her response was heartening.

One problem she continually faced was an insensitive attitude at her son's school. She repeatedly remarked that she felt the school was critical of her efforts and made her feel she was not a good parent. Teachers and staff often said her son needed to be in a special school. This upset her because she wanted her son to have the most normal experiences and opportunities possible.

As a service provider, I became aware that teachers often blame alcohol-affected children or their parents for difficult behavior because they do not understand the specific neurologically based deficits and problems associated with this condition. The need for more training in FAS/E seems critical in education, especially in school districts where increased numbers of alcohol-affected children have been documented.

Matilda's case reflects what can be accomplished by parents motivated to provide positive interventions. With her guidance, her son accepted discipline more easily, stopped hanging around the peers who created a bad influence, and began following Native American traditions under the tutelage of a medicine man.

Unfortunately, many children with FAS/E do not receive needed services. This was the case with Pat.

Pat is an adolescent with identifiable features of fetal alcohol syndrome. His grandmother raised him because his parents could not or would not. When he got older, his grandmother was unable to care for him adequately so he entered a residential facility for neglected or abandoned children. Pat spent his adolescence there and earned a high school degree.

Pat's parents did little with him or for him. This was puzzling because his father served on the tribal council and was active in tribal and Indian issues. For Pat, it seemed as if his parents were either too ashamed of having a child with FAS or were too immobilized by their own problems to care for him. Parents who are drinking have little or no time to give their children, and this makes children with alcohol-related birth defects vulnerable to a variety of problems, including an inconsistent diet and inadequate nurturing. Social problems include educational and behavioral difficulties and an increased risk of being victimized or exploited by others. Children in actively drinking families also face a greater risk of physical and sexual abuse, being responsible for younger siblings, having nowhere to turn for help, and being separated from their families and placed in foster care or residential facilities.

Some tribal groups do educate foster parents about these problems, although there are generally not enough special resources to train them. Consequently, alcohol-affected children are often placed in settings where providers do not fully understand or are incapable of effectively responding to their special needs. Care-givers may label these children as unmotivated, distractible, impulsive, demanding of too much attention, lacking common sense, dumb, lazy, and so on. These problems simply reflect the need for more education and understanding about fetal alcohol syndrome.

Why was Matilda able to help her son? In large part, she was able to focus on her son because she stopped drinking. She chose to commit herself to a treatment program, a decision prompted by a threat from State Social Services that she would lose custody of her children if she did not seek help.

Matilda entered a treatment program that stressed Native American values in addition to a sober lifestyle. During treatment, she felt she had found what she had been looking for—the tradi-tional values and cultural activities that reaffirmed her worth. This is significant because as a child, Matilda had been removed from her family, placed in a non-Indian foster home, later sent to boarding school, and upon graduation returned to her home reser-vation. These disruptive developmental experiences stole much of her Indian-ness from her. Her re-introduction to traditional culture allowed her to come home to herself.

Upon returning home, Matilda contacted several traditional people and began work with a medicine man. After a year's prepa-ration, she participated in the Sundance, an annual ceremony by the Lakota people that reaffirms the link between each member and the tribe and expresses commitment to the betterment and well-being of the tribe. This experience strengthened her abilities, her identity, and her determination to overcome the various problems life offered her.

Today, Matilda participates in a variety of traditional cultural activities ranging from the Sundance to ceremonies to the sweat lodge. She works actively with her son and began studying for a degree in human services from the local tribal college. She offers insight and assistance to other tribal members who have a family member with FAS or FAE. She has become an advocate not only for herself and her son, but for her community.

THE NATIVE AMERICAN RESPONSE TO FAS/E

The Native American community generally accepts people along with their strengths and weaknesses and tries to integrate them into the social fabric of the tribe. Most community members accept people's various limitations or idiosyncrasies. The extended family also acts to help protect vulnerable people from improper or exploitive situations.

Even though Pat did not benefit from a mother able to turn away from drinking, he benefited as a young adult from this Native American community attitude. After graduating from high school, he was too old to remain in residential care and was released, choosing to live with a relative in one of the reservation communities. Instead of drifting through life without any connections, however, Pat joined community life through employment, continuing education, and improved ties with his family and Native American culture. He lives independently, but members of the community subtly guide his social interactions through a sense of obligation and interdependence.

Pat found a job at a grocery store where he had worked during a high school work-study program. He stocks store shelves and carries out customers' groceries. This is work that his employer appreciates, that he finds satisfying, and that pays him well. Native American communities provide many such opportunities for disabled persons to find useful positions in tribal life. Work-study programs give adolescents with FAS/E the chance to learn through repetition what employers expect, to develop good work habits, and to manage themselves better. Usually vocational programs offer supervision and guidance that serve individuals with FAS/E well. Sometimes, however, people are given meaningless, low-skill jobs that can generate dissatisfaction and problems.

The community looks out for Pat in other ways as well. He has difficulty understanding some interpersonal and social codes, and he often speaks and behaves in ways that seem inappropriate or embarrassingly direct. Once, after seeing a picture of an embracing couple in sexual education materials, he used an obscene word to describe their activity—not because he wanted to shock anybody, but because he does not have the kind of internal monitor most people use before expressing their thoughts. Community members know his history and simply note that this behavior is typical for him: that is the way Pat is. No one criticizes, chastises, or shames him about his social mistakes. Rather, people often prompt or cue Pat to orient him more appropriately to the situation. "Hey, Pat, remember what we talked about?" someone might say, reminding him of a conversation about the proper way to speak or act in public. Through interaction and example, they gently offer guidance.

Teaching and reinforcing appropriate sexual behavior is an arduous task. In mainstream society, parents who deny the sexual stirrings of a child with FAS/E often stress celibacy rather than consider allowing for more intimate behavior. Accepting the normality of sexual drives in children with FAS/E is important so that parents can encourage suitable sexual expressions. In my experience, Native Americans tend to be less threatened or preoccupied with sexual behavior, making them easier to work with.

Native American families are concerned that their children are not sexually victimized or taken advantage of. Families with what the Sioux call *tiospaye*, or extended family, have numerous relatives available to prompt, guide, and protect the child with FAS/E. This role is regarded as a family and community responsibility rather than the problem of the affected person. People know who is vulnerable to exploitation, and they also know who will take advantage of young people with FAS/E. Tribal members who encounter someone in a potentially bad situation may say, "You shouldn't be hanging around with those people and I'm going to take you home," or they may call the child's family and say, "Your daughter's hanging out with so-and-so and you know how he is, so you'd better come and get her."

Presently Pat lives alone and works full-time, earning enough to pay his rent, buy his food, and, with careful budgeting, enjoy some spending money. He recently took a computer course at the tribal college, although he is not in a degree or educational program. Again, the community responded to his wishes as a tribal member. He has few friends, although he is interested in finding a girl friend and is distressed that he doesn't have one. His parents contact him more frequently, and he often accompanies his uncle to the sweat lodge. Like Matilda, Pat is increasingly aware and proud of his heritage, and he wants to join in more Indian activities.

In mainstream communities, young people with FAS/E often remain at home with their parents. Too often they are treated in terms of their condition, and they are pressured to prove themselves at work and at home. People with FAS/E tend to be protected from too much community exposure, are often avoided by community members, and are shielded from opportunities to develop sexual identities.

Most Native American cultures differ in that they do not label individuals with disabilities such as FAS/E. Although tribal members and the family know the diagnosis and the problem, this awareness generally does not result in a special status or an arbitrary separation from daily life. Rather, the community tries to integrate the person, use his or her strengths and contributions, and provide guidance and protection. The individual is a valued, accepted tribal member, one who contributes to tribal well-being.

↩ Epilogue ↪

Rodger Hornby died an untimely death, leaving the legacy of his students, his writing (two books, one on alcohol and one on human services, and numerous articles or book chapters), the many healthy individuals who had been treated by him, and a long standing commitment to prevention of fetal alcohol syndrome. At the time of his death, he was completing research related to understanding the predictors of health among the Rosebud Sioux. He will be remembered for his unique humor and long term commitment to education, prevention, and treatment in American Indian communities.

19

Relinquishing Our Christmas Child So We Could Reclaim Him

ANN MICHAEL[1]

Ann Michael is a registered nurse. She and her husband have six children, three of whom are adopted. Two of her adopted children have FAS. In addition to being a mother and partner to her husband, Ann works as a fetal alcohol educator and consultant. She presents workshops and consults with parents and professionals in an attempt to refer clients to appropriate service providers. At the same time, she offers encouragement, understanding, and hope. She leads monthly support groups for parents and is a contributing editor of the newsletter, FAStrack.

TWO WEEKS BEFORE CHRISTMAS 1979, I WAS READY FOR THE HOLIDAY. I had already baked the cookies, decorated the house, wrapped presents, and made new stockings for our three children. Then, on December 11, we received a Christmas present that would alter our lives forever. Knowing that we hoped to adopt an infant boy, a friend called to tell us about two brothers who needed a home immediately. In a moment I can only describe as "graced," I knew those boys were meant to be ours. Six hours later, they arrived. John was nearly five and his brother, Mike, was three and a half. My husband likes to tell people he went to work the father of three children and returned home the father of five.

In those exciting days, we could not know that despite our love for our new sons, we would one day relinquish John—who

---

[1] Ann Michael is a pseudonym.

had FAS, we learned much later—so he could receive help for inappropriate sexual behavior and other problems. We gave up John, but we never gave up on him. The support of friends, the dedication of professionals in our community, and faith in God sustained us as we searched for a place that could treat John while keeping him near our family. After a difficult period, we found an innovative community program that offered an array of services tailored to his needs, including medication to control his sexual urges and 24-hour supervision in an independent apartment. Gradually, John needed less full-time support and today he works, pays taxes, and most important, shares in our family's life.

John's troubles unfolded over many years, but I first realized we faced significant problems during that joyful Christmas when he and Mike came to live with us. Mike was not only bigger than John but looked older as well. Blond-haired and blue-eyed, John was thin, wiry and in constant motion, a problem later diagnosed as ADHD (attention deficit hyperactivity disorder). At first, he showed no emotion of any kind. When he finally skipped and sang his way through the kitchen six weeks after his arrival, I burst into tears. He did not speak intelligibly despite his age; the other children seemed to know what he wanted and translated for him. His sensitive gag reflex meant he could vomit at will, which he threatened to do when he didn't get his way. He almost always overate until he had a very distended abdomen. A pediatrician later learned he suffered from malnutrition, and one side of his chest was caved in. He wet the bed until he was 14.

Nevertheless, John was a spirited, fun-loving child who adored his new family. He rarely got angry, even when he was disciplined. He and I grew especially close, even though I sometimes joked, "My blessings are killing me." Every now and then he showed great insight. One day when he was 11 and the family was on vacation, I told him to sit still and read a detective book so the family could relax. When he asked me what a detective is, I explained that it is someone who solves problems. John said, "Mom could you hire a detective for me? I've got a lot of problems."

COPING WITH JOHN'S TROUBLES

John's problems isolated him from other children and became an emotional drain on everyone in the family. I became his primary companion, although I often felt overwhelmed, confused, and inadequate. My husband and I coped by consulting a case-worker and turning to chocolate—lots and lots of chocolate. We made many a midnight run for more. Keeping a journal also helped ground me, but it soon became one long prayer: Help us, Lord!

We took both boys to an early intervention program for a comprehensive evaluation, and John was then placed in a wonder-ful preschool program that included weekly home visits from his teacher. Before long I began to wonder if John's problems were not the result of early deprivation but of mental retardation, although many of his behaviors still didn't make sense. After a brief bout in school, John attended special education classes, moving to a new school every two years (a district policy) until we placed him in pri-vate school. As academic failure, lying, stealing, and other behav-ioral problems increased, specialists offered little help, and I continued to believe that somehow I was failing him. Well-meaning relatives suggested that John could do things if he wanted to, and all we needed to do was discipline him more consistently. We would get tough again, but nothing seemed to work. My husband and I suspected a deeper underlying problem.

OLD CONCERNS APPEAR IN A NEW LIGHT

As John grew, so did his problems. Incidents such as taking other people's things or doing silly pranks became more troubling in light of his advancing age. As John became an adolescent, he began making inappropriate sexual statements and behaving like a peeping Tom. When questioned about these statements, both boys said, "Daddy said it was okay." This led us to believe that John and Mike had been molested as well as abused and neglected in their birth home. Then one day a neighbor called to say John had taken down the pants of her toddler.

I was horrified, angry, and more frightened than I had ever been. Ashamed of my son and convinced I was an inadequate parent, I inflicted my feelings verbally on John. We punished John but knew we needed help in handling the situation. Today I realize that his behavior was an extension of his then-undiagnosed FAS coupled with probable early molestation in his birth home. When he was younger, I had dismissed similar behaviors as just childish or immature. Now they assumed an entirely different meaning.

After an unsuccessful attempt at therapy for John, several more incidents occurred in which he exposed himself or touched young children, generally males. One professional suggested homosexuality, but another noted that terms like pedophilia and homosexuality could apply only if John had the full range of choice and still chose males or children. This professional reminded us that John did not have sexual or social opportunities with peers because he functioned well below his chronological age. Yet his body was maturing and demanded sexual release. This professional's approach made sense to us but did not help us figure out what to do. We still had no idea that John had FAS.

MAKING THE HARDEST DECISION

Knowing that our family was so important to John made it even more painful when we considered placing him out of our home when he was 16. After I became pregnant again at the age of 43, my husband and I realized that having five teenagers and a newborn would make it nearly impossible to monitor John as much as necessary. During this time we dealt with many problems our other children were experiencing: chronic illnesses, learning disabilities, and drug and alcohol addiction. John's brother Michael was later diagnosed with FAE and borderline personality disorder. Those were dark days that only prayers, family, and friends saw us through.

Finally, after much anguish, we contacted the state department of children's services and asked to relinquish voluntarily our rights so John could find the help he needed in residential placement. We made it very clear that we were not giving up on our son, that we wanted to be an essential part of his care, and would do anything to help. I even helped search for the right facility. We became John's advocates as well as his parents.

FINDING A PLACE FOR JOHN

The new baby was nearly a year old before we could find the right place for John. We received help only because another crisis erupted. In July 1991, a police officer friend arrived at the door with bad news. John had exposed himself to four young boys he had lured to a more isolated area. Because he placed his hand on one boy's arm to urge him to follow, the police charged John with battery and disorderly conduct. He was not charged with any kind of sex crime because the courts understood he was mentally disabled and recognized that our caseworker and our family had been working hard to deal with this problem. John pleaded guilty to battery, and several days later he entered an adolescent psychiatric unit in the local hospital for diagnostic testing while a social worker searched for a placement. In about six weeks, he moved about 90 miles from home to a good residential facility for teenage male sex offenders.

After leaving him, I cried all the way home, wondering what kind of a parent does this to a child. I felt relieved to know he was safe and that we no longer had to police him 24 hours a day, and I felt guilty for feeling relieved. Soon the staff saw that John was not like their other clients. He did not understand that what he had done was wrong, and he did not know why it was wrong. He only knew he was in trouble and had to move away from the family he loved. Eventually the staff asked our caseworker to move him to a new facility, a place 500 miles away that treated developmentally disabled boys with sex-offender issues. We thought we had found the perfect place.

During those first few weeks after John left, I realized I wanted to use my pain to help others, so I volunteered at the local Association for Retarded Citizens. By chance I was placed on a committee to present FAS education in the schools and took material home to read about it. Suddenly, for the first time, everything made sense. I knew without a doubt that John had FAS. A specialist at a clinic near John's new facility examined him and officially diagnosed the disorder. Unfortunately, the staff at the facility was not interested in my new knowledge of FAS, and they seemed unwilling to consider his diagnosis.

After several runaway incidents and sexual episodes with other males, John was asked to leave, a pattern that repeated itself at several other facilities until he was finally hospitalized in an adult psychiatric unit in our town. None of the doctors and other professionals who worked there knew what to do; their experience dealing with FAS was not extensive, so their understanding of the syndrome was limited. We struggled again to find a residential facility that understood both FAS and sex offending. The only facility that seemed secure enough yet capable of handling the sexual issues and the mental retardation was more than 1,500 miles away and would cost $190,000 per year! This actually worked to our advantage because the cost was so high that it made people think that surely we could come up with something less expensive locally.

By this time, everyone seemed to understand John's need to be near his family and our desire to be an integral part of his treatment, even though we had officially relinquished him. This situation led to our participation in a new community-based program called Local Access Network System (LANS) that was appearing all over the country. John became the first client in our town. This system draws on existing services and the cooperation of many people to help a client function as well as possible within his own community. The wrap-around approach identifies and diagnoses the client's problems and then molds a plan of support around the person's needs. In some cases, this requires creating new programs that mesh with the treatment plan.

John's case was ideal for this approach. As one professional commented, "The current wrap-around program is the only way John could have been kept in the community. He seems willing to work on his problems, but there were no supports before. John

needs constant supervision—his own 'Jiminy Cricket,' if you will."
I was moved to tears when I entered the first meeting and saw
about 20 people—all professionals ready to try to help our son. I'm
sure everyone thought it would be easier than it was. Fleshing
out the system required several meetings. No single program
could house John due to the combination of his needs and the
problem of safety for other residents. The final plan worked this
way:

1. *Independent living.* John resided in his own apartment in a
rent-subsidized complex. He was eligible for this because he was
already receiving Social Security.

2. *Constant supervision.* John received round-the-clock
caregivers sponsored by the state. This supervision provided the
structure he needed and removed the opportunity to re-offend
until he demonstrated better social skills. Constant oversight also
gave him a full-time living classroom in which he was coached
in his own setting on any problems that arose. The State Department of Developmental Disabilities agreed to pay for this program
after John reached 21 even though his IQ was too high to qualify
for the subsidy. Later, John did so well that his caregivers spent
only 20 or 30 hours per week with him. Now, he needs caregivers
and supervision no more.[2]

3. *Cooperation between the caregivers and the family.* The
caregivers have done an outstanding job of learning all they could
about fetal alcohol syndrome (they actually wanted to hear what I
had to teach) and then creating a program unique to John's needs.
They soon learned it was extremely important for all of us to
work together as John can be manipulative and at first tried to
play all of us against each other. We talked with the caregivers frequently to check everything John told us, and we all worked on
particular issues simultaneously to present a united front. The
agency gave us copies of any programs they implement (such as
a point/privilege system) so we could further reinforce their

---

[2] This was a mistake. See epilogue, page 289.

program, using repetition as a strategy. The agency also provided John with a payee, an important service as he cannot handle his own money without help. We especially appreciated being relieved of this responsibility because it decreased tension for us and avoided conflicts.

As John began to improve, the agency used our family more and more as a critical part of the formula, and we were willing and happy to be there for John and to provide respite for the agency. Since John spent almost all holidays and many weekend days with us, this saved the agency from the need to staff these hours. Cooperation and respect for each other were critical.

4. *Self-support.* When the program began, Social Security paid for John's rent and food. But as he began working in a community job, he earned enough to pay these expenses on his own, and he no longer received Social Security benefits. This was a point of great pride for us. In fact, with the help of his payee, John contributed taxes instead of needing government support. He even had his own health insurance through work and no longer needed Medicaid. He also saved money extremely well with the help of his payee. He was willing to turn it over to her and let her save it for him.

5. *Employment.* Usually clients try various jobs to see what they can do. One of the staff members took a special interest in John and read everything we gave him about FAS. He understood the need to try differently, not harder, so he moved John from a job packaging materials—in which he was not doing well—to a job supervising other employees, where he thrived. Before long, John was named "Employee of the Month." More button-bursting pride for all of us. Then, he began working for a major employer in the community with the aid of a job coach. At first, the newness of everything frightened John, and he refused to stay. Staff came to the job site and calmed him down, and then he did very well. He started out doing dishes, was promoted several times, and later assisted with food preparation, cleaned rooms, refilled machines, and did other tasks he enjoyed.

Spurred by his success and by boredom after work hours, John decided he wanted a second job. He applied at a pizza parlor near his apartment and was hired. His employer did not know about his disability. I told John he needed to give his caregiver permission to talk to the employer, and finally John agreed to allow me to speak to his boss. However, he was doing so well that I decided to let it go rather than seem a dominating, overprotective mother. John did not handle free time well, and because he loves being busy and around people, the second job added even more structure to his life. Then he was fired. I called the employer, explained the situation, and apologized for not telling them earlier. John had not caused trouble; he simply could not function in as many positions as they needed, and since business was down, the employer could not afford an employee who could not do it all. I have since learned that employers are given tax breaks for hiring the disabled, so in the future there is every reason to tell an employer about John's disability. John started to look for a second job again. He enjoys the activity and companionship of the workplace.

6. *Recreation.* The program provided recreation by helping John plan activities beforehand and by using the Special Olympics. Such structured recreation programs helped him handle his free time productively and kept him from becoming bored and restless. John enjoyed basketball but continued to have great difficulty making friends. Family fulfills much of this need, but we know he needs more.

7. *A sexual treatment program.* Medication formed a critical part of the system. After consulting a sex specialist who evaluated John's degree of sexual dysfunction and risk of re-offending, we decided that, with John's consent, hormone therapy must be part of his program. Although his testosterone level was not high, the specialist decided to lower it in the hope of decreasing his risk of sexual offenses. Initially John received monthly injections of Depo-Provera, but later the injections stopped and his testosterone level did not return to its former level. His present level has no negative medical implications but may assist in his current ability

to control his sexual impulses. No sexual incidents have occurred despite his increased freedom.[3] John also took lithium to help control his impulsiveness.

Perhaps the most important part of John's sexual treatment program was individual attention from adult males of about age 25 who talked with him about normal sexuality and taught him about situations that are off limits for him, such as entering public bathrooms while children are inside. The staff learned to make everything concrete and to repeat lessons frequently. John really liked one of the young men and began asking him about how to dress "cool," as he put it, and how to talk to girls. This relaxed format seemed to work very well for John. He did attend more formal therapy briefly but was generally uncooperative with the therapist.

8. *Living skills.* The program taught John independent living skills from the beginning. He decided when he would do laundry or shop for groceries as long as he did it regularly. Supervisors made every effort to allow him to make as many choices as possible. Right after moving into his apartment, John invited his father, me, and his younger brother over for dinner. We were delighted to see how well he could cook, set the table, and act as host. Clearly he had gifts we had never discovered.

We have all learned so much from John that tentative plans call for replicating his program with others in a three-to-one client ratio that would decrease costs and allow for some greater social skills through interaction with others. We have also discovered the goodness that was in our child all along. Our whole family marvels at the way John phones his grandfather to see how he is feeling or remembers a sister's birthday. When he's not working, he joins us every Sunday for church and then comes home for breakfast. He mows our lawn and participates in other household chores. We also try to include him in some of our social events. One weekend we took him to a movie on Saturday afternoon and to church on Sunday. On Monday he called to thank us for a great weekend. Last

---

[3] This turned out not to be true, and ending the injections may have been a mistake. See epilogue, next page.

year for our birthdays, he took his father and me out to dinner and paid for it himself with money he had earned. This meant planning ahead to get extra money from his payee. He even asked the restaurant to bring us a cake—chocolate, of course.

CONCLUSION

Our family was named the local "Family of the Year." This honor came not because we are special or different. We believe we were recognized because we are committed to each other as a family, and we are committed to helping other families believe in themselves. We have come to see John less as a victim of FAS and more as a pioneer who teaches us all and touches the lives of many others with his courage and his spirit. That seems to be his mission—and our family's mission. John is our greatest source of hope.

↪ EPILOGUE[4] ↩

This is the saddest epilogue I have ever had to write. Four years after the Michael family was honored as "Family of the Year" for their unstinting generosity, John was jailed for sexual molestation. He faces a long prison sentence.

Why did this happen? John was a victim of his own success and of the philosophy of social service agencies to make its clients as independent as possible. John had been doing so well that the agencies removed the structures that had supported him. First, the 24-hour supervision was removed. Then he was moved into a new apartment and supervision was further decreased. With little if any supervision, John stopped taking the medication that had helped him keep his behavior under control. Lonely and isolated, he sought the companionship of young children.

"What did we learn?" asks his mother. "Don't remove the safety net!" Even though John had especially severe problems, the program had been working. John was employed, had stayed close to his family, and had gotten into no sexual trouble. Then the supports were kicked out, and John went down.

---

[4] Judith Kleinfeld interviewed the author for this epilogue.

20

Caring for the Caregivers: Family Support and Empowerment

GEORGIANA WILTON, RAYMOND KESSEL,

AND MOIRA CHAMBERLAIN CLARK

Georgiana Wilton, M.A., is the coordinator of the Family Empowerment Network (FEN),[1] a national network providng resources, referrals, and support to families affected by FAS/E and the professionals in their lives. Raymond Kessel, Ph.D., is a professor at the University of Wisconsin-Madison in the departments of Medical Genetics and Professional Development and Applied Studies. He is the director of FEN and related projects serving women and their families. Moira Clark is the parent of a child with FAS who has worked with FEN as a volunteer and staff person.

WHEN A CRISIS STRUCK A FAMILY WHO HAD KNOWN THEY WERE ADOPTING a child with FAS, they got this reaction from their own parents:

You did this to yourself by adopting THAT child. You knew he had problems. Don't come crying to us with your problems now!

Other people tell parents in exasperation:

If you didn't baby him so much, he wouldn't behave that way. A good old-fashioned spanking is what he needs!

---

[1] FEN thanks all the parents involved with the organization that led it in the direction of serving families. For reasons of confidentiality, individual contributors are not acknowledged by name; comments, however, are representative of the hundreds of families served by FEN. The chapter authors thank them all for welcoming them into their lives and taking the time to teach them.

Birth mothers of children with FAS/E see this reaction all too often when people discover who they are:

People ask me, "Are YOU the birth mother?" like they expect me always to be drunk! People don't seem to think someone can change.

Never has a group of individuals—that is, parents of children with FAS/E—deserved more accolades. They must face not only the ordinary challenges and rewards of raising a child, the missed school buses, the sizzled toast. They must face as well the myriad of information, much of it conflicting, regarding their children's diagnosis. They must face the problems of raising a child with a disability. They must face the misunderstanding and plain disrespect of the professionals who are being paid to serve them and of well-meaning family members as well.

The need for family support is great: Support in the form of information to combat confusion; support in the form of appropriate professional services to combat deterioration of the family; support in the form of an understanding ear to combat isolation.

From talking with hundreds of families and professionals on the Family Empowerment Network's toll-free resource line, we have gained insight into the issues families of children with FAS/E must deal with. Whether they are birth, adoptive, extended, or foster families, they face similar issues.

Validation

I just want to thank you for believing me. You were the first person I talked to that understood what I was trying to say and didn't think I was crazy. I've been told over and over that I am just making excuses for him. When I get tougher with him, he will come around. I was beginning to believe them and question myself as a parent.

First and foremost, families want their concerns validated. At some point in their lives, many families affected by FAS/E go through a stage where they just want to be believed. They want someone, anyone, to believe that their child is somehow different from other children, that FAS is a real disability. Parents have told us that if their children at least looked a little different, it would be easier to explain their behaviors.

Parents also want to be believed that they are not bad parents, but rather that traditional child-rearing strategies that they have used successfully with other children are not having the same results with this child.

GUILT

I feel so guilty most of the time because of the way I treated my son. If I only had known about FAS and the right intervention strategies I wouldn't have been so hard on him. I hope my actions then didn't contribute to his problems now.

Guilt turns out to be a common bond between adoptive and birth families, which many people find surprising. Birth parents feel guilt at having caused their child to have fetal alcohol syndrome. It may take many years for a woman—and other significant people in her life—to understand alcoholism not as a weakness but as a disease. Furthermore, not every child diagnosed with FAS is born to a mother who is clinically diagnosed with alcoholism. If a woman does continue to drink heavily while pregnant she truly may not have recognized the dangers associated with this drinking pattern. In this case, our public health messages and provider interventions have failed.

But adoptive families also feel guilt. They often feel that they were unnecessarily hard on their children with FAS/E because they did not understand that the child's actions were due to brain injury. They feel guilt about the punishments they dealt out. They feel guilt over making their children work harder in school. They feel guilt over showing their anger and frustration to the children. Feelings of guilt usually emerge after receiving the diagnosis of FAS for their child. Once parents realize that there is a biological reason for many of their child's actions, they understand the behavior in a new light.

Guilt is a universal emotion, because no parent, and especially the stressed parents of children with FAS/E can ever do enough.

Frustration

We've been so abused by the system, a system that doesn't understand FAS, that we can't even ask for help anymore. If we ask for help, we are offered parenting classes. The behaviors our children displayed as children are no longer acceptable as teenagers.

Frustration is another universal emotion. It comes from lack of educational services, lack of qualified medical specialists, lack of financial resources, and the unpredictable nature of FAS itself. Just when parents think they have taught a child to shop at the store or avoid disreputable strangers, their moment of triumph is snatched away. Something in the store changes and the child can no longer locate the milk. The child talks to a stranger at the bus stop and goes away with him because now the stranger is a friend.

Fear for the Future

Yes, some children do grow up to become success stories, but the reality is that many do not. The room was full of parents whose children have not.

Parents of children with FAS/E are united by this common fear: What will happen to my children in the future when I am no longer around? Even in supportive parent groups, some worries are shrouded in silence. Bill and Joan Smith from Ontario, Canada, were asked to chair a sharing session for parents of children affected by FAS over the age of 16. They decided to talk about an issue they had never seen addressed at any of the many conferences they had attended or either of the two support groups they had started. "We decided to talk about us, not our children. The problems parents of older children and adults face are totally different than those of younger children."[2]

---

[2] This is an excerpt and summary of a letter Joan and Bill Smith wrote to *FEN Pen* (Fall 1995).

The Smiths decided to pierce the veil of silence:

> Whenever parents of young FAS/E children are together these issues cannot be discussed. First we would frighten them with our stories and we would not want to take away their hope. It's all they have. It's what keeps them going. It's what kept us going. They are not ready, nor can they be expected to understand issues like children who are missing, children in jail, children who are alcoholics and addicts, or having to raise grandchildren because moms and dads are not capable.

Today children with FAS/E stand a much better chance of becoming successful adults, the Smiths point out. Many of these children had the advantage of a diagnosis in early childhood. Their parents and teachers have a better understanding of FAS/E and know many coping skills and instructional strategies. But the parents of the previous generation did not have the benefits of this knowledge:

> At this workshop we were able to share our innermost feelings with each other.... Things like the guilt we all have over the way we disciplined, punished, and often forced our children to do things in the hope that they would learn from their experience and how that must have affected them, the anguish we now live with as we watch our adult sons and daughters who are still children mentally and emotionally struggle in an adult world where they are not understood nor accepted, the hopelessness we feel when we think of what might happen to them over the next 40 or 50 years.

The families of children with FAS/E are shouldering an enormous responsibility. They need family assistance and they need respect.

FAMILY-CENTERED CARE

Families need support as family units. Children do not grow up and thrive in a vacuum so services or interventions that focus on the child or individual alone are doomed to failure. Families are a constant in a child's life whereas service systems and their personnel fluctuate. If the intervention is to be successful, the family must be at its center.

A national agenda for the support of families who have a child with special needs was articulated long ago under the exceptional leadership of the former Surgeon General C. Everett Koop. This agenda calls for services that are family centered, community based, comprehensive, coordinated and culturally competent. It is essential that we as parents and professionals working with FAS/E understand the meaning of these principles and advocate for them.

The key concepts of family-centered care are:

• *Strengths*: focusing on the strengths of the family and how to build upon those strengths

• *Respect*: an honest respect for the entire family system

• *Choice*: respecting a family's choice even if it doesn't fit into our own vision of what is right for a child

• *Information*: providing up-to-date information to the family to help with their decision making

• *Support*: providing support to a family and helping that family develop their own support system

• *Flexibility*: designing a system that remains responsive to individual family needs

• *Empowerment*: providing the resources that permit families to help themselves[3]

These concepts sound so straightforward: who could not agree with them? The reality is that these concepts will be hollow and meaningless and will not improve services and programs unless we make demands of ourselves: We must understand these principles and talk about them so we know how they should be applied. As an example, Moira Clark, a birth mother of a child with FAS, has organized a network of support, despite the limited resources of a small community. This community network includes her pastor, shopkeepers who know her son and understand his difficulties, an

---

[3] These are adapted from B. H. Johnson, E. S. Jebson, and L. Redburn 1992.

Alcoholics Anonymous group, other parents who are raising children with FAS, and even a janitor at her son's school.

FAMILY STRATEGIES

The parents we have worked with at FEN have taught us many strategies. Some seem so basic, but even these can make such an enormous difference in people's lives:

• *Take care of yourself, too.* Parents are much better equipped to take care of their children when their needs are also being met. Do not pour all of your time and energy and dreams into one child.

• *Deal with the guilt and transform it into something positive.* Guilt is a feeling that saps one's energy and anyone living with a child with FAS/E knows that energy is a precious commodity. To turn guilt into positive energy, do some self-examination and then move on. Use the energy that the guilt was robbing from you to be creative in discovering new avenues of support for your family. Advocate for your child (see "Advocacy Tips below, and on the following pages). Keep in mind: All families affected by FAS/E face guilt, not just birth parents.

ADVOCACY TIPS*

—*Before the Meeting:*

↬ Take someone to the meeting with you. It helps to have another person to listen and take notes for you. You can tape record the meeting to review later or share with your spouse, a relative, or your child's private service provider.

↬ Go to the team meeting (or any other conference about your child) *prepared.* Take information about your child's strengths and needs and what you see at home or in other settings.

—continues

---

* Reprinted by permission from *Washington PAVE* (Parents Are Vital in Education).

Advocacy Tips, continued

—At the Meeting:

⤷ The image you project makes a difference:

- Carry written information in a file folder, notebook, or expandable file to the meeting.

- Arrive promptly. Being on time shows that you feel that is an important meeting and that you are ready to conduct business.

- Shake hands or acknowledge other people at the meeting as you are introduced to them. If no one else begins the introductions, you do it.

- Sit with other team members. This shows that you are part of the decision making. Sitting between the people with power makes the statement that you are an equal in the process.

- Speak clearly and look at the other team members while you are talking.

- Make positive statements, such as "I expect....," "I understand...," "My child needs...."

⤷ Ask questions and ask for clarification of anything you do not understand.

⤷ Remain as friendly as possible. Separate the people from the problems.Do not allow yourself (or others) to deal in personalities.

⤷ Focus on the issue at hand. Do not be sidetracked by other issues such as past experiences, the district's lack of funds, or what all the other children are doing.

⤷ Make your proposal and expect to get what you child needs. Be flexible enough to accept minor revisions, but be firm about the major issues.

⤷ Feel confident enough to end the meeting if it seems that no more progress can be made. Tell the other team members that you would like to continue working with them and set up another appointment for a fresh start.

⤷ Sometimes it is necessary for team members to begin leaving the meeting before decisions have been made. If this happens, stop the meeting and reschedule a time when all team members can attend and finish the negotiations.

—continues

ADVOCACY TIPS, continued

—*After the Meeting:*

- Follow up with a letter. If you are satisfied, state what the agreements were. If you are not satisfied, explain your position, your understanding of their position, the next course of action, and your timelines.

- Remember that you are advocating for your child. If you do not do it, no one else will.

- *Develop trust.* Creating trust between yourself and other families and the professionals you work with can produce many benefits—more sensitive help for your child, a relaxation of arbitrary rules, the satisfaction of open and honest talk with others.

- *Make contacts everywhere.* Although time and energy are always in short supply, most parents find such contacts a great investment. Contacts quickly turn into a personal support network.

- *Structure.* For many families, structure is the key element. Living in the same place may help. Shopping at the same malls where you know the hiding places helps. Eating at the same restaurants where you are familiar with the menu helps. Most children affected by FAS/E are most comfortable when in familiar surroundings. And most parents are most comfortable when their children are comfortable!

CONCLUSION

Funding for family support programs in this country is inconsistent at best. Nonetheless, many parents of children with FAS/E have created parent support networks that provide them with information, with services based on the key concepts of family-centered care, and with support. These organizational achievements are one more tribute to the dedication and generosity of parents of alcohol-affected children.

21

Diagnosis and Thereafter: What We Know Now and Where We are Going

BARBARA A. MORSE

Barbara A. Morse, Ph.D., is an FAS specialist and consultant. She directed the Fetal Alcohol Education Program at Boston University School of Medicine, where she is also assistant research professor of psychiatry. Dr. Morse was past president of the Fetal Alcohol Study Group of the Research Society on Alcoholism. She has published extensively on FAS/E .

"I'VE CALLED AT LEAST 30 PLACES AND YOU'RE THE FIRST PERSON I've found who knows what I'm talking about!"

Many of my telephone calls from parents who have children with FAS/E begin this way. It is both puzzling and frustrating to families and professionals who work with families why the information on FAS/E is so hard to find. Families have often acquired considerable knowledge in the field, yet they find themselves forced to explain their child's difficulties over and over, redistributing materials on FAS/E at each grade level, trying to get professionals to see beyond an IQ score, or trying in vain to explain to a judge why prison is not the right place for their child. Even those of us in the field who regularly speak to professional groups find that the primary need in training seminars is for basic diagnostic and descriptive information, and secondarily for the latest in research findings.

The purpose of this chapter is to present what is known about FAS/E, to describe some of the more exciting work going on, and to discuss how families can contribute to increased understanding and improved intervention. In the end, I hope to leave families with a sense of competence about what they know and also to provide a scientific base of information from which they can advocate for their children.

FAS/E Characteristics and Their Development

The study of alcohol's effects on the developing fetus in utero is in its youth. The first contemporary reference to what we now call fetal alcohol syndrome (FAS) is from the late 1960s.[1] The term FAS was not used until two seminal papers from the University of Washington were published in 1973.[2] Physicians and researchers had noticed that infants born to alcoholic mothers failed to grow properly and shared a common pattern of birth defects. Following descriptions of many similar cases in medical journals, a set of criteria for diagnosis was established and standardized.[3]

A child could be considered to have FAS when he or she had signs (problems or unusual development) in each of the following three areas:

• Pre- or postnatal growth retardation: height, weight, or head circumference in the lowest tenth percentile of all children born in the United States.

• Central nervous system abnormalities: examples are neurologic abnormalities (changes in the size or formation of various brain structures), reduced learning ability, developmental delays (slower to acquire basic skills such as walking, talking, etc.) and microcephaly (head size in the lowest three percent of all children).

• Facial dysmorphology (a face that looks unusual because of the way it has developed): examples are a flattened midface (eyebrows to upper lip), broadened nasal bridge, small eye openings,

---

[1] P. Lemoine et al. 1968: 476–482.
[2] K. L. Jones and D. W. Smith 1973: 999–1001; K. L. Jones et al.1973a: 1267–1271.
[3] Clarren and Smith 1978; H. L. Rosett 1980: 119–122; R. J. Sokol and S. K. Clarren 1989: 597–598.

absent or flattened philtrum (the ridges which run from the base of the nose to the upper lip), and thin, straight upper lip. There are a number of additional features which are commonly seen, but this cluster of the midsection of the face is considered most characteristic of FAS.[4]

As the problems seen in FAS at birth were believed to be unique, knowing the mother's drinking history was not originally thought to be necessary for diagnosis. Dysmorphologists (a pediatric subspecialty which studies birth defects) believed that any time they saw a child with the cluster of features described above, it was FAS. We now know that several other conditions look very similar to FAS. These are discussed below.

To be diagnosed with FAS, a child must show signs in each of the areas described above. However, as the field grew and researchers and doctors began to share what they were learning about alcohol's effects on the fetus in utero, it became clear that some children had effects from maternal alcohol consumption, although they did not show all three diagnostic signs. The term "fetal alcohol effects" or FAE was used to describe these children. It has been estimated that there are probably three to four times as many individuals with FAE as FAS.[5]

The early literature had many case reports of children with FAS.[6] It became clear that alcohol could result in damage to a variety of developing systems, but the most serious impairment was to the brain. Reports often described children with mental retardation, usually severe, and multiple physical birth defects, and painted a very gloomy picture. The literature also focused

---

[4] These diagnostic characteristics and terms are in flux. A report issued by the National Academy of Sciences, Institute of Medicine, has suggested changes in the diagnostic terms to further clarify differences seen in individuals with prenatal alcohol exposure. These changes include dividing the diagnosis of FAS into "with" and "without" knowledge of how much the mother may have drunk, and adding the term "alcohol-related neurodevelopmental disorder (ARND)" to describe the behavioral problems commonly associated with prenatal alcohol exposure. For a fuller description of these diagnostic suggestions, see Stratton, Howe, and Battaglia 1996.
[5] H. L. Rosett and L. Weiner 1984.
[6] R. H. Palmer et al. 1974; J. J. Mulvihill et al. 1976; M. S. Tenbrink and S. Y. Buchin 1975.

predominantly on infants and young children with few or no descriptions of children over the age of 12. Research was begun to see if similar problems could be produced in animals. Animal research demonstrated conclusively that the problems seen in children indeed came from alcohol, and animal research continues to investigate how the damage is caused and how people with FAS/E might be helped. Although a small field, research on fetal alcohol syndrome is extremely active, involving several hundred scientists and resulting in a constant supply of new research.

As a result, increased understanding has broadened our knowledge of FAS. We now know that only some individuals are severely mentally retarded. Others have IQs in the average (100) to above average range; most have IQ scores in the low average to borderline range (80–95). The facial characteristics and physical problems, such as cardiac malformations and kidney abnormalities, may be very obvious or subtle. Diagnosis at birth is possible, and the sooner a diagnosis, the earlier intervention can begin. But it is often easier to diagnose FAS between the ages of 18 months and 8 years, when developmental and neurobehavioral problems are obvious. As individuals approach adolescence, the physical appearance may change. Both weight and height may increase, and distinctive facial characteristics of FAS become more subtle. It has also become clear that the damage which results in FAS is permanent, although intervention may improve a person's ability to lead a productive, successful life.

We have learned from observation that FAE is much more difficult to diagnose than FAS. Individuals with FAE seldom have facial characteristics like those with FAS, and are usually of normal height and weight. Their most serious problems are learning and behavioral. Yet because such problems can also arise from other causes, physicians may be reluctant to give a diagnosis of FAE. FAE is, by definition, less severe than FAS in its primary disabilities. The secondary disabilities like school problems may be equally or more severe, probably because it is much harder to access services if you have FAE and expectations may be higher.

While individuals with FAS/E can be similar to one another in terms of appearance and behavior, there can be wide variation in the specific disorders they have. Some children seem hyperactive, others do not. Some have difficulty with auditory learning, others with visual learning. Some grow up and appear to lead relatively successful lives using community structures and supports, and others are never able to do that. Although we are not yet able to predict who will be severely affected and who will not, we do know why some variation occurs. This includes:

• *Dose and pattern of alcohol use by the mother*: The effects of prenatal alcohol exposure are directly linked to the amount of alcohol a woman consumed during pregnancy and the pattern in which she consumed it. FAS is the result of excessive or heavy drinking, which is defined as a pattern of consuming five or more drinks per occasion, on a routine basis. However, heavy drinkers consume vastly different amounts and drink differently from one another. Some women drink every day; others drink only on the weekends, but consume large amounts (five or more drinks) per occasion. This is referred to as binge drinking. Every woman who drinks heavily is at risk for having a child with FAS; however, not every child born to a heavily drinking woman will have FAS/E. The newest animal and clinical research has shown that binge drinking is the pattern most likely to result in the birth of a child with FAS.[7] This is because binge drinking results in a very high level of alcohol in the blood (blood alcohol concentration or BAC). High levels take proportionally longer to be eliminated from the mother. The fetus must rely on the mother to eliminate alcohol from its system. Therefore, binges result in the fetus being exposed to high amounts of alcohol for a long period.

• *Metabolism*: The longer alcohol remains in the mother, the greater potential it has to change the development of the fetus. All of us vary in our ability to metabolize (eliminate) alcohol from our bodies; some people normally metabolize more quickly than others. As the liver is the most important organ for the metabolism of

---

[7] Sampson et al. 1989; West 1987; J. L. Jacobson et al. 1993.

alcohol, people with liver disease or other kinds of liver problems may take longer to eliminate alcohol than others. Women who have been drinking heavily for a long time (more than five years) may have developed liver problems that slow down their ability to metabolize alcohol. These differences in metabolism may explain why a group of children with FAS/E have different problems, even when their mothers were all heavy drinkers.

• *Genetics*: The differences seen in individuals with FAS and FAE may also be due to genetic differences in the mothers, possibly related to race or ethnicity. Recent studies have suggested that some ethnic and racial groups, those of African and Native American descent, may be at higher risk for FAS than others.[8] Differences are seen between fraternal twins; one twin is often more affected than the other,[9] suggesting that the different genetic pattern in each twin may have responded differently to the alcohol. A number of studies are underway to understand these differences more precisely.

• *Parity* (number of pregnancies): The risk for having a child with FAS or FAE goes up with each pregnancy.[10] Thus, it is more common for later born children to be affected than it is for first born. The reasons for this are not entirely understood but are probably influenced by the number of years of drinking by the mother,[11] an increase in amount consumed, decreased liver function, and the age of the mother.

• *Time during the pregnancy when drinking occurs*: There is no safe time during pregnancy to drink heavily, even though different effects may be seen based on when a mother was drinking. Heavy drinking in the first three months may result in structural abnormalities and changes to central nervous system organization, while during the last three months it may have the greatest impact on brain development and organization.

We also know that the mother's health and well-being during the pregnancy can interact with alcohol. Women who have untreated

---

[8] Sokol et al. 1987.
[9] Chasnoff 1985.
[10] Rosett and Weiner 1984.
[11] Abel and Sokol 1983.

medical problems, poor diets, extreme stress in their lives, such as homelessness or domestic abuse, or use drugs such as cocaine or heroin may have a developing fetus at increased risk from the alcohol they drink.

Recognizing all the different factors that contribute to the origin of FAS/E makes it easier to understand why there can be such variation in effects among children. For example, in a group of ten children with FAS, it is unlikely that any two share the same combination of dose, pattern of use, genetic history, or parity. These factors may help explain why not all children born to excessive drinkers have FAS. The best estimates are that 10 percent of children born to heavily drinking mothers will have FAS, another 30 to 40 percent will have FAE, and half are unaffected.[12]

In addition to all three diagnostic signs, individuals with FAS are more likely than those with FAE to have a variety of related problems. These problems occur more often in FAS but are not necessarily unique to FAS. Disorders commonly seen include physical ones such as myopia (nearsightedness), strabismus (when muscles in the eye do not work together resulting in crossed or double vision), cleft palate (failure of the roof of the mouth to close during fetal development), otitis media (middle ear infections), heart defects, urinary and kidney abnormalities, increased infections (especially respiratory infections), skeletal abnormalities, sleeping and eating disorders, and neurobehavioral disorders such as hyperactivity, attention, memory and focus problems, language processing disorders, speech and language delays, and learning disabilities (including mental retardation and difficulty with cause and effect, judgment, abstract learning or complex thought).

In some cases it is easy to understand why the person with FAS might be at higher than average risk for some problems. For example, anyone with dysmorphic facial structure is at higher risk for related physical problems occurring on the inside of the head, such as cleft palate or hearing loss. Other problems, such as hyperactivity, may result from many different causes. Any time the

---

[12] Rosett and Weiner 1984.

brain has been altered (whether from alcohol or something else like genetic differences, illness, or accidents), a person may be at risk for conditions like hyperactivity. Still other conditions, such as urinary tract abnormalities, may mean that those tissues are particularly susceptible to damage from alcohol during fetal development.

One of alcohol's effects on a fetus is to slow development. In some cases development may be slowed enough that an organ cannot develop properly. In other cases, development may slow, but may catch up when the alcohol is no longer present. Of all the organ systems, the brain is the most susceptible to damage from prenatal alcohol exposure, at least in part because its development takes place across the entire nine months of pregnancy.

Is FAS/E Unlike Other Developmental Disabilities?

Does this long list of problems suggest that FAS and FAE are unique, that they are unlike any other developmental disability? Not necessarily. While almost every parent has heard a professional say at one time or another, "Your child isn't quite like anyone else I've treated," such statements may reflect an unfamiliarity with FAS/E as much as it does a unique condition. Most disabilities have many associated problems. The long list of associated problems may simply be a result of the fact that FAS remains a poorly understood disorder, and individuals who have this condition receive inadequate early intervention and treatment. It is important to remember that most people with FAS or FAE don't look or sound as if they should have problems, and this contributes to the confusion over their disability.

It may be that eventually we will learn that FAS and FAE are totally different than other central nervous system disorders. However, it is more likely that FAS/E share common characteristics with other disabilities. For example, some scientists have suggested that some of the language disorders are like those seen in mild autism. This is possible because the brain can probably be affected in a limited number of ways, and many different causes can result in similar disabilities. Researchers are just beginning to look at similarities and differences between FAS/E and other disabilities. There is no question that this research will help us design effective interventions.

As we learn more about the individuals who have FAS and FAE, we are also learning more about the problems they encounter as they grow up. Recent data from the University of Washington has shown a high incidence of mental illness, substance abuse disorders, and involvement with the criminal justice system among adolescents and adults.[13] Some of these problems, such as mental illness, may be directly related to the nature of FAS and the specific effects it has had on the brain. Others, like some instances of involvement in crime, may be the result of the learning problems associated with FAS, such as difficulty in understanding cause and effect—how consequences are related to behavior. Some of the teenagers who end up in court lacked early and appropriate intervention, and still others may have lived in difficult environments. Further study over many years will be necessary to determine the effect of all of the influences on the lives of those with FAS and FAE, and to determine what effects early diagnosis, early intervention, and appropriate schooling can have on avoiding or ameliorating such problems.

DIAGNOSIS: WHY IS IT SO IMPORTANT BUT SO HARD TO GET?

Diagnosis is the first step in seeking to understand and treating any medical disorder. Typically, families seek health care advice when they are concerned about a child's development. They present a doctor with information about the child and expect him or her to have the expertise to understand and diagnose the problem. If the first physician doesn't have the answers, they expect to be referred to one who has more expertise. People use a diagnosis to help define the problem. It helps sort out related and unrelated conditions so that appropriate treatment can take place. In many cases, diagnosis ends the searching to recognize a disorder, helps create a

---

[13] Streissguth et al. 1996.

310 / Barbara A. Morse

sense of how various symptoms are related, and often suggests how medical and educational professionals can intervene.

The diagnosis of FAS often proceeds differently. The first question asked is who should, or who is expert enough, to diagnose. This condition was first identified and then named by dysmorphologists, a subspecialty of pediatrics. Dysmorphologists have remained active in the field, and many consider those who see patients as the experts in diagnosis. However, at least two other specialties often have expertise in the diagnosis of FAS as well. They are pediatric neurologists who specialize in disorders of the brain and geneticists, who understand genetic disorders and see individuals who may have a range of problems at birth. Some developmental pediatricians who have taken special training in changes in normal development of children are also expert in the diagnosis of FAS. Several questions can help determine how well a doctor understands FAS. These include:

1. Have you seen patients with FAS or FAE?

2. How many such patients have you diagnosed?

3. Do you provide followup care for diagnosed patients (helping with school plans, seeing a person on a regular basis, consulting with other professionals who also provide care)?

And even if you get a "no" to the first question, but the professional seems interested, you can always ask:

4. Are you interested and/or willing to learn about FAS/E?

Even with physicians who treat FAS/E, obtaining a diagnosis of FAS/E is not easy. Some doctors remain unsure about FAS, and many doctors question whether FAE exists at all. Even though animal research has shown that alcohol causes real and severe birth defects, it isn't always easy to know for certain that alcohol has caused the problems seen in these particular children or adults. FAS remains a clinical diagnosis, made on the judgment of an individual doctor; no single test or battery of tests can be done that confirms or denies the diagnosis. We have also come to recognize that the symptoms of FAS are very similar to several other conditions. For example, maternal PKU (resulting from a metabolic disorder in the mother) and fetal hydantoin syndrome (resulting from use of the antiseizure medication dilantin) can result in birth problems which are very similar to FAS. These conditions should always be ruled out when a diagnosis is in question.

Typically for FAS, a child receives a number of diagnoses—attention deficit hyperactivity disorder, oppositional defiant disorder—none of which fully describe the difficulties he or she is having. Often it is the parent who first suggests that FAS might be the correct diagnosis after having read descriptions in the media or having talked with other parents. Too often, families are told that a child cannot be diagnosed unless doctors have proof that the biological mother drank excessively during the pregnancy, and if so, how much and when. Even foster and adoptive parents, the largest group raising children with diagnosed FAS, seldom have such precise information. One parent who recently called our program had been told that the only way her adopted son could be diagnosed with FAS was if his biological mother had either delivered him while intoxicated or had died from her alcoholism!

In the north and southwestern United States over-diagnosis has been reported. For example, among Native peoples in both the United States and Canada, developmental problems are often assumed to be alcohol-related. Researchers in FAS seeing members of those groups describe the need to drop the diagnosis of FAS and to provide an accurate one.[14] In still other settings, families describe situations in which children who have been correctly diagnosed at several points in their lives suddenly have the diagnosis removed by a doctor who disagrees with the previous assessments or who is unaware of the time-dependent changes in FAS. Other reasons for a child's problems are often suggested, for example, illicit drug exposure, living in a dysfunctional home, a history of abuse, etc. While co-existing conditions such as poor parenting or multiple foster placements may complicate FAS, they do not cause it.[15]

[14] Nanson, personal communication, 1993; Aase, personal communication, 1993.
[15] Stratton et al. 1996.

The diagnosis of FAE presents even greater obstacles. The most common feature shared between FAS and FAE is neuro-behavioral disorders. Facial dysmorphology and growth retardation are rarely seen in FAE. The neurobehavioral disorders are often similar to problems seen in children with other histories, such as multiple foster placements, abuse, exposures to illicit drugs, or anything that can affect brain growth and development. Many physicians are uncomfortable diagnosing FAE in a child who has a complicated history, even if it includes prenatal alcohol exposure. They are concerned that it is too difficult to confirm that the child's problems are directly related to prenatal alcohol exposure and not to something else. Parents report that doctors tell them FAE is only a label that may cause more hurt for a child than help. Parents need to know that both FAS and FAE are medical diagnoses that describe neurological impairment resulting from prenatal alcohol exposure. In some states a diagnosis is necessary in order for a child to be eligible for services. And most frustrating to families is to be told that disciplining their child differently or better is all that is needed.

All of these problems contribute to delays in diagnosis, referral for intervention, getting an accurate count on the number of affected individuals, and the development of effective intervention strategies. The good news is that with increased understanding and recognition of FAS and FAE, the rate of accurate diagnosis is on the rise. Statistics from the Centers for Disease Control (1995) report that between 1979 (when few people outside of the research community knew about FAS) to 1993 there was a ten-fold increase in the number of diagnosed cases listed in birth defects registries around the United States. Several approaches are underway to improve diagnosis even more.

One approach is to clarify the guidelines that doctors use to diagnose FAS/E so that they are used uniformly. Sterling Clarren and Susan Astley from the University of Washington have developed a diagnostic grid that ranks growth, facial changes, brain functioning, and the mother's alcohol history from one to four (1= no problem, 4= the most severe problem). Very specific definitions are provided for each rating. The total score then reveals whether that person has FAS, FAE, or neither problem.[16]

Another approach to improve diagnosis is to find an objective technique that can identify FAS as unique from other disorders. Two promising approaches are currently being investigated. One uses a computer analysis of photographs to distinguish FAS from other disabilities.[17] Photographs of children suspected of having FAS are compared against a template for particular facial features. When the photo matches the computer template, it is highly likely that the child has the facial features of FAS. While this work is very preliminary and has been used on only a small sample of individuals, such an approach offers hope for a less subjective diagnostic measure which clinicians might feel more comfortable using.

An objective measure of FAS in children for the ages 9 to 14 is also being worked on. FAS specialists have been studying the corpus callosum, the band of fibers that connects and facilitates communication between the two halves of the brain, using very specialized magnetic resonance imaging (MRIs).[18] They have found that among children and adolescents very severely affected with FAS, the corpus collosum is significantly smaller (or in some cases missing altogether) than in a comparison group (see illustrations on page 314). Again, this study has been conducted only on a very small number of people and must therefore be interpreted cautiously. However, the findings may point to a test that might demonstrate specific brain abnormalities resulting from alcohol exposure.

An additional approach towards improving diagnosis is to provide better training to primary care physicians so that they are able to understand and recognize FAS more consistently and feel more comfortable addressing it with families. In a study of pediatric diagnosing practices, 10 percent of pediatricians who responded (N=234) to a survey stated that they were skeptical that FAS was a specific syndrome, and 57 percent said they felt unprepared to deal with the issues associated with alcohol-related birth defects.[19]

[16] Astley and Clarren 1997.
[17] Ibid.
[18] Mattson et al. 1994.
[19] Morse et al. 1992; Nanson et al. 1995.

THE PHYSICAL REALITY OF FAS

BRAIN SCAN OF A
NORMAL 13-YEAR-
OLD FEMALE. AN
ARROW POINTS TO
THE CORPUS
CALLOSUM.

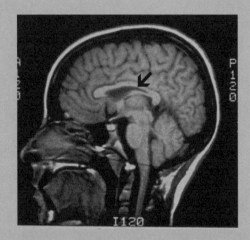

BRAIN SCAN OF A
14-YEAR-OLD
MALE WITH FAS
WHOSE CORPUS
CALLOSUM IS
ABSENT.

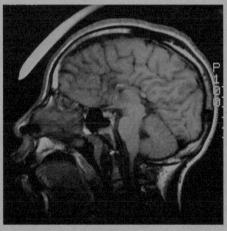

The brain scan of the child with FAS, above, reveals a serious abnormality: the corpus callosum—the band of fibers that connects and facilitates communication between the two halves of the brain—is absent. Parents may wish to obtain a copy of the article where these images are published* and use the images when discussing FAS/E with teachers and others to help them understand that FAS/E has physical reality.

---

* See S. N. Mattson, T. L. Jernigan, and E. P. Ripley, "MRI and prenatal alcohol exposure," *Alcohol Health & Research World* 18; 1 (1994): 49–52.

More than half of the respondents (56 percent) said that they had suspected FAS at one time or another but did not diagnose it. Additional training would be helpful, said 74 percent of the respondents, and 61 percent said that a listing of FAS/E specialists would be helpful.[20] A number of training curricula are available for health care professionals, and board certification for pediatricians now includes several questions about FAS. All of these approaches should help improve doctors' responses to alcohol-related birth defects.

There are other reasons why making the diagnosis can be a challenge. When the early studies first described FAS, their examples were infants and young children. As those children have grown and as older individuals have been identified, it has become clear that FAS looks different both physically and developmentally over time. For example, growth failure was once thought to be permanent; that is, individuals with FAS would always stay at the low end of the growth curve. However, observations and reports from clinics and families now suggest that both height and weight can improve during puberty. While individuals with FAS may always be smaller than the average adult, the improved growth may be great enough to raise questions about the original diagnosis.

Facial features also shift in adolescence and adulthood. The face becomes more proportional, and the diagnostic features become significantly more subtle. Both the changes in growth and in the face mean that the best time for diagnosis is after age one but before the changes of adolescence have begun. We often suggest that families seeking a first diagnosis in an adolescent bring photographs of the person as an infant or child to assist in assessing facial dysmorphology. In light of these new understandings, the research community has begun to discuss the need to describe more clearly how FAS looks at different ages—infancy, childhood, adolescence, adulthood—and to study groups of people with FAS to document how growth accelerates. Certainly clearer, more specific

---

[20] The Fetal Alcohol Education Program at the Boston University School of Medicine compiled a national resource guide to diagnostic and treatment services under a grant from the Health and Human Services Maternal and Child Health Bureau. This document is available from HHS-MCHB.

descriptions of the changes that take place would help the health care community decide when FAS might be considered the appropriate diagnosis.

While obvious physical abnormalities decrease at adolescence, many families report dramatically increased behavioral problems in the teen years, and many of these have been confirmed in recent research.[21] These problems include:

• difficulty with peer friendships or failure to form them, resulting in low self-esteem

• difficulty with the most basic daily living skills, such as hygiene, keeping appointments, dressing appropriately

• failure to discriminate between peer groups, making wrong choices in selection of peers, engaging in inappropriate activities with peers, the appearance of being taken advantage of by more competent peers

• continuing learning problems or school failure; in older people, difficulty in holding a job

• lying or stealing, with no apparent understanding of the consequences of behavior or the meaning of punishment

• inappropriate sexual behavior, ranging from peeping-Tom types of behavior to more serious offenses of molestation or rape

• involvement with the law, usually associated with one of the behaviors above

• mental health problems

• alcohol and drug use problems

Many of these problems are undoubtedly related to the learning and cognitive delays of individuals with FAS and FAE, as well as to ineffective intervention. All of these problems raise enormous concerns for families who have tried for years to get professionals to listen to them. However, there is also hope to be

---

[21] Steinhausen 1995; Streissguth 1996.

found in this research. Ann Streissguth's 1996 report not only identified significant problems in the group of adolescents and adults they studied, she also reported on what helped to protect a person from such negative outcomes. These factors include:

• living in a stable home for most of one's life, e.g., not moving from foster home to foster home

• being diagnosed before age six

• experiencing a home where a child's problems are recognized and help is sought for those problems

• having services for the developmentally disabled

• having the diagnosis of FAS rather than FAE. FAS is a more recognized diagnosis than FAE, is more likely to be diagnosed earlier allowing for better intervention, and is more likely to qualify a person for services. All these factors can contribute to a better outcome.

This study helps us recognize which factors are important to address in terms of improving the long-term outcome for individuals with FAS. Many of them could be addressed now with fairly minimal shifts in the way care is provided. For example, better diagnosis through training, increased awareness, and improved medical school curricula could benefit all affected children. Training and support for foster and adoptive parents could reduce the instability of some homes and the number of placements a child experiences before finding a permanent home. Advocacy by and for families could open access to services for the developmentally disabled.

It is also important to look at this information about the problems that FAS may cause from the opposite perspective—that is, not only what percentage of individuals are having severe problems, but what percentage are not, and what we can learn from them. These same data tell us that 70 percent have no substance abuse problems, 50 percent have not displayed inappropriate sexual behavior or been confined for mental health, legal or other reasons,

40 percent have had uninterrupted school experiences and have never been in trouble with the law. By studying those who have not experienced problems in these areas, we may be able to learn what can be done to prevent them in others.

It is also important to remember that the teenagers who were studied at the University of Washington may not be representative of most teens with FAS/E. As there are no studies of FAS/E in the general population, we have no way of knowing if this group includes individuals showing the broad range of effects, or if they represent only the severe end. Many in this study were diagnosed in the early years when little was known about FAS. If they received any intervention at all, those interventions could not have addressed all the problems that we understand today. *It is likely that children diagnosed today will have a much better chance for success than these early examples suggest.*

WE HAVE THE DIAGNOSIS; WHAT DO WE DO NOW?

While getting a diagnosis is an important first step, families and others realize that having a diagnosis of FAS or FAE does not solve the problems these disorders can present. Even the most sensitive parent, teacher, friend or family member can have a difficult time understanding that an attractive, well-spoken person with FAS or FAE may not be as competent as they appear. As I wrote in *Fantastic Antone Succeeds*,[22] the most important shift to make in understanding these problems is to move from seeing a person with FAS as someone who won't do something to seeing them as a person who can't do certain things. Once the shift has been made, there remains the difficult task of convincing others. So how can you help your child cope and convince others that your 16-year-old still has real and significant problems?

1. *Discuss the diagnosis with your child in terms which he or she can understand.* Many people with FAS/E find it an enormous relief finally to understand that there is a reason why life is so much more difficult for them than for others.

---

[22] See Barbara Morse, "Information Processing," in Kleinfeld and Wescott 1993, 23.

2. *All parents (birth, foster, adoptive, guardian) need to have a good understanding of the nature of addiction and how difficult it is to stop drinking when you are addicted.* It is also helpful to explain the role of addiction in FAS and FAE. Remember that no mother drinks with the intent of having a child with birth problems. When a child is a victim of FAS or FAE, his or her biological mother was a victim of alcohol addiction.

3. *Explain the diagnosis and stress the word "diagnosis" as opposed to "label" to emphasize the medical nature of the problem.* Provide brief amounts of reading material to every professional with whom your child interacts. Highlight or underline the sections that apply most to your child. When possible, provide concrete examples of behaviors which your child has exhibited as they relate to the material you provide, and any learning or behavioral tips you have found helpful ("She learns best when her work space is quiet and when you check in with her every half-hour or so"). When you know your child's birth history, share that as well.

4. *As early in the child's school career as possible, seek specialized testing focusing on learning disabilities (especially auditory and visual learning abilities, organizational and sequencing skills, memory and ability to focus), expressive and receptive language, sensory integration and activities of daily living.* These tests can help locate the reason for the specific problems a person is having and may suggest treatment or services that could help. Tests can also help track progress and tell you whether an intervention is having the desired effect. When presented with an overall test score, ask to see all the subtest scores and discuss the wide range (or scatter) between various skills.

5. *Take an advocate, a person trained to speak up for someone with disabilities, with you when you go to discuss educational, medical or social service plans.* An advocate will often understand the ins and outs of a system better than you do. They may know which questions to ask and what information is important for you to have. An advocate may also listen differently than you do, hearing or interpreting information in a different way. Bringing another person

along also gives you someone with whom you can discuss any suggested treatment or plans. Agencies such as The Arc can often help you find advocates.[23]

6. *Contact agencies in your area that deal with developmental disabilities.* Inquire about school-to-work transition programs, particularly those that involve concrete or repetitive activities, where people work with their hands rather than with ideas. Use some of the chapters in this book as examples of the types of programs that can be helpful.[24]

7. *Provide as much structure in your child's life as possible and is feasible, given that you have an adolescent!* Choose activities that have built-in structure such as religious youth groups, scouting, or sports. If you see a particular talent in your child such as art, pottery, cooking, etc., find classes or activities where your child can develop these skills. Inquire if elementary schools, day care centers, nursing homes, or hospitals could use volunteers. Describe your child's strengths and difficulties to whoever is in charge, and share the techniques that you have found to be most helpful to keep your child focused and successful.

8. *Begin sex education early and repeat the information often.* Recognize that adolescents have normal sexual urges even if their cognitive levels and hormonal levels don't match. Focus on appropriate outlets for sexual feelings. Use a variety of teaching methods to explain sexual feelings and concepts. If this topic is difficult for you to approach, find outside expertise—clergy, school counselor, a developmental disabilities specialist—who will help you.[25]

9. *If your child shows especially low levels of self-esteem, seems depressed, or shows any other signs that concern you, find a counselor with whom he or she can meet regularly.* FAS and FAE are enormously frustrating disorders, and having someone with whom to discuss that frustration can make a big difference. As in a medical consultation, ask about a counselor's knowledge and

---

[23] See Appendix 2. See also "Advocacy Tips," in Wilton, Kessel, and Clark, chapter 20.
[24] See Malbin, chapter 10.

experience about FAS/E before meeting with them. It is also help-ful to find a counselor who is willing to meet with you periodically to review progress and discuss mutual concerns.[26]

10. *Make arrangements for guardianship or care for the time when you are no longer able or willing to make decisions for your child.* Knowing these arrangements are in place can do a lot to relieve stress even long before they will be needed.

11. *Find support for yourself.* This can be through a support group with other parents who have a child with FAS/E, through involving yourself in activities related to FAS/E that help raise awareness of the need for treatment and intervention, or simply by taking time off from the topic altogether. While the problem will often dominate your life, try to make sure it does not rule it.

12. *If the opportunity presents itself, participate in research. People with FAS or FAE who are willing to tell researchers about their lives can contribute greatly to understanding and treating this disorder.* A number of research registries have been started, and families are under no obligation to participate in any study even after they have inquired about it.

13. *Be hopeful.* Research in this field is increasing rapidly. Parents are becoming more vocal about their needs, teachers are asking for information, physicians are learning, and the government is recognizing the need for better and more intervention research. I predict that in the next 5 to 15 years there will be significant advances made in diagnosis, prevention, and treatment of FAS and FAE. Keep speaking out, keep making your needs known, keep educating others and you will help lead this movement forward.

---

[25] See Miranda and Levine, chapter 13.
[26] See Baxter, chapter 11.

References

J. Aase, personal communication, 1993.

E. L. Abel and R. J. Sokol, "Maternal and fetal characteristics affecting alcohol's teratogenicity," *Neurobehavioral Toxicology and Teratology* 8 (1986): 329–334.

S. J. Astley and S. K. Clarren, *Diagnostic Guide for Fetal Alcohol Syndrome and Related Conditions* (Seattle: University of Washington Press, 1997).

"Centers for Disease Control and Prevention Update: Trends in fetal alcohol syndrome—United States, 1979–1993," *Morbidity and Mortality Weekly Report* 44 (1995): 249–251.

I. J. Chasnoff, "Fetal alcohol syndrome in twin pregnancy," *Acta Genet Med Gemellol* 34 (1985): 229–232.

S. W. Jacobson, J. L. Jacobson, R. J. Sokol, S. S. Martier, J. W. Ager, and M. G. Kaplan-Estrin, "Teratogenic effects of alcohol on infant development," *Alcoholism: Clinical and Experimental Research* 17, 1 (1993): 174–183.

K. L. Jones, D. W. Smith, C. N. Ulleland, A. P. Streissguth, "Patterns of malformation in offspring of chronic alcoholic women," *Lancet* 1 (1973a): 1267–1271.

K. L. Jones and D. W. Smith, "Recognition of the fetal alcohol syndrome in early infancy," *Lancet* 2 (1973): 999–1001.

P. Lemoine, H. Harousseau, J.-P. Borteyru, and J.-C. Menuet, "Les enfants de parents alcooliques: Anomalies observéas. À propos de 127 cas (Children of alcoholic parents: anomalies observed in 127 cases)," *Ouest Medical* 21 (1968): 476–482.

S. N. Mattson, T. L. Jernigan, and E. P. Riley, "MRI and prenatal alcohol exposure," *Alcohol Health and Research World* 18 (1994): 49–52.

B. Morse, "Information Processing: Identifying the Behavioral Disorders of Fetal Alcohol Syndrome," in Kleinfeld and Wescott, eds., *Fantastic Antone Succeeds* (Fairbanks: University of Alaska Press, 1993), 23–36.

B. A. Morse, R. K. Idelson, W. H. Sachs, L. Weiner, and L. C. Kaplan, "Pediatricians' perspectives on fetal alcohol syndrome," *Journal of Substance Abuse* 4 (1992):187–195.

J. J. Mulvihill, J. T. Klimas, D. C. Stokes, and H. M. Risemberg, "Fetal alcohol syndrome: Seven new cases," *American Journal of Obstetrical Gynecology* 125 (1976): 937–941.

J. Nanson, personal communication, 1993.

J. L. Nanson, R. Bolaria, R. E. Snyder, B. A. Morse, and L. Weiner, "Physician awareness of fetal alcohol syndrome: A survey of pediatricians and general practitioners." *Canadian Medical Association Journal* 152 (1995): 1071–1076.

R. H. Palmer, E. M. Ouellette, L. Warner, and S. R. Leichtman, "Congenital malformations in offspring of a chronic alcoholic mother," *Pediatrics* 53 (1974): 490–494.

H. L. Rosett, "A clinical perspective of the fetal alcohol syndrome," *Alcoholism: Clinical and Experimental Research* 4 (1980): 119–122.

H. L. Rosett and L. Weiner, *Alcohol and the Fetus: A clinical perspective* (New York: Oxford University Press, 1984).

H. L. Rosett, L. Weiner, and K. C. Edelin, "Treatment experience with pregnant problem drinkers," *Journal of the American Medical Association* 249 (1983): 2029–2033.

P. D. Sampson et al., "Neurobehavioral effects of prenatal alcohol: Part II," *Neurotoxicology and Teratology* (1989): 477–79.

R. J. Sokol and S. K. Clarren, "Guidelines for the use of terminology describing the impact of prenatal alcohol on the offspring," *Alcoholism: Clinical and Experimental Research* 13 (1989): 597–598.

H. C. Steinhausen, "Children of alcoholic mothers: A review," *European child and Adolescent Psychology* 4, 3 (1995): 143–152.

K. Stratton, C. Howe, and F. Battaglia, eds., *Fetal Alcohol Syndrome: Diagnosis, epidemiology, prevention and treatment* (Washington, D.C.: National Academy Press, 1996).

A. Streissguth et al., "Understanding the Occurrence of Secondary Disabilities in Clients with Fetal Alcohol Syndrome (FAS) and Fetal Alcohol Effects (FAE)," *Final Report, August 1996,* Seattle: University of Washington.

M. S. Tenbrinck and S. Y. Buchin, "Fetal alcohol syndrome: Report of a case," *Journal of the American Medical Association* 232 (1975): 1144–1147.

J. R. West, "Fetal alcohol-induced brain damage and the problem of determining temporal vulnerability: A review," *Alcohol and Drug Research* (1987): 423–41.

Conclusion:
What the Wisdom of Practice
Teaches Us About FAS/E at
Adolescence and Young Adulthood

JUDITH KLEINFELD

SO WHAT HAVE WE LEARNED?

What can we say to Sally Caldwell, the mother of Antone, who asked us, as her son careened toward adolescence: Where are the stories of adolescents who are succeeding, the stories of parents who have sustained effective parenting strategies when their children turned into teenagers, the stories of teachers who have figured out how to accommodate students with FAS/E in high school?

We have found these stories, these cases.

Parents, practitioners and people with FAS/E possess valuable knowledge, drawn from experience, what we have called the "wisdom of practice." Their knowledge is rich and concrete, practical and particular. Their knowledge has been put to the test in the tough experiments of everyday life. Researchers are learning to respect this knowledge, to draw upon parents' observations and their insights. No one cares more about the children. No one observes so closely. No one has such creative imagination.

Such wisdom of practice offers more than information about techniques. It offers also mature understanding—*wisdom*. I am awed by the strength of so many of the parents and young people with FAS/E we have featured in this book. Life has dealt them a tough hand, but they play it with zest and verve. So many turn their personal sufferings into larger purposes. They give workshops, organize support groups, staff hot lines, advocate for each other, and raise the consciousness of their communities about FAS/E. "Anyone who loves a child with FAS/E dreams of that child's life as it would have been without drug and alcohol exposure," writes a devoted sister. "The only way I can live with Eric's FAS/E is to dream of preventing it in other children by educating women about the consequences of drinking alcohol during pregnancy."

Some draw their strength of spirit from religious faith—raising children with FAS/E is a kind of ministry:

> *How do we support our children and love them and totally accept them knowing that getting arrested is part of their lives?*
> *My husband and I have a very deep faith in God. We have asked for this assignment. We feel that the children are our ministry, a kind of offering. We feel that it is a spiritual thing, part of our relationship with God. Because it's a spiritual thing, we don't have to win. We forgive ourselves for things we don't do well. We don't mind apologizing to the children for things we don't do well.*

> —Interview with *Jocie DeVries*, executive director of the FAS Family Resource Institute in Seattle, Washington

These parents have made choices, spiritual choices, philosophic choices, about the kinds of people they are going to be. Despite the fact that her son with FAS is in jail for sexual molestation, yet again, Ann Michael takes control of how she is going to live:

> *My Dad used to quote Abraham Lincoln, "You are as happy as you choose to be." The more I play act, the more I actually feel better. At the moment, I was shopping, buying pillows. So I say to people I meet, "Yes, he's in jail. Now tell me about your family."*

> —Interview with Ann Michael

I try to sum up in this concluding chapter what parents, practitioners and people with FAS/E themselves have learned about how to deal with this disability. I try to offer the wisdom of practice—what happens when young people with FAS/E hit adolescence, what success looks like, what courage looks like, what strategies and attitudes help people cope. But I offer a caution: A conclusion offers generalities, and generalities can not capture the wisdom of practice. This kind of knowledge dwells in concrete experiences, in the stories of what life is like and what problems come up and what people do and how they feel about it. Please…, read the chapters.

But I have my responsibility, too, and that is to try to put into a few words what we have learned from this project. We began by asking parents in FAS/E support groups what questions troubled them the most as their children entered adolescence. We then asked these parents, other parents, and researchers who study FAS/E to recommend people who could address these questions through hard-won experience. This is what we have found.

1. Why do the problems of FAS/E so often become much worse at adolescence?

Many parents succeed in providing the structure and routines, the visual and experiential approaches to learning, the fierce love and security, that enable children with FAS/E to thrive. But their sense of success is tempered by the anxiety that adolescence lies ahead, blocking the road like a gigantic boulder. They know from other parents that, at adolescence, so often, things fall apart.

Adolescence hits some children with FAS/E far harder than others. This is important to remember: While some children head down dangerous paths at adolescence, others continue to make steady gains. All but one of Jan Lutke's seven teenagers with FAS/E, for example, are thriving. Their youngest teenager, Katie, has severe alcohol-related problems but she is a delight, the beneficiary of all the Lutkes have learned about raising children with FAS/E. A "freckle-faced, red-headed dynamo" at 13 years old, Katie won an election to represent her class on the student council, uses a computer to cope with bad handwriting, and looks out for classmates who are left out of basketball games. Katie relies on her teaching aide, "Mrs. G." to run interference for her. When the class-room noise level reaches threatening levels, for example, Mrs. G., with exquisite tact, says *she* can't stand the noise and asks Katie to accompany her out.

Other children with FAS/E have far more difficulty at adolescence. One adoptive father describes how his son, yearning for friends, got in with a bad crowd:

> *Bill obtained funding for decent housing and soon discovered he had something that other young people wanted. He hung around the local shelter for runaway or homeless teens and offered others a place to stay.... His apartment quickly turned into a flophouse as those he invited to stay brought other friends and then held disruptive parties that created unhappy neighbors and an angry landlord. In Bill's mind, he was not participating in the disturbance.... He couldn't tell the partygoers to leave for fear of losing all the acceptance he thought he had gained. Eventually he was evicted, labeled as "trouble" or a "gang member."*

—Interview with Jim Slinn

Adolescence is so difficult for young people with FAS/E because this stage of life brings expectations for independence and achievement beyond what most can achieve. Adolescence brings with it a host of difficult tasks: establishing independence from your family; learning to rely on peers for friendship and emotional support; coping with sexual drives; developing romantic relationships; coping with the academic rigors, noise, and commotion of a comprehensive high school; figuring out who you are and what you want to do with your life; getting a job and starting to support yourself. These tasks are difficult for any young person, and they are beyond the capacities of many young people with FAS/E. Many know it. They watch other teenagers moving on, leaving home for college, finding romance, getting married. Many adolescents with FAS/E know full well what they are missing and this terrible knowledge brings on depression and rage.

Another difficulty—problems that are small in childhood can turn serious at adolescence. When a child takes what he wants at four years of age, it is annoying; When a young person takes what he wants at 14 years of age, it is stealing. Seeking physical closeness with a stranger can be appealing at four years of age but is sexually dangerous at 14 years of age.

The troubles of adolescence seem to subside when young people with FAS/E enter their late twenties. Alcohol delays development within the uterus, and children with FAS/E are often developmentally delayed throughout their childhoods. The cases we portray in this book raise a promising possibility: Adolescents with FAS/E may also be developmentally delayed. To some degree, they may grow out of the emotional and behavioral turmoil of the teenage years. Janeen Bohmann points out that her brother Eric, who fits the "worst-case disaster scenario," has gotten better as he has gotten older. Yet, he seems to have aged out of the extreme troubles and emotional turmoil of adolescence. At 27 years old, he is much less angry and depressed than he was five years before, she observes. His mistakes are less severe and dramatic. He understands his limitations better and is better able to cope.

Keith Wymer, a middle-aged adult with FAS who gives presentations and workshops on FAS/E across the country, makes a similar observation about his own development. "Somewhere along the line I stopped doing dangerous things to gain approval," he observes; "I gave it up." His stealing and lying, he says, were just adolescent attempts to get acceptance from others. ("If I stole my mother's silver dollars and gave them away, maybe people would like me.") Now he no longer does such things.

The problems of adolescence subside, we suspect, not only because the children mature but also because the families gain perspective. Parents learn to accept what they can not change. Parents tell us that they learn to accept the fact that they cannot control what happens to young adults with FAS/E and they learn to stay out of many of their problems. "We don't bail them out," says Jocie DeVries. "If you bail them out of these things, you get angry

because you don't have a life. We had to teach ourselves that."
This, too, is the wisdom of practice.

2. What does success look like for adolescents and adults with FAS/E?

Many of the young people in these chapters defy the disastrous stereotypes. They are not in jail. They are not selling themselves on the streets. Some have achieved conventional success—a job, a marriage. Many are coping, with support, with all the tasks of living on their own.

• Cindy Gere graduated from college with a bachelor's degree in art, got her teaching certificate from a graduate program, and became a certified art teacher. She worked in a teaching team in a Native American charter school.

• Stef Pummell married a navy man whom she describes as "patient, kind, loyal, and smart." After difficult bouts of anger and depression, she learned to cope through more effective medications and the support of her church group. When her husband is away on an aircraft carrier for two months at a time, she shoulders the full responsibility of a full-time job, managing a household, and caring for a young boy. She is happy with herself: "He has a full chance at a full life because of the choices I have made."

• Dave Jones has worked at the same job for three years and has earned several pay raises because of his excellent job performance.

• Pat, now a young adult in a Sioux community, works full-time at a grocery store, stocking the shelves and carrying out customers' groceries. He enjoys the work, he is paid well, and he is appreciated. He lives alone and wants, most of all, a girl friend. In this community, people are aware of problems like FAS/E and fit him in. His uncle, for example, takes Pat with him to the sweat lodge.

I had hoped to find many such examples of conventional success for young adults with FAS/E. I regret to say that I have not. I have come across several instances of adults who are doing well and suspect they have FAS/E. Ken Dietrich (a pseudonym), for example, owns a fishing boat in Alaska. He has always had difficulty with arithmetic, but his wife takes care of the business end. He knew his mother was a heavy drinker but he did not suspect he had FAS until they tried to adopt a young boy with FAS. Then he watched movies of himself as a child and saw in his own face and movements the characteristic signs of FAS. Some children diagnosed with FAS/E today may not have been diagnosed 20 years ago, and they may find ways to accommodate their disability, like Ken Dietrich. The situation for this generation of young people with FAS/E, who are more likely to have gotten a diagnosis, may be more hopeful than we realize.

While conventional career success eludes most young people diagnosed with FAS/E, many do manage the daily tasks of living on their own—driving a car, cooking for themselves, cleaning their homes, doing their laundry and maintaining their personal hygiene. Many families use modeling, practice, and repetition to teach systematically the skills their children will need to live on their own. Marceil Ten Eyck, for example, showed her daughter Sidney how to clean and cook and get the oil changed on her car. Her mother then left Sidney on her own, first for a weekend, then for a week, then for two weeks. She did fine. Most young people with FAS/E cannot handle all the routine tasks of adult life without some external support. Balancing a checkbook, for example, eludes Sidney, who calls the bank to find out how much money she has in her account before writing checks. But she has never bounced a check, she informed me with pride.

Success must be redefined for young people with FAS so we can see and celebrate their progress and achievements. Few young people with FAS/E are going to graduate from college. Few can hold a full-time job; the stress and stimulation are more than they can manage. But many do well at work, if they get job coaching and adjustments in work hours and demands. Job coaches, trained for this purpose, are especially effective in smoothing out problems at work. They can work out routines that protect young people with

FAS/E from too many simultaneous demands or from lines of authority that are unclear to them.

Many young people with FAS/E do valuable work, both for pay and as community service. Karen Lutke, for example, works part-time as a dog groomer. She is so good at caring for animals that family friends bring their pets to her house and pay her for her work. She also takes pride in her accomplishments as a public speaker who informs people about FAS/E. When a well-meaning therapist in the audience once asked her about her plans for further education, she drew herself up and said, "For me, FAS means I can't do college work, but I am a very good dog groomer."

Not only her daughter Karen but also her other teenagers with FAS/E have made steady progress, Jan Lutke points out. Patsy has an IQ measured at 47 and has numerous alcohol-related birth defects, but she has learned to take care of herself and is learning sign language to help a deaf and autistic friend. Ken lost his job at the car dealership because he didn't think to look behind him when asked to back up a car. But he has a new job now working for an automatic door installer and he is a hard worker.

I have used Jan Lutke's words as the epigraph for this book— her point that "success has many definitions" because she reminds us to think in more flexible and generous ways about the meaning of "success"—not only for young people with FAS/E but also for ourselves.

Adolescents with FAS/E often have a special sweetness. They remind us all to savor the daily moments of life, the small delights. Children with FAS/E do not let life just pass them by, Pamela Groupe Groves reminds us. Many know how to take delight in the beauty of a rose bush, the shape of the clouds, the dash into the woods. "Living in the moment," Groves observes, "is the flip side of not living in the future."

Many parents appreciate the joys that children with FAS/E have brought them. "When I took Ryland his lunch at the gas station, he always kissed me in front of all the mechanics," writes

Mary Lou Canney. "He possesses all those qualities we so often miss in the world today—a sense of loyalty and sweetness, the ability to be nonjudgmental and accepting."

Children with FAS/E teach us to enlarge our vision, to go beyond conventional definitions of success and think in more profound ways about what counts as success.

The young people in this book give the lie to the perverse and wrong-headedness stereotype that people with FAS/E lack conscience and empathy for others. Helping others is important to many and is an important source of their sense of self-worth. To be able to cope every day with so much confusion, so much misunderstanding, so much failure, so much blame requires a bedrock sense that you are a worthy person, facing difficulties well. Virtually all the families we have worked with emphasize this point: Their most important task is to help children with FAS/E develop the sense that they are good and valuable people who contribute to the world. For this reason, many parents made sure that their children have the opportunity to give help, not only receive it. Ryland's mother volunteered both of them, for example, to help remodel the building for the Resource Center for Parents and Children. Ryland liked the feeling of being valuable, useful, and important. Dave Jones volunteers for several agencies one or two days a week. He does odd jobs, yard work, and landscaping. Dave prides himself on his thoughtfulness. Elisabeth Groves demonstrated compassion by leaving flowers at the home of friends who died tragically. Soon, others began to do the same. She tended the flowers and worked through her grief. Her example inspired and guided family and friends through their own grieving process.

What will happen to a young person with FAS/E is difficult to predict because so many different influences affect their life chances. The bad news is that the neurological damage, at this point in our medical knowledge, is not reversible. The good news is that much can be done to improve the odds that life will go smoother. Parents and teachers want to know what the chances of success are for young people with FAS/E. But the outcomes are difficult to predict, especially when children are very young. Many parents recall the dismal predictions that they first received, and the way their children leaped beyond what professionals saw as their limits.

Why are the outcomes so difficult to predict? First of all, prenatal alcohol damage is quite variable in its neurological effects. Even fraternal twins, in the same womb at the same time, can show quite different degrees of biological damage from excessive drinking. The exact effects of alcohol on the fetus depend on many influences—how much the mother drank, whether drinking took the especially damaging form of bingeing, what organ systems were developing during the periods of heavy drinking, the mother's ability to metabolize alcohol, and the genetic characteristics of both the mother and the developing child.

Second, what happens to alcohol-affected children depends on the kind of family the child is raised in. Alcohol-affected children are far better off when they are raised in stable, nurturing families, research shows, where parents have a diagnosis of FAS/E. The cases of effective families in this book show why the quality of parenting matters so much.

Third, it is essential to recognize that young people with FAS/E are distinctive people quite apart from prenatal alcohol damage. Some are more sociable than others. Some are more physically attractive than others. It may be unfair, but we know both from scientific research and from our own experience of life that good looks and an outgoing personality are apt to be advantages. We know from research on resilient children that such children are especially apt to be good-looking and outgoing. Why do these children do better in poverty or catastrophe? The answer is that they are better able to attract nurturant adults. But the die is not cast. *Many parents are able to teach children with FAS/E how to spot adults who are willing to help them, giving them the advantages that good looks and sociability brings.*

No matter what the biological damage from prenatal alcohol abuse, we can shift the odds toward the child's favor.

3. Can parents, practitioners, and people with FAS/E develop strategies that enable them to cope with the problems?

I am in awe of the imagination, the ingenuity, the sheer intelligence that many people show in devising strategies to deal with the everyday problems of FAS/E. The chapters in this book offer a cornucopia of practical ideas.

Effective parents prepare young people for adulthood by encouraging them to take control of their own problems. Katie Lutke was thrilled to be asked to be a junior bridesmaid for her brother's wedding. But she worried that she would get get overexcited and start "hyping" (her expression for hyperventilating due to overstimulation and perseveration). Her solution—bring along track pants and running shoes so she could run between the wedding ceremony and the photography session. Physical activity, she realizes, calms her down. "She made this decision after working through why she couldn't wear the running clothes under her formal gown— a process that took about an hour from the time she started talking about it to the time she figured out the reasons," her mother remarked. Her mother let Katie do this thinking.

Many young people with FAS/E delight in developing strategies on their own. Cindy Gere, for example, describes the wealth of ways she has developed to cope with her memory lapses. Her basic principle is: If you think you may lose it, tie it on. "If you lose your purse, wear a fannypack. If you lose your keys, wear them as a necklace or tie them to the pocket of your jeans with a safety pin and string."

Effective parents teach their children self-advocacy at an early age. While the children are young, the parents serve as their advocates, battling the school system, the social service agencies, the medical profession. But parents are all too aware that they are aging, that their children will soon be adults and their children must learn how to advocate for themselves. Learning how to tell people you have a problem, and learning how to ask for help courteously are important skills. These skills are especially important for young people with FAS/E because they so often show no outward physical signs of their inner disabilities and because their verbal skills make people overestimate what they can do.

Parents lay the groundwork for self-advocacy early in life by allowing children to answer for themselves questions that are put to them. Parents make sure the children know the right words to label their problems. They develop with their children "scripts" for getting help. Marceil Ten Eyck, for example, worked with her daughter Sidney on The Plan. If her daughter was having trouble in a class, the first stage was to ask for help from the teacher in an assertive manner. If that didn't work, the second stage was to make an appointment with the school counselor and be explicit about her needs. The Plan had four stages and could be adapted to different situations.

Self-advocacy is a crucial skill for young people with FAS/E. "Tell people when you can't listen any more to the torrent of words coming at you," Mary Lou Canney advised her son. "Learn to tell people you have a problem," Cindy Gere tells other young people with FAS/E. "If you want to tell a teacher about FAS and make sure you are not embarrassed in front of the class, learn to say, 'This is a private matter. I want to keep this problem between you and me.'"

Most young people with FAS/E will always need outside help, an "external brain." At adolescence, young people with FAS/E still need the structure, support, and supervision they required as young children. As adolescents, however, many want independence. Many resent the structure and supervision they still need.

The noted physician Sterling Clarren at the University of Washington, who has pioneered techniques for diagnosing FAS/E, has coined an apt phrase for what people with FAS/E need throughout life—an "external brain." Sometimes parents are able to provide this guidance to children who accept their help. Anne Gere managed, from thousands of miles away, to guide her daughter Cindy through registration and course selection at the University of Alaska. She helped her complete term papers and helped her find substitute courses when the mathematics requirements exceeded her capabilities. "My mom and I are a team for the rest of my life," as Cindy put it. In other cases, the external brain consists of many service providers as with Kim, a woman alone, who drank and used drugs, and who gave birth to a daughter with FAS.

Parents often have to exercise tact and ingenuity to guide adolescents with FAS/E chomping to get free. When her son Ken wanted to buy a used car that did not back up (Ken said that he would never need to put the car in reverse), Jan Lutke asked his older brother, Paul, who worked at a car dealership, to stop by. Paul went to look at the car with Ken and together they reached the conclusion that this particular car was not a good buy. External structure at adolescence, says Lutke, may need to take the form of an "invisible guidance system."

Once an effective external structure is in place, beware of pulling it up in the misguided belief that supervision is no longer needed. The most tragic problems I have come across, working with the families in this book over several years, took place because effective supervision was withdrawn. Ann Michael had developed a "wrap-around" program, for example, that was successfully controlling her son's temptation to sexually molest young boys. The program featured round-the-clock supervision and hormone therapy to reduce John's sex drives. John did so well that he created the illusion he did not need so much supervision. When it was withdrawn, John relapsed, molesting several children, including one of Ann's young sons. Other families have learned a similar lesson: Supervision is a bearing wall. Do not tear it down.

Parents, practitioners, and young people have worked out ways to deal with the characteristic secondary disabilities of FAS/E which become pronounced at adolescence.

Parents and practitioners and people with FAS/E have developed a wealth of concrete ideas for dealing with such problems as trouble in school or trouble with the legal system. I offer here a sampler of the ideas parents and practitioners describe in useful detail in their chapters.

Problems with High School

Substitute experiential education in small, personalized school settings for the lectures, turbulence, and anonymity of a large comprehensive high school.

The problems of young people with FAS/E are especially hard to address in large comprehensive high schools. Such schools are busy institutions with large numbers of young people who have many diverse problems. Educators in such schools, no matter how big-hearted, find it hard to keep in mind the needs of alcohol-affected children. Even if inservice education on the disability did occur, perhaps a year or so ago, the school by now has experienced many changes in staffing. Teenagers with FAS/E so often look like everybody else. Early in life, some children with FAS/E have distinctive facial features and are small in stature. Young children sometimes look like cute little elves. At adolescence, these features fade and their height and weight become more typical of teenagers. In a large, comprehensive high school, young people with FAS/E are hard to spot. In a small school with just a few teachers, such young people stand out.

Many young people with FAS/E find the noise, turbulence, and commotion of comprehensive high schools impossible to cope with. "When Ryland hit junior high school, he had a different teacher for every class, different expectations in every class, a different schedule each day and three different combinations to memorize—one for his hall locker, another for his gym locker, and a third for his bicycle," said his mother. The students jamming the hallways and running into him especially upset him, since he is sensitive to touch. He came undone. Even at home, he became angry and aggressive.

Many parents have found alternatives to standard high school programs for children with FAS/E. Some are able to design an individualized program within the public school system. Jan Lutke convinced the vice principal, for example, to let her organize a program for her daughter Karen which did not require Karen to change classes every hour. Karen studied mathematics and English but dispensed with social studies and the sciences. She learned practical subjects like cooking and woodworking, and focused on sewing, where she had genuine talent.

Other parents, like Diane Malbin, find no satisfaction within the school system. In "Finding the Right School for Devorah," she describes how she withdrew her daughter from a large middle school where failure overwhelmed her. She and her mother did home schooling for a year, and they then located an alternative school, the Pacific Crest Community School, where Devorah thrived. A year before, Devorah had hated school so much she said she didn't want to live. At Pacific Crest Devorah hated to miss school so much that she wanted to tape record a class she had to miss. At Pacific Crest, if the subject was geology, students went to the mountains. If the subject was biology, they visited the wetlands. If the subject was history, they dramatized the event. At Pacific Crest, Devorah no longer believed she was stupid. She discovered her strengths, like building a kayak. "Mom, I have smart hands," she said.

The schools where adolescents with FAS/E thrive have common features:

• Small number of students and teachers so students receive personal attention and the entire school staff can be educated on FAS/E

• Stress on projects, experiences, life skills, and activities rather than books, lectures, and abstractions

• Group work where everyone contributes as they can and students are not singled out for evaluation.

Adolescents with FAS/E still need the visuals, the hands-on learning, the scripts and structure and role plays and routines that they needed as small children. Such experiential approaches to education are emphasized in elementary schools. The problem is that teaching becomes progressively less visual and more abstract in high school. But many teachers, parents, and young people themselves have developed more experiential ways of learning for

340 / Judith Kleinfeld

adolescents. Computers can offer the movement, music, visuals, and sound that young people with FAS/E need in a hip, teenage way. Cindy Gere got videotapes on historical events to help her understand college history lectures. Steff Pummell found she could learn just about anything if she could substitute a visual image for the verbal abstraction.

Brian, a student who didn't know how to maneuver his way around the cafeteria at lunchtime, learned the routine just fine through a visual, experiential approach. When educational consultant Debra Evensen asked him to say the cafeteria rules, he could state them faultlessly. When she asked him to show her what he was supposed to do in the cafeteria, he didn't even know where to sit. So first she walked him through the routines. Next they practiced what to do when routines failed: What if someone was sitting in his usual seat? Then she got a Polaroid camera and took pictures of Brian doing everything right—a visual reference Brian could use to refresh his memory.

MENTAL HEALTH PROBLEMS

Contrary to common stereotypes, insight therapy can be effective for young people with FAS/E, but therapists need to use visual therapeutic methods to make abstractions, such as feelings and friendships, concrete.

The common idea that insight therapy is ineffective for young people with FAS/E unfortunately means that therapists can be reluctant to treat them. But insight therapy can be adapted to the visual, experiential learning styles of adolescents with FAS/E. Therapist Susan Baxter describes the techniques that succeeded with Sarah, a young woman with FAS whose rages were so intense that she knocked holes in her bedroom wall. Baxter used Sarah's baby book, for example, to show Sarah in a tangible way that her adoptive parents loved her and not only their biological daughter. Baxter drew diagrams of Sarah's friendship networks to show Sarah that, indeed, she had friends. In fact, when Sarah's friends changed, Sarah asked for the diagrams so she could change the pictures. Over time, Sarah's rages subsided and she did better at school and at home.

TROUBLE WITH THE LAW

Families can prepare themselves and their children to deal with the legal system by: (1) documenting patterns of behavior likely to cause trouble with the law, and (2) using advocates and information to convince judges and others that FAS/E is a neurological disability that requires special approaches.

Young people with FAS/E are at much higher risk for breaking the law. Many are intellectually and socially immature and do not understand what committing an offense means. Desperate for friends and wanting to fit in, many young people can be easily persuaded to do something illegal. Sexual molestation becomes a serious worry. Adolescents with FAS/E develop the sex drives typical of teenagers. Since many are socially immature themselves, they may spend time with children considerably younger than they are. Sexual exploration and touching with young children have severe legal consequences.

The American legal system does not have an appropriate way to deal with young people with FAS/E whose mental defects and state of mind do not fall into ordinary legal categories. On the one hand, the disability caused by fetal alcohol syndrome makes the person far less blameworthy. On the other hand, it makes them more likely to repeat the offense—and in some cases thus more dangerous. Parents and their lawyers may face an expensive legal ordeal that can last for years.

Advocates for people with FAS/E are trying to change the way the legal system treats people with these types of mental defects. The Alaska Court System has started two projects in the Anchorage District Court, for example, for offenders who are mentally disabled and have committed misdemeanors. The Court has developed:

1. The Coordinated Resources Project, a specialty court which provides a more individualized approach for mentally disabled

offenders. This court relies on carefully selected judges with special training in mental health issues.

2. The Jail Alternative Services Program within the Department of Corrections, which develops community treatment programs for mentally disabled offenders.

Such programs offer promise for young people with FAS/E who commit offenses. But what to do remains difficult even when judges do understand the nature of fetal alcohol syndrome, have great sympathy for the young people, and are genuinely trying to do the right thing for both them and for the community. The Honorable Judge C. Cunliffe Barnett offers an example in the case of Ida: He calls for a psychological case report on Ida, a woman suffering from FAS who also has a chaotic family background. Ida has knifed an acquaintance in a rage. Despite Judge Barnett's understanding of FAS, he can not find an appropriate and effective sentence.

Families experienced with FAS/E have developed ways to cope with the legal system. Anticipate that your child could be arrested and be prepared, Jim Slinn advises. Arm yourself with material on FAS/E and professional observations of your child. Insist on joint meetings with the district attorney, the judge, and probation officer where everyone goes over the material together. The information in *Fantastic Antone Grows Up* may be useful and persuasive to those in the legal system, particularly Judge Barnette's court decision (Appendix 1) and the information on FAS/E by Dr. Barbara Morse (which includes photographic evidence of the brain damage alcohol can cause) for people who doubt the very existence of the disability.

Marie Jones describes how she was able to protect her son, even after he was sent to jail. "His childlike nature, his desire for friends, his willingness to please, and his difficulty in distinguishing friend from foe and safety from danger made him extremely vulnerable," she writes. "Through the efforts of our pastor, prison officials acknowledged the threat and assigned Dave a single cell." With the help of FAS professionals and friends in the community, the family succeeded in getting their son's sentence reduced. Even while he was in jail, Marie Jones and her husband were able to make Dave feel safe and that his parents were still there and in charge.

Marie Jones intends her chapter to prepare other families to deal more effectively with the legal system. Since Dave had not been in trouble with the law before, they were naive. Her husband, for example, did not protest when the police wanted to interview Dave alone. When his mother asked him later if they had told him his rights, Dave replied, "They told me I could leave at any time, but, Mom, he had a gun." Young people with FAS/E should carry a card in their wallets that explains what to do and what to say if arrested or questioned by a police officer. The card should include the name and telephone number of an attorney experienced in dealing with people with such disabilities.

Parents must also remember that they cannot anticipate every situation. "Be gentle with yourself," Jim Slinn advises. "Don't wallow in guilt should your child run afoul of society's laws."

INAPPROPRIATE SEXUAL BEHAVIOR

• *Head off anticipated problems before adolescence.*

Many parents anticipate the problems of adolescence and teach children with FAS/E habits that are apt to reduce their risk of getting into trouble. One father told me he never relieved himself while hiking with his son in the woods because his son might not realize that he could not relieve himself on city streets. Some parents use games to show young children the location of "private parts" that cannot be touched. Develop useful habits early on, Pamela Groupe Groves advises parents. Remember that behavior which may not be a problem in a small child, like running around without clothes, can become a serious problem in a teen-ager.

• *Teach young people with FAS/E the scripts for romance.*

At adolescence, young people with FAS/E seek romantic partners and seek ways to satisfy sexual needs. But their isolation from other teenagers means that many have not learned the dance of romance. Some parents walk their teenagers through dating situations. One mother had her son practice dating with his sister. When he was ready to put the show on the road, she called the mother of the young woman he was asking out and discussed the situation with her. The boy's mother accompanied them on their date, walking a few paces behind. Gradually she withdrew from the scene. Teaching teenagers how to act on a date is a lot like teaching them how to act in a play—they need to learn the lines and rehearse their roles. Even so, it's best to try out the play in Boston before you hit New York.

• *Find a teen mentor who can teach a teenager with FAS/E how to handle the adolescent social world.*

School programs in social skills did not teach her son Tony how to handle himself with teenagers, says his mother Janet Adams. But she developed an ingenious strategy. She used a state-funded program for "personal care assistants" to get Tony a teenage mentor. Nick showed Tony how to act like a teenager. They went together to basketball games, to the beach, and to the grocery store. They hung out with Nick's friends. With less than a year of mentoring, Tony could strike up a conversation, something he couldn't do after four years of social skills training in the school-room. Other parents report similar success with older male coaches whom their sons admire, such as a Big Brother from the Big Brothers/Big Sisters Program or a cool young male caretaker in a "wraparound program." Such mentors can teach social skills and appropriate sexual behavior in the situation.

• *Keep in mind that love and marriage may be wonderful for a young person with FAS/E. Do not discourage romance for fear of sexual problems.*

Most of us want a loving, committed relationship and young people with FAS/E have similar yearnings. Marriage can provide young people with FAS/E the affection, structure and guidance that they need, that their parents provided before. Marriage can provide for their spouses a loving and devoted mate. Sidney Guimont's

HOW A GROUP HOME HELPS JOHN
by Nancy Harrison *

John started on a downhill course—shoplifting from stores, sexual exploration with the dog, running away from home. Nancy Harrison and a group of other parents who had children with FAS/E developed a proposal for a group home for children growing up and careening out of control.

Their proposal was turned down. But life has its quirks. When John turned 19 years old, his misbehavior brought him under the supervision of a social agency. This agency created the type of group home his mother had wanted from the start.

The social services agency found an apartment for John and another young man with FAS. Each boy has his own bedroom and they share a living room and kitchen. A policeman was hired during his off-duty hours to be an advocate for the boys. He takes them on trips, counsels them, and helps when trouble arises.

John works half-time at a restaurant under a special employment program. His job placement coach counsels him on how to get to work on time and how to spend his money.

> "John is happy and moving in the direction he wants to go," says his mother. "He wants to be independent, a self-sufficient person. To me, being an adult means getting an education, getting a job, and living in your own place.
> Unbelievably, it means the same to him."

_____

* Judith Kleinfeld interviewed Nancy Harrison for this sidebar.

FINDING A GROUP HOME FOR DAVID
by Adam McRoy*

A year after being arrested for car theft at age 17, my son David, who has FAE, entered a group home supported by a program through the Provincial Government's Human Resources Department. The home is on a farm and is run by a woman with extensive experience with FAS/E. David thrived.

When he reached age 19, David had to leave the home because the government considered him an adult. I attempted to set him up in an apartment in the small community where he grew up, hoping that he would have fewer distractions there. The experiment was a disaster, however, as David quickly gravitated to the drug and alcohol crowd and was evicted from his apartment. His problems became more serious; he ran afoul of the law, violated probation charges, and couldn't stay out of trouble.

Despite everything, David is an eternal optimist. He is currently awaiting sentencing for theft and breach of probation. He is supposed to be checking in regularly with his probation officer, a task that would be difficult for any adult with FAE. I support him by contacting lawyers, probation officers, and police officers in an attempt to educate them about the consequences of FAE and to discuss other avenues than jail.

David may never be able to live an independent life. He is so bright, and yet he cannot put it all together. What precious few studies or statistics there are seem to suggest that the prognosis is not good. I am not, however, going to give up on him. He is my son, I love him, and he deserves too much more than he has received in life.

Society as a whole should be prepared to offer the services that David and others like him need, because we will pay for him whether we want to or not. A protected home environment that is loving, structured, and removed from urban dangers and distractions is certainly less expensive than jail. And we will all save on the costs, both economic and social—the cost to victims, the cost of police and the courts, not to mention the $40,000 per year that it costs to keep them in jail. As a comparison, the woman who runs the farm receives about $12,000 per year for the children in her care.

What is really required is a full scale political assault to educate politicians and bureaucrats in both the judicial and human resources ministries about the costs of FAS. We need to show the true cost of ignoring these people and funneling them through the courts and jail instead of providing the environments they need.

---

* Adam McRoy is a pseudonym.

husband, for example, found in her a wife who took the greatest joy in his company and who was willing to go with him anywhere he chose. Yes, happy endings do happen!

4. What do families of young people with FAS/E need from the community?

When a family adopts a child with FAS/E, they are taking on themselves, in their own home, 24 hours a day, the responsibility for children with great needs. Children with FAS/E did not cause their own neurological damage. They are the victims of others' bad choices. These children need help and most of us feel keenly our responsibility to help such children. The families who adopt children with FAS/E are thus shouldering our community responsibility. They are helping the children lead happier and more productive lives. They are also helping the rest of us by warding off the kind of damage that unsocialized and unloved young people with FAS/E might otherwise do in the community.

We owe these parents. It is as simple as that.

How can we repay our debt to these families? What do families most need from the community?

• *The greatest public policy need is the development of group homes for adults with FAS/E near their families.*

Michael Dorris, whose search for what was wrong with his adopted son, riveted public attention on FAS. If he had a magic wand, said Dorris, he would create group homes in the country where people like his son could do useful work far away from drugs and alcohol, enjoy each other's company, and enjoy a nonstop cartoon channel.[1]

Parents of alcohol-affected young people wish for the same magic wand. "David is so bright and yet he cannot put it all together," his father says. "He deserves so much more than he has received in life." Society will find it far cheaper to head off the havoc that young adults with FAS/E can cause than to pay for it

---

[1] Nancy White, "Michael Dorris: A messenger of hope, prevention," *Iceberg* 7, 1 (1997): 3, 5.

later. "Funding a group home, a protected environment, that is loving, structured, and removed from urban dangers, is certainly less expensive than jail," points out David's father.

Some families have managed to find appropriate adult homes for their children. But the search is arduous and homes near enough for families to visit are hard to come by. Where the families did find good group homes for adults with FAS/E, they described these places in such similar terms that I had to check to make sure that they were not talking about the identical place. They were not. The group homes where adults with FAS/E thrived, however, had common features:

• *Small and family-like setting:* Young people with FAS/E need the loving atmosphere of a family to provide the encouragement they need. The staff need to understand FAS and to realize that the young people's misbehavior comes from brain damage, not defiance.

• *Peers who do not model delinquency:* Young people with FAS/E want desperately to fit in, to be like everybody else. The group home should not expose them to delinquent models.

• *Sheltered employment and job coaching:* All of us need something useful to do, work that we can take pride in.

• *Lots of activities:* Since many young people with FAS find it hard to structure their time, they need organized things to do. Many successful group homes are on farms, where the children are far from urban dangers, and have animals to care for.

• *Close to families:* Even if they have had to relinquish their adopted children to get the expensive services their children need, many parents want to continue to stay close to them and advocate for them.

We are a compassionate, rich, and generous society. Providing group homes is the least we can do for the children and the families who care for them.

Group homes for adults with FAS/E is the most pressing need. But there are others:

FINDING THE RIGHT GROUP HOME AND
FINDING OUR DAUGHTER AGAIN
by Julie Davis*

Like other parents, the Davises tried different group homes until they found one right for their daughter Emily, a young woman with FAS who did not get into serious trouble until adolescence.

Our daughter Emily was a happy and loving child when she was young, but her adolescence arrived with a bang. At age 14, she became friends with a girl who used drugs and got into trouble. Emily began to copy her friend. She skipped school and left home for days on end, used drugs and alcohol, and stole my credit card and the key to my new truck. We tried to rescue her, but she was a different person. She rejected her family and was hostile. We couldn't understand her new language and attitude and were deeply hurt by this new behavior. My husband was dreadfully ashamed of what was happening, and our other children were angry with her for what she was doing to the family. I found myself wishing we had never adopted her. We were exhausted and needed respite.

We arranged for Emily to live in a group home. The first home didn't serve Emily well, however. Discipline was too loose, she copied troubling behaviors from other youths, and the staff was not experienced with FAS/E. We needed to find a home with supervision, structure, and other people like herself.

Fortunately, we found one through our local support network. The group home was run by a family who lived in the country. The foster mother, who cared for other alcohol-affected young people, understood FAS/E and the need for structure and supervision all the time. If necessary, those teenagers who were having trouble in school could stay at home and focus on learning life skills. All the children took care of animals and enrolled in 4-H, attending agricultural fairs

—continues

* Julie Davis is a pseudonym.

—Finding the Right Group Home, *continued*

during the summer to show their animals. My husband and I visted this home and felt it was exactly what Emily needed. Emily entered this home when she was in the eighth grade, and during this time she was diagnosed with FAS/E.

But Emily hated it—at first. She described it as a boot camp because she wasn't free to catch a bus and go downtown whenever she wanted. After a year in the home, however, she was once more the Emily we knew. She had chores as well as fun activities to keep her busy, and peers who she could talk to. She was treated with respect and praised for her progress. Finally, she was laughing and happy again. She even made the honor roll at school and got a job working in the community for three mornings a week.

Emily has her ups and downs, but overall she has made a lot of progress in one year, a change that would not have happened had she remained in the first group home. Although we are not caring for her daily, we feel we have an important role to play as her advocates.

We understand now that her actions stem from FAS/E and not from defiance; she doesn't mean to hurt us but has strong, inappropriate impulses and requires supervision. Now that we understand her behavior, we no longer blame her and can put our anger and hurt behind us. She is a highly vulnerable, loving, happy, sociable young lady who will always need help, and we will forever do our best to provide it.

• *Expand people's understanding of FAS/E and destigmatize it.*

Prevention and educating people about the risks of drinking while pregnant is the first priority. Many are working hard to get the message across. Judges and others in the legal system, doctors and health care workers, teachers and day care workers, health care providers and social workers—all need to understand FAS/E and the kinds of problems this disability can cause. They need to be able to spot young people whose misbehavior may be the result of neurological damage, not deliberate wrongdoing, and to know how to go about getting a medical diagnosis. They need to recognize that FAS/E is not a shameful state but a neurological disability, which the young people themselves did not cause. Such education is a never-ending task. People who have been educated in FAS/E move on and others replace them. People forget. Educating people about FAS/E needs to go beyond the flurry created by an emotionally moving book like Michael Dorris' *The Broken Cord* and become a routine part of professional education.

• *Establish clearer definitions of FAS/E and improve diagnostic methods.*

Dr. Sterling Clarren and others at the University of Washington have pioneered methods of diagnosing FAS/E and they and others are educating professionals on their use. But we have not yet developed agreed-upon definitions and we have not yet developed diagnostic methods that are appropriate for people of different ages and different ethnic origins. Often professionals like judges and teachers suspect FAS/E and want to take it into account but lack the diagnosis they need.

• *Establish educational programs, from early childhood through vocational training, that are suited to the learning styles of those with FAS/E.*

We know a great deal about the educational approaches appropriate for young people with FAS/E. We know that teaching should emphasize life skills, that teaching should be done in real-world situations, that teaching should emphasize visual methods, role plays, and projects. We know that young people with FAS/E often have special talent in art and music and a special gift for working with animals. The wisdom of practice has taught us much about effective schooling. But school systems rarely offer programs suitable for young people with FAS/E. Parents are too often on their own, left to try to work out something for their children. School systems should shoulder this responsibility.

↪ EPILOGUE ↩

As we finished this book, I got a telephone call from the FAS/E parent support group in Fairbanks, Alaska. The parents had been talking about how they wanted me to end it.

"We want you to end the book with stories about the children," they told me.

> We are so scared. Our children are growing up and we are terrified of what could happen to them. When we get together, we laugh at so many of the things our children say and do. The stories keep the fear at bay.

So I drove out to Chena Hot Springs, 30 miles from Fairbanks, where the FAS/E parent support group was holding its annual summer camp. The families knew each other's children and watched out for them. We sat on a rickety porch with cups of coffee and swatted the mosquitoes. I took out my notepad.

৯৬

"I told my son he had 50 dollars in his checking account," said Jim Slinn. "I told him, over and over again, that he should never write a check for more than 50 dollars."

Then his checks started bouncing and I asked him what had happened.

"I did just what you told me, Dad," he said. "I wrote a lot of checks—but none for more than 50 dollars."

৯৬

"That's like the year we had two birthday parties for my son Tony," said Lisa Lovell. "He thought he was two years older! We couldn't talk him out of it."

≈

"We had the opposite problem," said Vickie Horodyski. "When Teena was living with her first family they didn't celebrate her eleventh birthday."

"She would tell everyone. "'I am 10 years old, even though I am really 11.' We couldn't talk her out of it."

≈

"Antone was giving me a tour of his youth camp and showed me the gravel drive he had helped build," said Sally Caldwell.

"I worked on this," he said with pride.

"You did!" I said, impressed. "Did you do it? By hand?"

"Oh, no, Mom. How silly. We used shovels."

≈

"My daughter Teena had been reading books about the Hardy boys and she decided she now knew how to survive anything," said Vickie Horodyski.

"So she decided to leave home. She was going from Alaska to Ohio to visit her Grandpa—on her bicycle.

"The police went out looking for her. When they spotted her, they turned on a search light. Teena was terrified and outran them. We finally found her at two in the morning.

"The next day we took her to the police to explain to her what could happen to a young girl who ran away.

"Well, she wanted to give the police officer who had chased her a gift.

"So she got a photograph of herself from her soccer team and put it in this gorgeous frame she had gotten from her godparents. The frame had a picture of a guardian angel on it.

"And she gave it to the policeman so he would always remember her."

❧

"All these things happen to us," said Betty Taafe, president of the FAS/E Support Group. "They happen all the time."

Afterword:
Broken Beaks and Wobbly Wings

Teresa Kellerman

Teresa Kellerman is an adoptive parent of John, a young adult with fetal alcohol syndrome. As coordinator of the FAS Community Resource Center in Tucson, Arizona, Teresa advocates for families, consults with professionals, publishes a newsletter, facilitates support groups, produces workshops, and offers classroom presentations to students of all ages. ° *She serves on several boards and helped organize FASWORLD, an international organization that promoted the first worldwide FAS Awareness Day.*

"HONEY, YOU MUST GIVE YOUR CHILDREN ROOTS, BUT YOU ALSO NEED TO know when its time to give them their wings!"

I often think of this with our children, and little by little I am trying to do that. I am learning to let go with my teenager who doesn't have FAS. I know I can trust him to make his own mistakes and be his own person and grow up the way he decides to grow up. I can let him learn to fly on his own. And I can allow him to become the person he is, not the person I want him to be. And that's okay. One of these days he will leave the nest and I will be so sad, grieving the departure of my baby. I know he will fly just fine, because he has good roots and strong wings. He will soar to heights I can only dream of.

I want my son with FAS/E to have the same chance for independence. But I know it will take longer before he is ready to leave

---

°Teresa Kellerman can be reached by e-mail at tkj@azstarnet.com or on the Internet at http://www.come-over.to/FASCRC.

the nest. After he leaves, when I can't be with him, he will need a support network to help him manage.

Steve Neafcy—whose words inspired my avian metaphor—describes what happened when he tried to leave the nest too soon:

> *My problem was not knowing I had FAE until age 43 years. I was expected to fly with the flock when I had a broken wing! Using this broken wing to try to glide with all my peers was a living hell but the worst was failing and seeing the disappointment in Mom and Dad's eyes...*

Our alcohol-affected baby birds, like all other baby birds, eventually want to leave the nest. Everyone (family, society, school, psychologists) seems to say we should give them their independence, even if they have disabilities. If we don't, we are called "overprotective" and "hypervigilant" and accused of not allowing our children to enjoy the freedom that other kids have, and that our kids should have, too. We should let them fly, so we're told.

Let's look at those wings. They *look* normal. Hmmmm. The wings aren't broken, they just didn't develop fully, they are stunted at baby bird size underneath all those feathers, and cannot support an adult bird in flight. But nobody realizes that until the grownup baby bird takes a flying leap out of the nest and lands on his little beak!

Oops. Too late.

Now the wings really are broken. So we take baby bird back into the nest, but now we have a baby bird that's a grown-up bird with a bent beak, wobbly wings, and a taste of the freedom of flying through the air. And he wants to taste that freedom again, so he flies again, even knowing he might crash again. So it goes.

Now, what if we can't take baby-boy-man-bird back into our nest? Or what if we can't keep him there now that he has been out of the nest? With broken wings and a bent beak, he will be the laughingstock of all the other birds and he will also be a candidate for becoming cat food. Yeah, there're cats out there, and dogs, and coyotes, just waiting for our little birdies who try to fly but can't.

I'm not going to explain who the predators are; you can figure that out. Vulnerability is a secondary disability, remember? So is arrested social development. These are not conducive to flying freely in those tempting blue skies. When our birdies fly, they see lots of pavement and never a mountain top.

This message is not a slam to the moms and dads of birdies who have flown and crashed. They didn't know this was going to happen. They all tell me that if they had known then what they know now, they would not have cared if they were called "overprotective" or "codependent" or "hypervigilant" or "neurotic" or whatever else we've been called. They would be even *more* protective and vigilant.

This message is not meant to squelch any parents' hopes for their child's future. The failed flights that we see today are due to lack of adequate intervention in the early years but also were fueled by false hopes fed to us by the disabilities community and others who, meaning well, have pushed independence and inclusion and mainstream as though our kids could just sail right along with their peers if we only "let go."

Maybe some of the little ones really will be able to fly when they are older. The chances for independence in living and employment for kids with FAS/E growing up in the eighties was very low, according to Ann Streissguth, but I'm sure that chances will increase as we learn more about effective intervention strategies for FAS/E. We also need to work on selling the importance of these interventions to the "system" so that our birdies get the support they need to fly, even if it means flying with them to support them when they start to veer off course or take a dip too low.

Even if only some of those birdies with bent beaks and wobbly wings are able to fly, that means that some might be able to make it. We know that the range of alcohol effects is wide, and each child has unique abilities and disabilities. We know that there are many problems inherent with the syndrome. But we also know that a few can function somewhat independently.

Parents can draw from the wisdom of those who have traveled this path before, but in the end they will need to rely on their own judgment to determine if and when that time to fly may come. Every child has the right to earn whatever degree of independence he or she is capable of without jeopardizing the loss of that indepencence. The child also has a right to safety and quality of life. It is crucial to be able to recognize the limitations without losing hope of fulfilling the child's potential, in order to find the balance that offers the greatest chance for success.

We need to be realistic in the hope we offer to younger families. It is not fair to encourage parents to have unrealistic expectations for the future of their children. Hope that is built on false ideas today will be crushed mercilessly in failed attempts to fly tomorrow. I think it is healthier to give parents a realistic hope mixed with warnings of the dangers inherent in FAS/E that might be a little hard to swallow now. In the end, a lot of pain and grief can be avoided for families.

I was fortunate enough to have as good information available to me as I did during Johnny's adolescent years. And I had the foresight, even before Streissguth's reports were released, to know that Johnny would never be able to fly on his own. So I prepared him for this, starting way back when he would talk about "when I grow up, I want to drive (marry, be a daddy, become a famous drummer in a band that makes millions of dollars, and so on)." Now, I was careful enough to not burst his bubbles completely, but I also loved him enough to not let him believe that all those dreams would come true. Instead of taking away his dreams, I changed his dreams a little. He can learn to drive (way out in the middle of nowhere), and marry (if he ever finds someone who will have him), or stay single (no shame in that, I learned), be a daddy (to a puppy or two), make lots of money (70 percent of minimum wage *is* a lot of money in John's eyes), and become a famous drummer (almost everyone in Tucson has seen his video or has seen him on TV or in the newspaper, so he feels famous).

Does he want to fly? Of course he does! But he knows his abilities and his limitations. I remind him of both as often as I need to in order to keep him balanced between reality and dreams. He accepts his disability, with moments of frustration occasionally expressed with verbal outbursts that are not unlike those of my non-disabled son (non-abusive and quite appropriate). For every moment of frustration with not being able to fly, John has several moments of appreciation, joy, excitement, expectation, hope, and happiness about living his life in this nest.

And I take him flying with me as often as I can. No real independence is in John's future, but he feels free at times and he feels happy most of the time, and he is safe and secure within the limitations of the home nest and accepts the restrictions of flying only when he has his wing supports on (mom, brother, mentor). This boy-man-birdie has a straight beak and a strong body and a bright mind and a happy spirit. The wobbly wings don't really bother him that much, because they just aren't an issue. But we never forget for a moment that those wings will not carry him farther than he can fall.

My job as mama bird was never to prepare John to fly off on his own. My job has been to ensure that the proper supports are in place so John never has to experience the pain of hitting that pavement or the fear of being confronted by predators. My job is not done yet, so I'm keeping this little bird right here under my wings, that have become stretched and strong over the years of being what some call overprotective.

> Somewhere over the rainbow, bluebirds fly.
> Birds fly over the rainbow.
> Why, then, oh why can't I?

Let's find some rainbows! And lets help our kids fly, but never, never alone. I made a promise to John once. He came to me with such anxiety and fear. He said, "Mom, I know I can't behave when I'm on my own, and that I need you there to remind me of what I forget. Mom, I'm afraid that someday when you aren't here to be with me, that I won't be able to help myself, and I will do something bad and get in trouble, and I will go to jail. Mom, I don't want to go to jail. I think I would be better off dead than going to jail." I made a promise to John that day. I said, "John, I will not let you go to jail. I will do everything in my power to keep you safe and to protect you from your disability. You know you need someone to be with you all the time, every minute, in order to stay safe." "Yes, Mom, I know." So we work together to educate the "system" and to look for alternate means of support, because these old wings aren't going to hold up forever.

Some birds don't need too much support, and some can actually fly with minimal assistance, but there has to be some kind of safety net in place just in case. Hurray for the few who can make it and thrive. May they see all the rainbows and mountain tops they long for. Remember though, this is the exception, not the rule. I'm not being pessimistic, just realistic. I feel fortunate in that it is relatively easy for me to provide John with wing supports (for now, anyway). Some birds are heavier, so to speak, and need stronger supports than parents can offer.

Sometimes the community is not willing or able to help with those supports. I want to reach out to some of those parents and offer help. That is so hard to do so far away. That is why I do everything I can to gather twigs of information and tips on building stronger nests. Let's all work together to strengthen our communities so we can take our kids over the rainbows and up to the mountain tops. Let's work on making our own nests secure. And let's be careful about false hope that is given as misguided encouragement that could result in parents pushing the birdies out without safety supports.

During the early years of my parenting John, there was not much information available on what to expect for his future. I had to wing it, so to speak, and had to rely on basic good parenting and my own maternal instincts. There is so much more known today about what intervention strategies work best. Even though we can't change the primary disabilities of impaired neurological function that stunt social development, we can learn how to parent in ways that minimize some of the more avoidable pitfalls, and increase the chances of success in school and on the job, with relationships, and with life in general.

We might not be able to strengthen those wings, but we can strengthen the safety nets, and we can encourage our young to fly tandem, with mentors and coaches, who can accompany them as they discover all that life's expansive horizons have to offer.

Appendix One:
The Case of Ida

THE HON. JUDGE C. CUNLIFFE BARNETT

C. Cunliffe Barnett, who retired from the bench in 1997, was appointed a judge and moved from Vancouver to Williams Lake in central British Columbia in 1973. He has traveled throughout British Columbia and the Yukon Territory on court circuits. Much of his work has been done in aboriginal communities. He has had an interest in FAS issues for 15 years and most recently organized a seminar presentation for all the judges of the Provincial Court of British Columbia.

THE STORIES HEARD BY JUDGES ARE ENDLESSLY SAD AND DISTURBING. Ida's story, which I shall recount here,° is one of the saddest and most disturbing that I have heard during more than 20 years of judging.

Ida is a small and artless woman, not quite 24 years old. She is a Sekani Indian whose home community is the Indian reserve at Fort Ware, British Columbia. Life is harsh in Fort Ware, and Ida's life has been marked by an uncommon number of tragedies. Her father was killed in 1975. Her sister was sent to prison for manslaughter in 1992. And later in 1992 her sister was killed by the man who had killed their father. Other members of Ida's immediate family have been sentenced for violent offenses. All of the killings and other violent incidents were fueled by alcohol.

° Judge Barnett slightly revised and edited his decision for this book. Because this case is a matter of public record, the name of the defendant has been retained.The decision is available in unedited form as R. V. Ida Lucille Rose Abou, January 24, 1995, British Columbia Decisions/Criminal Sentence Cases #7100-02.

Ida was raised by her alcoholic grandparents. She is mentally handicapped. She claims to have a Grade 2 education, or perhaps it was Grade 4 or 5. She really cannot remember. (The Department of Indian Affairs ran the school in Fort Ware until June 1994. The educational standards were notoriously and abysmally low, and services for students with special needs were essentially nonexistent.)

Ida has given birth to seven children; it appears that all are FAS or FAE and all are "in care." Ida's children demonstrate that she is a severe abuser of alcohol. When she is under the influence of alcohol, she has a distinct inclination to act impulsively and violently.

The author of a pre-sentence report written in August 1993 summarized matters by saying that Ida's life has been "punctuated with poverty, alcoholism, violence, and death." And when that report was being prepared, responsible persons in Fort Ware expressed the thought that "it is as though she has never been taught right from wrong."

There is more.

Ida herself is almost certainly afflicted with FAS, a fact that apparently went unrecognized until a court-ordered report was written in July 1993. FAS has been the subject of comment in only a few reported Canadian court decisions, and it is not well understood by most judges, lawyers, probation officers, corrections officers, social workers or other persons likely to encounter it in the context of the justice system.

It is not a new notion that the taking of strong drink by pregnant women endangers unborn babies. People understood this truth in biblical times. But ancient wisdom was largely forgotten or ignored until about 20 years ago, when the first reports of modern studies were published. We have now come to understand that fetal exposure to alcohol is the leading cause of mental retardation in Canada. Moreover, fetal exposure to alcohol causes actual brain damage and the long-term effects of fetal exposure to alcohol are more severe than those of other drugs, including heroin and cocaine.

People whose brains were damaged by alcohol before they were born are entirely likely to have behavioral characteristics that will bring them into conflict with other persons and the criminal law or will set them up to become victims of crimes, particularly sexual crimes. Ida is prone to becoming frustrated and then to overreacting in impulsive, violent ways. Behavior like this is entirely consistent with her affliction and it is not merely willful misbehavior by a woman who refuses to mend her ways. People with FAS have brains that simply do not "work right." They cannot be made to learn and change by the punishments that are the traditional tools (or weapons) of our criminal justice system. They may, however, cope pretty well and be considered model inmates in the highly structured environments of prisons and penitentiaries.

Ida is in court today because I must sentence her for two criminal offenses:

• Assaulting M. C. at Fort Ware on February 8, 1994.

• Assaulting and causing bodily harm to R. P. at Fort Ware on February 12, 1994.

The circumstances of these offenses are not extraordinary. On February 8, 1994, Ida got into a trivial argument with another young woman, M. C., whom she then beat up. Ida put M. C. down and kicked her in the head. A few days later, at a time when she had reason to be upset with R. P., who was making a drunken nuisance of himself, Ida grabbed a kitchen knife and slashed R. P.'s leg with it. He was hurt, but not terribly seriously. Ida pled guilty to the assault upon M. C. She was tried and found guilty of the assault upon R. P.

These offenses were not Ida's first. In September 1992, Ida got into a trivial argument with C.P., who had merely wanted to borrow some cigarettes. When C. P. departed the scene Ida grabbed a knife and followed her. Ida slashed C. P with the knife and inflicted a significant wound. On that occasion Ida had been drinking home brew and was not sober. She was similarly under the influence when the present offenses were committed.

I sentenced Ida for the assault upon C.P. in September 1993. At that time officials within the Corrections Branch were unwilling to extend a helping hand to permit a form of sentencing that might have been constructive, a situation that I said was a "shameful mistake."

Mr. Justice David Vickers has recently spoken strongly about the difficulties people with FAS and other handicapped persons encounter in Canada. He says (in the case of Victor Williams) that our model of service delivery is "counter-productive, judgmental and nonsupportive."

One real tragedy of cases like those of Victor Williams and Ida is that nobody made any effort to provide any meaningful help until it was, perhaps, too late. We must all pay a very real price for these and other similar failures, and persons whose handicaps might have been addressed are now stigmatized as criminals.

I do not mean to suggest that Ida should not be held responsible and sentenced for her actions. That is not the law in Canada and she is clearly capable of seriously threatening the safety and well-being of other persons. A judicial response is rightly demanded. But what might be a fair, reasonable, and hopefully constructive response?

When crown counsel spoke to sentence before Mr. Justice Vickers in the case of Victor Williams, he said the court's principal consideration should be general deterrence. And when crown counsel spoke to this case in November 1994, I heard a similar submission. Mr. Justice Vickers rejected this concept in the Williams case, and rightly so. I reject it in the present case. It is, I believe, simply obscene to suggest that a court can properly warn other potential offenders by inflicting a form of punishment upon a handicapped person who has, indeed, committed an offense for which some sanction must follow. That is not justice. That is unthinking retribution. If it were inflicted upon Ida she could not fully comprehend it or possibly learn from it.

I believe that in sentencing Ida I must focus upon two essential needs:

1. It is necessary to provide a measure of protection for other persons.

2. It is necessary to provide a realistic framework for her possible "rehabilitation."

When Ida's trial was completed in Fort Ware on November 3, 1994, the case was adjourned for sentencing in Williams Lake on January 24, 1995. There were three reasons for doing so:

1. An updated pre-sentence report was required.

2. I considered it essential that Ida complete a substance abuse treatment program and that the correctional center program mentioned by the probation officer was the most appropriate in her circumstances.

3. I hoped that during the remand period Ida could be seen and fully assessed by an FAS expert or experts. I said I believed their recommendations would greatly assist any persons who might be tasked with supervising or assisting Ida during the term of a probation order. I now have a report jointly authored by Dr. Christine Loock (a pediatrician and clinical assistant professor at University of British Columbia) and Dr. Julianne Conry (an assistant professor in the Department of Educational Psychology and Special Education at the University of British Columbia). This report contains a wealth of information. It is helpful to me and will, I very much hope, assist those who must help Ida and her children in the future.

The Case Report

Drs. Loock and Conry cannot be absolutely certain in their assessment of Ida. They observed a number of physical characteristics that strongly suggest FAS but these features, which may be very pronounced in childhood, are masked and subtle in adults such as Ida. They observed psychological indicators also, but there are other possible causes of mental handicaps such as Ida's, including events such as head injuries. There is a report that when Ida was a child she was hit on the head with a hammer by an abusive relative. Most important, Drs. Loock and Conry were not able to confirm the various reports that Ida's mother was actively drinking when she was pregnant with Ida. They say that "a definite diagnosis cannot be made without prenatal history and documented maternal drinking." That is a very proper approach for conservative clinicians to take.

But while Drs. Loock and Conry cannot be definitive in stating the cause of Ida's handicaps, FAS is clearly the most likely cause and there is no doubt concerning the nature and extent of her handicaps. The observations of Drs. Loock and Conry are stark. Many of their recommendations are specific and practical. The recommendations, quoted here in their entirety, are:

1. *Medical follow-up.* Follow-up is needed for the following concerns.

> a. Counseling with respect to family planning. Ida is at very high risk for very serious obstetrical complications if she were to become pregnant again, due to her large number of pregnancies in a short period of time. She is at high risk for having more children with FAS. She has apparently expressed the desire to not bear any more children. She would not be able to reliably use methods of birth control that depend on her ability to remember or plan ahead. Consultation with a gynecologist is needed to improve her general state of health.

> b. Ida's children, who are described as being alcohol-affected, should be assessed, tracked, and have access to early intervention as appropriate.

2. *Cognitive limitations.* Ida has a significant mental handicap making her eligible for the benefits available to individuals with disabilities. She is severely limited in her understanding of what is being said to her or asked of her, with the result that her responses do not follow logically. She does not indicate (and maybe she is unaware) when she doesn't understand, but may respond affirmatively with "uh-huh." She has a severe memory deficit, such that basic requirements of day-to-day living must at times be very difficult. Basic academic skills are the end of Grade 1 level.

Treatment and educational programs should be those designed for individuals with mental handicaps. These are characterized by concreteness, simplicity, constant repetition, and supervision.

3. *Alcohol and drug treatment.* Our understanding is that the program Ida is completing at the Burnaby Correctional Centre is only the first step in recovery for Ida. It is imperative that she not return to a drinking environment. (The probation officer's report indicates that the grandparents' home is the center of a great deal of drinking.) She needs continued and intensive treatment. Due to her cognitive limitations, a Native culture/traditions approach may be most beneficial; her partner should attend with her.

4. *Care of her children.* Ida has a better chance of participating in the care of her children if her postpartum health improves and alcohol/drug treatment is successful. In the best of situations, children with FAS are very difficult to parent, but this is made all the more difficult when the mother lacks parenting skills. Ida says she would like a house and her children returned. It is unlikely that Ida could ever, independently, look after the needs of her children, but she should participate in their care. When queried, she said she didn't find it difficult to care for children. By report, it does not appear she has ever had the responsibility of caring for her children. When the children have been in her grandparents' home, others have taken care of their basic needs. Attending a child care program, if designed for her ability level, would not be sufficient, but it would be desirable.

5. *Basic life skills.* The AIMHI program described in the probation officer's report is appropriate (life-skills worker for four hours per day/five days a week) but there needs to be routine to fill the rest of the day. The life-skills worker can assist in putting such a routine in place. The life-skills workers for AIMHI are presumably skilled in teaching individuals with handicaps.

One important life skill is handling money. Living in Fort Ware has not provided Ida with basic learning and experience due to the fact that most purchases are made on a credit basis at the store. Ida does not have the basic computational skills to understand simple transactions. She does have a sense of greater and lesser values of things. For shopping, she could be taught to use a basic list (the same list every time) that will allow her to shop within a budget. Teaching Ida to use a calendar to schedule day-to-day tasks such a shopping and cleaning, and recreational activities, helps organize and fill her day.

The Association for People with Mental Handicaps could be helpful with regard to possible employment and recreational opportunities. Routine and repetitive jobs, such as cleaning, would be suitable. Ida says she likes cleaning. She learns best by being shown, rather than being lectured. Any job would require supervision and reminding with an employer who understands Ida's limitations in language, memory, and basic literacy.

Ida doesn't seem to have a concept of "doing things for fun," but she expressed an interest in sewing and beading. She has taken an interested in Native culture through the Burnaby program and so programs at the Native Friendship Centre would support some of the gains made in Burnaby.

6. *Living arrangements.* The ideal living arrangement, sometimes provided for people with handicaps, would be an apartment complex where she is able to maintain her own suite, but where there is general supervision of the house. This would help control the problem of "friends" coming by late at night pressuring her to party. A curfew would be appropriate for the duration of her probation.

7. *Care of her grandparents.* Ida has a somewhat romanticized view of returning to Fort Ware, which has been her home. Ida insists she needs to be back in Fort Ware in order to look after her grandparents who are "pretty old." She describes them as having physical problems (grandmother's problems with movement in hands/wrists, grandfather's problems in walking/moving about) and she worries that no one is helping them with their day-to-day needs: cutting firewood, washing/cleaning. They don't know how to read

and they can't use the washer/dryer. We understand that the band can provide some homemaker assistance, and so that situation is not as dire as she has convinced herself it is. As guardians of two of Ida's children, it would seem they are more capable than Ida believes. Also, she is unrealistic in her belief that the chief will have a house built for her, if she is there to ask for it. She needs to be told clearly, there is no way.

When Ida is residing in Prince George, regular day-only visits to Fort Ware (as there is no way to provide overnight supervision of drinking) could satisfy her concern and allow the Prince George program to be more successful.

8. *Need for regular assistance.* It is easy to anticipate that Ida could be set up for failure in meeting conditions imposed by the Court unless there is someone to help her meet those conditions— especially those associated with remembering and reporting on a particular schedule. On a very frequent and repetitive basis, she needs to review what she is doing to meet the conditions and why these conditions are imposed. Adults with the limitations of FAS often present as not appreciating the seriousness or the importance of conditions set out for them.

Clearly the prohibitions spelled out in the probation officer's report—especially abstaining from alcohol—are critical. As Ida seems to think that drinking in Fort Ware is less of a problem than drinking in Prince George, she may have a distorted idea that not all alcohol is equally harmful: beer, hard liquor, home brew, Lysol. With regard to all the prohibitions, they need to be spelled out in black and white. A simple message is best: e.g., If you keep drinking you will die.

9. *Comprehending the meaning of violence.* Ida's apparent lack of remorse over the violent incidents, including expecting that her victim would forget about it, is something consistent with what is described for individuals with fetal alcohol syndrome. In this instance, the additional factor is that violence has been a way of life for Ida. She describes how the Burnaby program has included anger management, but this is of minimal benefit when the violent

episodes are associated with drinking. Obviously, the only hope in changing the cycle is successful drug treatment.

The Sentence

The British Columbia Court of Appeal has said many times that persons who hurt other persons with knives or other weapons must anticipate serious jail sentences. Ida has been sentenced before for a violent offense. It would be wrong if she were now sentenced to serve a year or more in jail. That, of course, would very obviously limit her freedoms for a period of time.

I do not intend to send Ida back to jail. Hers is a special case and counsel are agreed that is appropriate today to suspend the passing of sentences and to place Ida on probation for three years. The terms of probation are very specifically intended to create a measure of structure in Ida's life. They limit her freedoms, but much less drastically than jail sentences would. And there is some real reason to hope that the period of probation will be a constructive experience for Ida.

I have very deliberately stated the probation conditions in plain language. I want Ida to understand these conditions when she signs the probation order. The probation conditions are:

1. You must report forthwith to a probation officer in Prince George.

2. You must report to your probation officer every day or faithfully meet with your AiMHi life-skills worker at least five days each week.

3. You must reside at a place in Prince George.

4. You will live at the Phoenix Transition House until Judge Barnett changes this order.

5. You must not drink alcohol. This includes whiskey, wine, beer, and home-brew.

6. You must never go to beer parlors, pubs, or bars.

7. You must never carry a knife.

8. You must not go to Fort Ware unless it is necessary for you to appear in court there, or unless you go to Fort Ware in the morning and leave before it is dark that same day.

9. You must appear in court at Prince George on June 30, 1995, for a review of this order.

When Ida moves from the Phoenix Transition House, it will likely be appropriate to add alcohol counseling and curfew conditions to the probation order.

⤳ EPILOGUE ⤳

At this writing, nearly two years have passed since I wrote the decision in Ida's case. Things have not gone well. Ida very quickly pushed past the abilities and resources of those who were expected to help her. Within a few months she was drinking, fighting, battered, essentially homeless, and pregnant all over again. She gave birth to another afflicted child in November 1995. She failed to attend a treatment center as she had promised and was required to do in January 1996. She also failed to attend court, and her frustrated probation officer lost all contact with Ida after December 1995. At least for now it seems that Ida is, quite literally, a lost soul.

The developments in Ida's case have been discouraging. But one needs always to search for the silver lining, and some other things happened following the decision in Ida's case:

The principal of the school in Fort Ware used the decision as a key element in his successful campaign to persuade the Department of Indian Affairs to fund the purchase of computers for the school. I am told that many special needs children who were previously almost hopeless as students are now making truly remarkable progress.

I am told that my decision in Ida's case has been cited to judges in distant places and that it has helped them search and push for creative solutions.

The decisions in the cases of Victor Williams and Ida Abou received significant media attention in British Columbia and that was a real factor in persuading our judicial education committee that more judges needed to learn about FAS/E. In the spring of 1996 Dr. Diane Rothon made a seminar presentation to all the judges of the Provincial Court of British Columbia, and she was exceptionally well received. To my knowledge, her presentation was a Canadian first.

Ida's children were all assessed. They are now all in permanent care and hopefully, their futures will be at least a little brighter.

The path was made a little less rocky for Robert, who appeared before me in the fall of 1995. He was 15 and had already incurred the wrath of quite a few judges, probation officers, and social workers because he steals, had failed to obey probation orders, and appeared very defiant, even in court. I was urged to "lock him up" and thus "teach him a lesson." I read his doctor's FAS assessment and I read my own decision in Ida's case again and I said "no." I insisted that everybody try harder and suggested that I favored the notion of Robert attending a specialized treatment center in Alberta, something I was told was "impossible." When I refused to accept that answer, things began to happen and funding was somehow found. Robert did go to the treatment center and it was a very positive experience for him.

There are lessons for all of us in these stories. I am reminded of events that surrounded the making of Robert Flaherty's 1922 classic documentary, *Nanook of the North*. An earlier version had been destroyed and Flaherty himself was badly burned when, while smoking, he accidentally lit the highly inflammable celluloid film on fire. Flaherty's reaction to this disaster was a determination to return to the Arctic and to make a film of Eskimo life "that people will never forget." And he succeeded.

Appendix Two:
Resources

GAIL S. AND DAVID A. HALES

Gail S. Hales is coordinator of FAS consulting and training with HCI Associates, Sandy, Utah.

David A. Hales is professor emeritus of Library Science, University of Alaska Fairbanks, and director of the library at Westminster College of Salt Lake City, Utah.

IN THE FEW YEARS SINCE PUBLICATION OF *FANTASTIC ANTONE SUCCEEDS*, the volume of materials relating to FAS/E has greatly multiplied. New organizations, family support structures, educational accommodations, research findings, networking capabilities, training programs, multimedia presentations, public policy proclamations, even new terminology have emerged. Numerous handbooks, guidebooks, guidelines, resource guides, manuals, assessment tools, strategic plans, newsletters, and fact sheets are available.

The purpose of this selected resource list is to aid parents and professionals in finding materials specific to adolescents and adults with fetal alcohol syndrome or fetal alcohol effects. This list emphasizes practical information for parents and professionals and is organized by the following categories: newsletters, organizations, books, articles, videos, FAS Sites on the World Wide Web, and databases.

NEWSLETTERS

About FAS/E

Available from the FAS/E Support Group of B.C., 151-10090 152 Street, Suite 187, Surrey, BC, Canada V3R 8X8. Telephone: (604) 589-1854. Subscription: $30.00.

This newsletter, published quarterly, includes information about conferences, workshops, and resources. It also includes a variety of articles. For example, the spring 1999 issue contains the following articles: "Binge Drinking During Pregnancy: Who Are the Women at Risk?" "Janet's Story," written by a recovering alcoholic, "Pregnant Women Told Wine is Worse than Cigarettes," and "Reflections from Becky," written by a teenager with FAS/E. The editors write, "We endeavor to inform, in the belief that everyone has the right to information. We try to promote and generate open, frank discussion." Others are encouraged to write letters to the editor and to submit articles to be considered for publication.

Action News: Official Newsletter of the Canadian Centre on Substance Abuse

Available from 75 Alberta Street, Suite 300, Ottawa, ON, Canada K1P 5E7. Telephone: (613) 235-4048. Fax: (613) 235-8101. Subscription: Access is through the website, URL: http://www.ccsa.ca/aneng.htm. You can receive this newsletter electronically by sending your e-mail address to rgarlick@ccsa.ca.

This newsletter is devoted to all aspects of substance abuse. Articles specific to FAS/E are included in some issues.

Clean Water

Richard and Kelly Wicklund, editors. Clean Water International 9077-161st St. W. Lakeville, MN 55044.
URL: http://www.shadeslanding.com/clean-water/news.html
Subscription: Free.

This newsletter, available in hard copy and on the World Wide Web, focuses on disseminating basic information about FAS/E in general. The editors are attempting to reach an international audience.

FANN (Fetal Alcohol Network Newsletter)

Hank and Linda Will, editors. Available from Fetal Alcohol Network, 158 Rosemont Ave., Coatesville, PA 19320-3727. Telephone: (610) 384-1133. Subscription: Free. Contributions welcome.

This newsletter focuses on disseminating information and support to parents and caretakers of individuals with FAS/E. Articles are well written, clear, and concise. It includes information about conferences, workshops, organizations, support groups, and resources.

F.A.S. Times

Jocie DeVries, editor. Available from FAS/Family Resource Institute Newsletter, P.O. Box 2525, Lynnwood, WA 98036. Telephone: (253) 531-2878. Subscription: $15 Family, $25 Professional.

Advocacy, support services, and information for individuals, families, and professionals is the major focus of this excellent publication. From early beginnings as the FAS Adolescent Task Force in Washington State, this group of creative, highly-trained, insightful professionals (who once claimed to be "just concerned parents") have created a structure of services and service delivery worthy of duplication throughout the United States, Canada, and beyond. Although much of the information on FAS/FRI's variety of activities and educational endeavors is focused on activities in and around the state of Washington, the newsletter also provides helpful general information on national and international conferences and resources.

FEN Pen

Georgiana Wilton, editor. Available from Family Empowerment Network, University of Wisconsin-Madison, 5221 Lowell Hall, 610 Langdon St., Madison, WI 53703-1195. Telephone: 1-800-462-5254. Subscription: $5 Family, $10 Professional.

From the original summer 1993 issue, FEN Pen has provided an excellent resource for families. Its main objective is and has always been "to provide families with a vehicle for networking, support and receiving information on relevant topics." Information on upcoming conferences, public policy issues, and available resources covers both the U.S. and Canada. Although much of the information understandably relates to the Midwest, *FEN Pen* was designed to have broad international appeal and not to focus only on regional issues.

Growing With FAS

Pamela Groves, editor. Available from 7802 SE Taylor, Portland, OR 97215. Telephone: (503) 254-8129. Subscription: $2.00 for a sample copy. Contact the editor for current rates.

This enduring newsletter provides information for families and care providers of people experiencing FAS/E. It includes helpful information on advocacy, family support, research findings, and resources. Readers are encouraged to submit letters, articles, or questions.

Iceberg

Janice Wilson, editor. Fetal Alcohol Syndrome Information Service (FASIS), P.O. Box 95597, Seattle, WA 98145-2597. Subscription: $12 Family, $25 Professional.

Iceberg describes itself as "An educational newsletter for people concerned about fetal alcohol syndrome (FAS) and fetal alcohol effects (FAE), because the problems we see are only the tip of the iceberg." This excellent quarterly publication is one of the oldest, most widely circulated, and most respected of all the FAS newsletters. Feature articles, written by professionals and parents, are usually timely and well documented. The Parent's Corner column provides a vehicle for family support issues. A listing of the FASIS Board of Directors reads like Who's Who in FAS identification, research, education, and advocacy. Reprints of articles from previous issues are available for the nominal cost of $1.00 each. Some materials may be available elsewhere but *Iceberg* articles are concise, easy to use, and easy to understand.

Reprints from issues of *Iceberg* specifically relating to adolescents and adults with FAS:

• "An Adult Has Been Diagnosed as FAS or FAE - Now What?" by Diane Davis

• "Fetal Alcohol Syndrome: A Letter from a 16 Year Old," by Sydney Helbock

• "Fetal Alcohol Syndrome in Adolescents and Adults: First Major Study of Long-Term Consequences," by Ann Streissguth

• "The FAS Adolescent Task Force: An Army of Velveteen Rabbits," by Jocie DeVries

• "Gratitude and Grief—Coping with a Teenage Son with FAS/FAE," by Sherry Jo Roth

Lifeline: A Newsletter for Parents/Caregivers of Children with Fetal Alcohol Syndrome/Effects

Available from Fetal Alcohol Assessment and Treatment Program, St. Catherine's Center for Children, 40 North Main Avenue, Albany, NY 12203-1425. Telephone: (518) 463-3730. Fax: (518) 463-3750. Subscription: Free.

Helpful information on specific topics such as impulse control, ear infections, and making transitions, among others, is available through this site.

Manitoba F.A.S. News

Available from Coalition on Alcohol and Pregnancy, c/o Association for Community Living Manitoba, 210-500 Portage Avenue, Winnipeg, MB, Canada R3C 3X1. Telephone: (204) 786-9850. Fax: (204) 789-9850. URL: http://www.ccsa.ca/fasnews/html. Subscription: $15.00, payable to Association for Community Living Manitoba

A noticeably higher proportion of prevention information sets this newsletter apart from most of the others mentioned here. Family support issues, upcoming conferences, and selected resources are also highlighted.

Notes From NOFAS

Available from National Organization on Fetal Alcohol Syndrome, 216 G Street NE, Washington, DC 20002. Telephone: (202) 466-6456 or 1-800-66-NOFAS (1-800-666-6327). Fax: (301) 468-6433. E-mail: nofas@erols.com. Subscription: Free.

The information in this publication includes coverage of what activities legislators in Washington, D.C., and other supporters are doing to promote FAS prevention and intervention issues on a national level. It also includes public policy updates and resource information.

ORGANIZATIONS

The Arc of the United States

Address: 1010 Wayne Avenue, Suite 650, Silver Spring, MD 20910. Telephone: (301) 565-3842. Fax: (301) 565-3843. E-mail: Info@thearc.org. URL: http://www.thearc.org.

The Arc is a national, nonprofit organization with local chapters throughout the country. Goals include improving quality of life for retarded persons as well as encouraging research and education to prevent mental retardation.

Arium Foundation, Inc.

Address: 17A-218 Silvercreek Parkway North, Suite 318, Guelph, ON, Canada N1H 8E8. Telephone: (519) 837-1124. E-mail: fetal@hotmail.com. URL: www.arium.org.

Arium is a nonprofit organization dedicated to the prevention of addictions and their effects upon individuals through the provision of resources, information, and research. The website offers articles, personal experiences, FAS resources, and interactive discussion forums.

Clean Water International

Address: 9077-161st St. W., Lakeville, MN 55044
E-mail: wicklund@tc.umn.edu

URL: http: //www.shadeslanding.com.clean-water

Clean Water International is a nonprofit organization dedicated to protecting the environment in which the human fetus grows. This international organization was founded by Richard and Kelly Wicklund. Membership is free and registered members receive a pin, a certificate, and the quarterly newsletter. The website provides some basic information about FAS/E, a full text of the newsletter, and access to an idea book where individuals can share experiences, express concerns, and request information.

Family Empowerment Network (FEN)

Address: University of Wisconsin-Madison, 610 Langdon St., Room 519, Madison, WI 53703. Telephone: (800) 462-5254 or (608) 262-6590. Fax: (608) 265-2329.
E-mail: fen@mail.dcs.wisc.edu

From its very beginnings, FEN has been an impressive national resource for parents and professionals caring for people experiencing FAS/E. In addition to the *FEN Pen* newsletter, FEN also sponsors an annual conference, the Educational Teleconference Series, a FAS resource file for every state in the United States, a video-lending library, great networking opportunities, and much more.

FAS/E Support Network of B.C.

Address: 151-10090 152 Street, Suite 187, Surrey, BC, Canada V3R 8X8. Telephone: (604) 589-1854. Fax: (604) 589-8438. E-mail: fasnet@istar.ca.

This organization provides information, support, and services for families, professionals, and the broader community. It highlights prevention, intervention, and treatment issues pertaining to alcohol related birth defects, including FAS/E and other disabilities caused by drug use during pregnancy. FAS/E Support Network provides training programs and a 24-hour warm line. It researches, designs, and develops resource materials, workshops, and participates in public awareness campaigns.

Fetal Alcohol Assessment and Treatment Program

Address: St. Catherine's Center for Children, 40 North Main Avenue, Albany, NY 12203-1425. Telephone: (518) 463-3730. Fax: (518) 463-3750. E-mail: fetalalcohol@st-cath.org. URL: http://www.st-cath.org/fetalalcohol.htm

The Fetal Alcohol Assessment and Treatment Program, in collaboration with Center Health Care, provides comprehensive assessment and treatment services to children and families affected by fetal alcohol and drug exposure. The program aims to provide families with a comprehensive array of services, support, and education to assist in meeting the multiple needs of their children, with or without FAS/E, so all can reach their greatest potential. The official newsletter is called *Lifeline*.

Fetal Alcohol and Drug Unit

Address: Department of Psychiatry and Behavioral Sciences, University of Washington School of Medicine, 180 Nickerson, Suite 309, Seattle, WA 98109. Telephone: (206) 543-7155. Fax: (206) 685-2903. URL: http://dept3.washington.edu/fadu

Much of the information currently available on FAS/E was gleaned from data collected by this research group. Workshops, training, and lectures are offered on a limited basis. Articles, resource lists, and FAS/E information packets are also available. This web page provides links to many resources.

Fetal Alcohol Network International

Address: 158 Rosemont Ave., Coatesville, PA 19320-3727. Telephone: (610) 384-1133.

Hank and Linda Will are the founders and driving forces behind this nonprofit parent group, established to provide support and information to parents coping with FAS/E. Their newsletter, *Fetal Alcohol Network News*, is described in the "Newsletters" section of this resource list.

Fetal Alcohol Syndrome Consultation, Education, and Training Services, Inc.

URL: http://www.fascets.org/

This organization is dedicated to prevention of FAS/E, Alcohol-Related Neurodevelopmental Disorders (ARND), and other birth defects resulting from prenatal alcohol and other drug exposure. Programs and services are designed to meet the needs of this high risk population and facilitate realization of their full developmental potential.

Fetal Alcohol Syndrome Family Resource Institute (FAS/FRI)

Address: P.O. Box 2525, Lynnwood, WA 98036
Telephone: (253) 531-2878 or in Washington, (800) 999-3429
E-mail: delindam@accessone.com
URL: http://www.accessone.com/~delindam

Formerly known as the FAS Adolescent Task Force, FAS/FRI provides advocacy, support, prevention, and educational services for teens, parents, and professionals. In addition to the *FAS Times* newsletter, the group provides a "Warm Line" for birth parents, offers training workshops and curricula, develops information packets, organizes local support groups, and willingly shares ideas to assist formation and development of other FAS advocacy and support programs throughout the country.

Fetal Alcohol Syndrome Clinic

Address: University of Washington, Child Development and Mental Retardation Center, Children's Hospital and Medical Center, 4800 Sand Point Way NE, P.O. Box C-5371, Seattle, WA 98105. Telephone: (206) 526-2522.

A multidisciplinary team of pediatricians, a dysmorphologist, a geneticist, educational and clinical psychologists, a family therapist, a communication specialist, a social worker, and a public health nurse provide diagnostic, evaluative, and referral services to people experiencing prenatal alcohol exposure. The clinic convenes weekly. Appointments and fees are required, but ability to pay is not an absolute prerequisite for services.

National Clearinghouse for Alcohol and Drug Information (NCADI)

Address: P.O. Box 2345, Rockville, MD 20847-2345. Telephone: 1-800-729-6686 or 1-877-767-8432 (Spanish). Fax: (301) 468-6433. E-mail: info@health.org URL: http://www.health.org

NCADI distributes information nationwide on prevention, intervention, and treatment of substance abuse. Staff also produce and distribute information on specific issues such as FAS/E. The website is current and provides access to a wide variety of materials including databases and the full text of articles. Assistance in Spanish is also available.

National Organization on Fetal Alcohol Syndrome (NOFAS)

Address: 216 G Street Northeast, Washington, DC 20002. Telephone: (202) 785-4585. Fax: (202) 466-6456. E-mail: nofas@erols.com. URL: http://www.nofas.org

The goals of NOFAS are to raise public awareness of FAS/E, to implement prevention and intervention strategies, and to influence public policy decisions. In addition to an annual conference and a quarterly newsletter, *Notes from NOFAS*, NOFAS also sponsors books, posters, videos, public service announcements, T-shirts, and bumper stickers.

BOOKS

ABCs of Fetal Alcohol Syndrome/Effect: A Handbook For Middle-Junior-Senior High School Teachers

Authors: Jerry Chavez and Elizabeth Chavez. Published and distributed by the National Organization on Fetal Alcohol Syndrome, 1996. Address: 216 G Street, NE, Washington, DC 20002. Telephone: (800) 666-6327 or (202) 785-4585. Cost: $3.95

This informative booklet includes basic information on characteristics and behaviors of affected individuals. Designed for educators by educators, it presents helpful strategies for working with adolescents and teens in the classroom, including behavior management techniques and life skills development.

The Art of Making a Difference

Published and distributed by: FAS/E Support Network of B.C., 1997. Address: #151—10090 152 St., Suite 187, Surrey, BC, Canada V3R 8X8. Telephone: (604) 589-1854. Fax: (604) 589-8438. E-mail: fasnet@istar.ca

This book provides essential information to parents on what they need to know about working with school systems in general: how to get what they need for their children, how to understand and interpret psychological/educational tests that should be administered to children with FAS/E.

Assessment and Resource Guide for FAS/E

Authors: Mary Wegmann, Linda Colfax, and Mark Gray, and Barbara Reed. Published and distributed by Pen Print Inc., 1995. Address: 230A East First, Port Angeles, WA 98362. Telephone: (360) 457-3404. Fax: (360) 457-6958. Cost: $15.47

This helpful booklet was designed to assist professionals and lay persons working with persons affected by prenatal alcohol exposure. It is in no way intended to be a diagnostic tool for FAS/E. The authors state their intent "is to share condensed and compiled information from many excellent resources." Significant sections on diagnostic procedures for adolescents and adults as well as psychological and behavioral issues of adolescence and adulthood provide clear, concise resources for families and professionals.

The Challenge of Fetal Alcohol Syndrome—Overcoming Secondary Disabilities

Edited by: Ann P. Streissguth, Ann and Jonathan Kanter
Published and distributed by University of Washington Press, 1997. Address: P.O. Box 50096, Seattle, WA 98145-5096. Telephone: (800) 441-4115. Fax: (800) 669-7993. Cost: $17.95

This volume is the result of a four-year study, funded by the Centers for Disease Control and Prevention, that followed

473 clients ranging from age 3 to age 51, documenting the impact of FAS/E throughout the lifespan. Dr. Streissguth, the principal investigator, and her team of associates identified some of the most significant secondary disabilities experienced by people with FAS/E. They assembled practical solutions and management strategies for dealing with them, including advice by experts from such diverse fields as education, human services, and criminal justice. The book provides a valuable resource for families and professionals working with people experiencing FAS/E.

"Clinical considerations pertaining to adolescents and adults with fetal alcohol syndrome." (Chapter 4 from T. B. Sonderegger, ed., *Perinatal Substance Abuse: Research Findings and Clinical Implications,* pages 104–131)

Authors: R. A. LaDue, A. P. Streissguth, and S. P. Randels. Published and distributed by The Johns Hopkins University Press, 1992. Address: 2715 N. Charles Street, Baltimore, MD 21218-4319. Telephone: (410) 516-6900 or (800) 537-5487. Cost: $95.00 (for the book).

Information for this publication was based on findings from a study of 61 adolescents and adults to determine long-term effects of FAS.

Dear World—We Have Fetal Alcohol Syndrome: Experiences of Young Adults.
Published and distributed by FAS/E Support Network of B.C., 1999. Address: 151-10090 152 Street, Suite 187, Surrey, BC, Canada V3R 8X8. Telephone: (604) 589-1854. Fax: (604) 589-8438. E-mail: fasnet@istar.ca. Cost: $10.00.

This book was written with the help of a group of young people with FAS/E. It is meant to be a guide to help other young peple with FAS/E understand what fetal alcohol syndrome is and what it means to them.

A Family Handbook on Future Planning
Published by The Arc of the United States, 1991. Address: 1010 Wayne Avenue., Suite 650, Silver Spring, MD 20910. Telephone: (301) 565-3842. Cost: $16.61 (order #10-2)

This handbook by The Arc (formerly known as the Association for Retarded Citizens) is designed to aid parents in understanding and organizing a future plan for a son or daughter with mental retardation. Helpful information on wills, government benefits, support services, financial arrangements, guardianship, and working with an attorney are some of the areas covered. Includes forms, checklists, outlines, and completed examples to assist parents in organizing an estate to help meet the long-term needs of a child.

A very helpful and comprehensive list of future planning resources compiled by The Arc is also available from the address listed above.

FAS/E and Education: The Art of Making a Difference

Published and distributed by FAS/E Support Network of B.C., 1997. Address: 151-10090 152 Street, Suite 187, Surrey, BC, Canada V3R 8X8. Telephone: (604) 589-1854. Fax: (604) 589-8438. E-mail: fasnet@istar.ca. Cost: $15.00.

This is a parent's handbook that provides information about what parents need to know to advocate within the education system. It is helpful for parents with children at all levels including the middle and upper grades.

FASNET Assessment Tool—For Use With Children Aged 14–18 Years; and FASNET Assessment Tool—For Use With Adults (19 Years of Age and Up)

Published and distributed by FAS/E Support Network, 1995. Address: 151-10090 152 Street, Suite 187, Surrey, BC, Canada V3R 8X8. Telephone: (604) 589-1854. Fax: (604) 589-8438. E-mail: fasnet@istar.ca. Cost: $8.50

Two of a series of six assessment tools developed by the FAS/E Support Network, these booklets were designed for both parents and professionals. This series of assessment tools is not intended to be used to make an FAS diagnosis. Such a diagnosis requires an extensive medical evaluation. These assessment tools are intended to be used by nonmedical professionals and parents to identify individuals who may be at risk for experiencing FAS/E. Information is intended to indicate whether or not a person should have further evaluation by a medical professional with specific training to diagnose FAS/E. *FASNET* has developed very helpful, user-friendly materials.

Fantastic Antone Succeeds! Experiences in Educating Children with Fetal Alcohol Syndrome

Edited by: Judith Kleinfeld and Siobhan Wescott. Published and distributed by University of Alaska Press, 1993. Address: P.O. Box 756240, Fairbanks, AK 99775-6240. Telephone: (907) 474-5831; toll free in U.S. (888) 252-6657. Cost: $20

This groundbreaking work, based on the concept of parents as researchers, includes numerous selections from parents and professionals who provide practical solutions for education and effective parenting. Stories highlight school-age children and young adults who are achieving varying degrees of success through appropriate and effective strategies by families, experts, and educators. The book provides lists of important resources, organizations to contact, and descriptions of effective classroom practices for teachers.

Fetal Alcohol Syndrome: A Guide for Families and Communities

Author: Ann P. Streissguth. Published and distributed by Paul H. Brookes Publishing Co., 1997. Address: P.O. Box 10624, Baltimore, MD 21285-0624. Cost: $22.95

This is an excellent resource work covering the spectrum of FAS knowledge from causes, impact, and advocacy, to prevention, services, and public policy. Several chapters deal directly with adolescent and adult issues.

Recognizing and Managing Children With Fetal Alcohol Syndrome: A Guidebook

Author: Brenda McCreight. Published and distributed by Child Welfare League of America Press, 1997. Address: CWLA, P.O. Box 7816, Edison, NJ 05818-7816. Telephone: (800) 407-6273. Fax: (905) 417-0482. Cost: $16.95

This publication includes development and management information spanning the stages from infancy through late adolescence. Because adolescents experiencing FAS/E confront and present enormous challenges, management strategies can and do improve the quality of life for individuals and their families.

A Manual on Adolescents and Adults with Fetal Alcohol Syndrome with Special Reference to American Indians (2nd ed.)

Authors: A. P. Streissguth, R. A. LaDue, and S. P. A. Randels. Published and distributed by the Indian Health Service, 1989. Address: Indian Health Services, FAS Project, 5300 Homestead Rd., NE, Albuquerque, NM 87110. Telephone (505) 837-4228. Cost: Free.

This work includes general FAS/E information, presents research findings, and makes recommendations for helping Native American adolescents and adults with FAS/E. Illustrations, graphs, photographs, and a bibliography are included.

Reaching Out to Children with FAS/FAE: A Handbook for Teachers, Counselors, and Parents Who Work with Children Affected by Fetal Alcohol Syndrome and Fetal Alcohol Effects

Author: Diane Davis. Published by: Center for Applied Research in Education (West Nyack, NY), 1994. Distributed by: Prentice Hall, P.O. Box 11071, Des Moines, IA 50336. Telephone: (800) 288-4745. Cost: $30

Davis suggests numerous successful strategies for families and therapists working with adolescents and adults experiencing FAS/E. The book is well organized, easy to use, and filled with practical suggestions Davis has developed over many years of working with individuals, families, and service providers.

ARTICLES

"Fetal Alcohol Syndrome in Adolescents and Adults"

Authors: A. P. Streissguth, J. M. Aase, S. K. Clarren, S. P. Randels, R. A. LaDue, and D. F. Smith. Published by: *Journal of the American Medical Association*, Vol. 265, No. 15 (April 17, 1991): pages 1961–1967.

This study of 61 adolescents and adults diagnosed with FAS found characteristic facial malformations grew less distinctive after puberty. Growth deficiency was still evident in head circumference and height but weight deficiency was less significant. Central nervous system damage was most evident in academic functioning and in maladaptive behaviors such as poor judgment, distractibility, and inability to perceive social cues. The study concludes FAS has predictable, long-term effects extending into adulthood.

"Indian adolescents and adults with fetal alcohol syndrome: Findings and recommendations."

Authors: A. P. Streissguth, R. A. LaDue, and S. P. Randels.
Published by: *The IHC Primary Care Provider*, Vol. 12, 1988, pages 89–91.

This publication reports on the research findings used in the compilation of *A Manual on Adolescents and Adults with Fetal Alcohol Syndrome with Special Reference to American Indians*, cited earlier.

VIDEOS

David with F.A.S.: A Story of Fetal Alcohol Syndrome

Length: 44 ½ minutes. Produced by Kanata Productions, 1996. Distributed by: (in Canada) National Film Board of Canada; (in the U.S.) Films for Humanities and Sciences. Telephone: Canada: (800) 267-7710; U.S. (609) 275-1400. Cost: $129 (U.S.).

David Vandenbrink is 21 years old. He experiences permanent brain damage due to FAS, but his condition was not diagnosed until he was 18. His misunderstood behavior and the devastating impact it has had for him and his adoptive family is a story repeated time and time again in families living with FAS/E.

Fetal Alcohol Syndrome: Adolescence and the Future

Length: 22 minutes. Produced by: Visions Video/Altschul Group, 1992. Distributed by: Altschul Group, 1560 Sherman Ave., Suite 100, Evanston, IL 60201. Telephone: (800) 323-9084. Cost: $345.

The advantages of a sheltered environment for some individuals affected by FAS/E are explored in this video spotlighting a 13-year-old youth and a 22-year-old adult and their families. The film promotes the importance of community-based programs emphasizing job skills and independent living skills to instill a sense of positive self-esteem and self-confidence.

Fetal Alcohol Syndrome and Effect: Stories of Help and Hope

Length: 45 minutes. Produced and distributed by Hazelden, 1993. Address: P.O. Box 176, 15251 Pleasant Valley Rd., Center City, MN 55012. Telephone: (800) 328-9000. Cost: $225.

Articulate young people, their families, and professionals share insight about the day to day struggle of coping with FAS/E. Effective intervention strategies are outlined. Format of this video is extremely flexible for presenters as well as informative for all audiences.

Influences: Innocence Betrayed—The Long-Term Effects of Prenatal Substance Exposure

Length: 24 minutes. Produced and distributed by: Pyramid Film and Video, 1992. Address: P.O. Box 1048, Santa Monica CA 90406. Telephone: (800) 421-2304. Cost: $295.

This presentation of case studies, which include adolescents and young adults experiencing the affects of prenatal substance exposure, describes the learning and behavior problems and poor socialization skills characteristic of affected individuals. As a result of such challenges, they are at high risk for criminal behavior, victimization, substance abuse, and much more. A discussion guide is included.

Training tapes for living with FAS/E: Independence, ages 12 to adult

Length: 32 minutes. Produced by: Visions Video/Altschul Group, 1992. Distributed by: Altschul Group, 1560 Sherman Ave., Suite 100, Evanston, IL 60201. Telephone: (800) 323-9084. Cost: $249.

Strategies to help adolescents and adults with FAS/E develop social and adaptive living skills are presented in clear, easy-to-follow steps. The importance of early diagnosis and intervention for best outcomes is discussed.

FAS/E Sites on the World Wide Web

The World Wide Web provides an easy way to update and distribute new information about FAS/E. Listserve and e-mail services tied to websites allow users to download information and communicate with others interested in FAS/E issues. Most sites listed here are compiled by organizations and individuals knowledgeable about FAS/E.

Sites vary in the amount and timeliness of information provided. Look at the end of the site for the compiler's name and for the date when the information was last revised. Most information is general enough to be helpful for everyone, although some material may be duplicated elsewhere or may include meeting notices or seminar information specific only to a geographic region.

Information about FAS/E can be found by doing a word search when an exact URL (Uniform Resource Locator) is not known. Users need to remember the various search engines don't always contain all the websites on a subject. When searching by subject, the user needs to search various search engines in order to find the available sites on the subject. Websites come and go depending on funding and many other factors.

If a URL address is known, be sure to use upper and lower case as given; URLs are case sensitive.

Another helpful source of information on the World Wide Web is Nancy White's article, "Finding a Wealth of FAS-Related Information on the Internet," *Iceberg*, Vol. 9 (December 1999), pages 4–5.

Alcohol Related Birth Defects

URL: http://www.worldprofit.com/mafas.htm

This site contains some excellent information about FAS/E although the information provided is not as extensive as that found on some of the other sites. Included is excellent information for individuals or groups seeking involvement with advocacy issues. Information about additional sites, links to other sites, and educational opportunities is included.

The Arc's FAS Resource and Materials Guide

URL: http://the arc.org/misc/faslist.html
E-mail: the arch@metronet.com

This is one of the most comprehensive sources of information about FAS/E available on the World Wide Web. The site includes detailed and comprehensive information about FAS/E. The development of the available material was made possible by a grant to The Arc from the Center for Disease Control and Prevention. Information is divided into major subject headings—Medical Overview Materials, FAS Overview Materials, Prevention Campaign Materials, Families With FAS Child Materials, Instructional Materials, Funding Resources, and Other Resources (a list of national organizations and agencies along with their mailing addresses and telephone numbers).

Included is an extensive listing of FAS/E sources arranged under broad subject headings. A description of the source, cost, and ordering information. Dozens of links to important sites are also provided. The Arc's Discussion Board is also a valuable resource for communicating with others regarding all aspects of FAS/E.

Arium

URL: http://www.arium.org/fas.html

This is an excellent website. The major sections include "An Anthology of FAS Resources," "FAS Links," "FAS Poster Gallery," "FAS Discussion Forums," "FAS Authors," "FAS Terms," and much more.

Canadian Centre On Substance Abuse

URL: http://www.ccsa.ca/fasgen.htm

This is another source of detailed information about FAS/E. This site provides the full text to the newsletter, *Action News: Official Newsletter of the Canadian Centre on Substance Abuse.* The newsletter is also available in French. Information is available on their FAS listserve (FAS forum conducted via e-mail). Also included is information about upcoming seminars and conferences, publications, and other resources. While the general information is helpful to everyone interested in the subject, most of the announcements regarding seminars, conferences, etc., are about activities in Canada. The listserve is especially helpful for communicating and sharing with others about various FAS/E issue and concerns.

Clean Water

URL: http://www.shadeslanding.com/clean-water/about.html
E-mail: wick1004@umn.edu

This provides some general information about FAS/E. It also includes the full text of their newsletter, *Clean Water*, and e-mail access to an idea book where individuals can share, express concerns, and request information about FAS/E.

Colorado FAS/ATOD Prevention Program

URL: http://www.hsc.colorado.edu/ahec/fas/index.htm
Address: Mail Stop F433, P.O. Box 6508, Aurora, CO 80045-0508. Telephone: (303) 724-0330. Fax: (303) 724-0891. E-mail: Sean.Clark@UCHSC.edu

This site was established by the Fetal Alcohol Syndrome/Alcohol Tobacco and Other Drug Prevention Outreach Project in Colorado in conjunction with the Colorado Area Health Education Center. It is a collaborative effort involving numerous community sectors and health, education, social service, law enforcement and community groups. The major sections within the site are: "Facts About FAS," "FAS Guides," "Web Resources," and "Training and Events." A wealth of information about FAS/E is available here and is useful to everyone interested in the subject. The training and events relate to activities and programs in Colorado.

Creative Consultants, Inc.

URL: http://members.aol.com/creaconinc
Address: P.O. Box 6028, Laramie, WY 82073. Telephone: (307) 745-3435. Fax: (307) 745-3415. E-mail: CreaConInc@aol.com.

Creative Consultants, Inc., specializes in the education of children who were prenatally exposed to alcohol and other teratogenic drugs, especially children affected by FAS/E. The organization is owned and managed by Cheryl A. Schroeder, Ed.D.

The website includes extensive information about FAS/E. Users can select from the following areas: "What Everyone Needs to Know About Pregnancy and Health," "Learn About FAS/E in our Brief Overview of FAS/E," "Find Aids to Help you Teach About FAS/E in our Product Guide," "Obtain Professional Consulting on FAS/E," and "Link to Other FAS/E Web Sites."

Family Village

URL: http://www.familyvillage.wis.edu/lib_fas.htm
E-mail: rowley@wasiman.wis.edu

Family Village is a global community from the Waisman Center, University of Wisconsin-Madison, that integrates information, resources and communication opportunities on the Internet regarding mental retardation, including FAS.

Fetal Alcohol Syndrome Resource Center

URL: http://www.azstarnet.com/~tkj/fashome.htm

This is an extraordinary website. In addition to general, more commonly found information, the site includes posters, brochures, handouts, award-winning newspaper reprints, pictures and stories of families living with FAS/E, links for sending messages to your congressmen, information about legislation related to FAS/E, and much more.

Fetal Alcohol Syndrome/Effects

URL: http://www.taconic.net/seminars/fas01.html
E-mail: swks@taconic.net

This is another outstanding website that provides comprehensive information about FAS/E compiled by Kathryn Shea, a certified social worker. She has had over 20 years of experience working with children with special needs. The resource information is located under the following subject headings: "Facts About FAS/E," "Treatment of Children with FAS/E," "Educating Children with FAS/E," "Parenting Children with FAS/E," and "More Information on FAS/E." A link to "Parenting Tips" from the St. Catherine's Center for Children is also provided.

Fetal Alcohol Syndrome Family Resource Institute

URL: http://www.accessone.com/~delindam/
Address: FAS Family Resource Institute, P.O. Box 2525, Lynnwood, WA 98036. E-mail: delindam@accessone.com.

This site is made available by the FAS Family Resource Institute, a nonprofit corporation. Their mission is to identify, understand and care for individuals disabled by prenatal alcohol exposure, and to protect future generations with this disability.

The site is divided into four major sections: "Services," "Membership," "Free Materials to Order," and "Behavioral Symptoms of Adolescents with FAS/E." Much of the information concerns the organization, the services they offer, and how to contact them for further information.

Fetal Alcohol Support Network

URL: http://netaccess.on.ca/~photobyt/fas/fasmenu.html

This is a nonprofit Canadian site which include approximately a dozen lengthy articles about FAS/E along with the citations and abstracts to an additional 250 articles about the subject. Easy access to other websites is also provided.

Fetal Alcohol Syndrome/Effects Information Homepage

URL: http://members.aol.com/jshawdna/fashome.htm
E-mail: shammer@initco.net

The website is provided by the Department of Medical Genetics, Shodair Hospital, Montana. It includes a fact sheet about FAS/E, a diagram of possible facial characteristics, resource materials, common cycles of individuals with FAS/E, and the full text of *FACETS*, a newsletter. A listing and links to other sources of information regarding FAS/E and substance abuse available on the World Wide Web are also included.

La bebida y su embarazo

URL: http://members/tripod.com/~sober joe/ embarazoniaa.htm

This site provides information about FAS/E in Spanish.

National Organization On Fetal Alcohol Syndrome

E-mail: nofas@erols.com. URL: http://www.nofas.org/

This is one of the most comprehensive and up-to-date sites available. The major sections are: "What is Fetal Alcohol Syndrome?" "What is NOFAS?" "NOFAS Strategies for Working with FAS Children," "NOFAS Medical School Curriculum," "FAS Resources," and "Talk to NOFAS."

Ratgeber zur Alkoholembryopathie: Alkoholschaden bei Kindern

URL: http://www.uni-essen.de/~ibp010/alkemb/

This site provides information about FAS/E in German.

SAF/EAF

URL: http://www3.sympatico.ca/fio.steve/saf.htm

This site provides information about FAS/E in French.

SAFERA

URL: http://www.safera.qc.ca/

This Canadian site provides information about FAS/E in French.

DATABASES

The following databases provide up-to-date access to the body of literature available regarding FAS/E:

CANBASE

Contact: Canadian Centre on Substance Abuse, Nation Clearinghouse, 75 Albert St., Suite 300, Ottawa, ON Canada K1P 5E7. Telephone: (613) 235-4048; in Canada only, (800) 559-4514. Fax (613) 235-8101.
URL: http://www.ccsa.ca/canbsrch.htm

This database contains over 10,400 bibliographic records from Canadian sources, published elsewhere about all aspects of substance abuse and treatment in Canada. CANBASE is created from records contributed by the libraries and resource centers comprising the Canadian Substance Information Network. Although not limited to FAS/E, numerous references are included.

ETOH—The Alcohol and Alcohol Problems Science Database

URL: http://etoh.niaaa.nihigov/

For more information, contact the National Institute on Alcohol Abuse and Alcoholism, 6000 Executive Blvd., Willco Building, Room 409, Bethesda, MD 20857. Telephone: (301) 443-3860; Fax (301) 443-6077.

This database, developed by the National Institute of Alcohol Abuse and Alcoholism, is the most comprehensive online index to information on alcohol-related research available. Begun in 1972, ETOH covers literature from the late 1960s to the present and includes over 110,000 bibliographic records. Topics include all aspects of biomedical and behavioral alcohol-related research, including psychology, psychiatry, physiology, epidemiology, sociology, animal studies, treatment, prevention, accidents, safety, legislation, criminal justice, and public policy.

In addition to the scientific and technical journal articles, books, monograph, reports and hard-to-find sources of alcohol research are included. The database is unique in that it offer entries for articles or book chapters in edited works. The database is updated monthly.

FASLINK Listserve

The Canadian Centre on Substance Abuse, FAS/E Information Service, offers FASLINK, a listserve providing an electronic forum for the discussion of FAS/E issues. Topics addressed to date have included conference announcements, new research, and alternative therapies. Individuals interested in joining the list should send an e-mail message to <list@ccsa.ca> and type <join faslink> (in lowercase letters) in the body of the message.

Works Cited

Abel, E. L., and R. J. Sokol. "Maternal and fetal characteristics affecting alcohol's teratogenicity." *Neurobehavioral Toxicology and Teratology* 8 (1986): 329–334.

Arbogast, D. *Wounded Warriors: A time for healing*. Omaha: Little Turtle Publications, 1995.

Astley, S. J., and S. K. Clarren. *Diagnostic guide for fetal Alcohol syndrome and related Conditions*. Seattle: University of Washington Press, 1997.

Borjenson, M. C., and J. Lagergren, "Life conditions of adolescence with myelomenin gocele." *Developmental Medicine and Child Neurology* 32 (1990): 689–706.

"Centers for Disease Control and prevention update: Trends in fetal alcohol syndrome—United States, 1979–1993." *Morbidity and Mortality Weekly Report* 44 (1995a): 249–251.

Chasnoff, I. J. "Fetal alcohol syndrome in twin pregnancy." *Acta Genet Med Gemellol* 34 (1985): 229–232.

Cole, J. *How you were born*. New York: William Morrow and Co., 1998.

Coles, C. D. "Prenatal alcohol exposure and human development." In *Development of Central Nervous System: Effects of Alcohol and Opiates*, 9–36. Wiley-Liss, Inc., 1992.

Dorris, M. *The Broken Cord*. New York: Harper and Row, 1989.

Elliott, G. R., and S. S. Feldman, "Capturing the adolescent experience." In S.S. Feldman and G.R. Elliott, eds. *At the threshold: The developing adolescent*. Cambridge: Harvard University Press, 1990, 1–13.

"Evidence and implications for society." *Alcohol Health and Research World* 15, 3: 239–248.

Hallum, A. "Disability and the transition to adulthood: Issues for the disabled child, the family and the pediatrician." *Current Problems in Pediatrics* (January 1995): 12–50.

Hornby, R. *Competency Training for Human Service Providers*. Mission, SD: Sinte Gleska University Press, 1993.

Ingerman, S. *Soul Retrieval: Mending the Fragmented Self*. San Francisco, CA: HarperCollins, 1991.

Jacobson, S. W., J. L. Jacobson, R. J. Sokol, S. S. Mariter, J. W. Ager, and M. G. Kaplan-Estrin. "Teratogenic effects of alcohol on infant development." *Alcoholism: Clinical and Experimental Research* 17, 1 (1993): 174–183.

Jones, K. L., and D. W. Smith."Recognition of the fetal alcohol syndrome in early infancy," *Lancet* 2 (1973): 999–1001.

Jones, K. L., D. W. Smith, C. N. Ulleland, and A. P. Streissguth. "Patterns of malformation in offspring of chronic alcoholic women." *Lancet* 1 (1973a): 1267–1271.

Kleinfeld, J., and S. Wescott. *Fantastic Antone Succeeds! Experiences educating children with fetal alcohol syndrome*. Fairbanks: University of Alaska Press, 1993.

Kohn, Alfie. *Punished by rewards*. Boston: Houghton Mifflin, 1993.

LaDue, R. A., A. P. Streissguth, and S. P. Randels. "Clinical consideration pertaining to adolescents and adults with fetal alcohol syndrome." In T. Sonderigger, ed. *Perinatal substance abuse: Recent findings and clinical implications*. Baltimore, MD: Johns Hopkins Press, 1992.

Leffert, N., and A. Petersen, "Patterns of development during adolescence: An Overview." In M. Rutter and D. Smith, eds. *Psychosocial Disorders in Young People*. Chichester, England: John Wylie & Sons, Ltd., 1995, 67–103.

Lemoine, P., H. Harrousseau, J. P. Borteyru, and J. C. Menuet. "Les enfants de parents alcooliques. Anomalies observéas. À propos de 127 cas (Children of alcoholic parents: anomalies observed in 127 cases)." *Ouest Med* 21 (1968): 476–482.

Lemoine, P., and P. H. Lemoine. "Avenir des enfants de mere alcooliques (étude de 105 cas retrouvés à l'âge adulte) et quelques constatations d'interet prophylactique [Follow-up of children of alcoholic mothers (study of 105 cases seen in adulthood) and some recommendations about prevention]." *Annales de Pediatrie (Paris)* 39 (1992): 226–235.

Locust, C. S. American Indian beliefs Concerning Health and Unwellness. *Monograph of the Native American Research and Training Center*. University of Arizona: Tucson, 1985.

May, P. A. Alcohol Abuse and Alcoholism Among American Indians: An Overview. In Watts, T. D., and R. Wright, eds. *Alcoholism in Minority Populations*. Springfield, Ill.: Charles C. Thomas, 1989.

———. Fetal Alcohol Effects Among North American Indians. 1991.

May, P. A., K. J. Hymbaugh, J. M. Aase, and J. M. Samet. "Epidemiology of Fetal Alcohol Syndrome of the Southwest." *Social Biology* 30 (1983): 508-518.

May, P. A., C. Clericuzio, K. Hymbaugh, D. Monteau, and M. Weller. Suggested Curricula for Fetal Alcohol Syndrome Prevention Education. *Report*. The National Indian Fetal Alcohol Syndrome Prevention Program, Albuquerque.

Mattson, S. N., T. L. Jernigan, and E. P. Riley. "MRI and prenatal alcohol exposure." *Alcohol Health and Research World* 18 (1994): 49–52.

Morse, B. A., R. K. Idelson, W. H. Sachs, L. Weiner, and L. C. Kaplan, "Pediatricians' perspectives on fetal alcohol syndrome." *Journal of Substance Abuse* 4 (1992):187–195.

Mulvihill, J. J., J. T. Klimas, D. C. Stokes, and H. M. Risemberg. "Fetal alcohol syndrome: Seven new cases." *American Journal of Obstetrical Gynecology* 125 (1976): 937–941.

Nanson, J. L., R. Bolaria, R. E. Snyder, B. A. Morse, and L. Weiner. "Physician awareness of fetal alcohol syndrome: A survey of pediatricians and general practitioners." *Canadian Medical Association Journal* 152 (1995): 1071–1076.

Palmer, R. H., E. M. Ouellette, L. Warner, and S. R. Leichtman. "Congenital malformations in offspring of a chronic alcoholic mother." *Pediatrics* 53 (1974): 490–494.

Park, Clara Claiborn. *The Siege: The first eight years of an autistic child*. New York: Little Brown & Co., 1990.

"Pathways through adolescence: An overview." In L. Crockett and A. Crouter, eds. *Pathways Through Adolescence: Individual Development in Relation to Social Context*. Mahwah, N.J.: Lawrence Erlbaum Ass., 1995, 1–12.

Patterson, J., and R. W. Blum. "Risk and resilience among children and youth with disabilities." *Archives of Pediatric and Adolescent Medicine* 150 (1996): 692–698.

"People with work disability in the U. S." Disability Statistics Abstract, Vol 4. Disablity Statistics Program, University of California, San Francisco: U.S. Department of Education, NIDRR, May 1992.

Rosett, H. L. "A clinical perspective of the fetal alcohol syndrome." *Alcoholism: Clinical and Experimental Research* 4 (1980): 119–122.

Rosett, H. L., L. Weiner, and K. C. Edelin. "Treatment experience with pregnant problem drinkers." *Journal of the American Medical Association* 249 (1983): 2029–2033.

Schopler, E., and G. Mesibov. *Autism in adolescents and adults.* New York: Plenum Press, 1983.

Shaywitz, S. E., D. J. Cohen, and B. A Shaywitz. "Behavior and Learning Difficulties in Children of Normal Intelligence Born to Alcoholic Mothers." *Journal of Pediatrics* 95, 6 (1980): 978–982.

Snyder, L. Fetal alcohol syndrome resource guide. *Report.* Albuquerque, NM: Department of Health and Human Services.

Sokol. R. J., and S. K. Clarren. "Guidelines for the use of terminology describing the impact of prenatal alcohol on the offspring." *Alcoholism: Clinical and Experimental Research* 13 (1989): 597–598.

Spohr, H., J. Willms, and H. Steinhausen, H. "Prenatal alcohol exposure and long-term developmental consequences." *Lancet* 341 (1993): 907–910.

Standing Bear, L. *Land of the spotted eagle.* Lincoln: University of Nebraska Press, 1978.

Steinhausen, H. C. "Children of alcoholic parents." *Acta Paediatrica Scandinavica* 82, 2 (1993): 208–209.

Streissguth, A. P. "Maternal alcoholism and the outcome of pregnancy: A review of the fetal alcohol syndrome." In M. Greenblatt and M. A. Schuckit, eds., *Alcohol problems in woman and children.* New York: Grune & Stratton, 1976.

———. "Fetal alcohol syndrome: An overview and implications for patient management." In N. J. Estes and M. E. Heineman, eds., *Alcoholism: Development, Consequences, and Interventions,* 196–206. St. Louis, MO: C.V. Mosby, 1986.

———. "Drinking during pregnancy decreases word attack and arithmetic scores on standardized tests: Adolescent data from a population-based prospective study." *Alcoholism: Clinical and Experimental Research* 18, 2 (1994): 248–254.

————. "A long-term perspective of FAS." *Alcohol Health and Research World, Alcohol-related Birth Defects*, PB94 213 725. Washington, DC: National Institute of Health, 1994.

Streissguth, A., and J. Kanter. *The Challenge of fetal alcohol syndrome. Overcoming secondary disabilities.* Seattle: University of Washington Press, 1997.

Streissguth, A., H. Barr, J. Kogan, and F. Bookstein. "Understanding the occurrence of secondary disabilities in clients with fetal alcohol syndrome (FAS) and fetal alcohol effects (FAE)." University of Washington School of Medicine Department of Psychiatry and Behavioral Sciences, 1996.

Streissguth, A. P., R. A. LaDue, and S. P. Randels. *A manual on adolescents and adults with fetal alcohol syndrome with special reference to American Indians.* Rockville, MD: U. S. Department of Health and Human Services, 1988.

Streissguth, A. P., P. D. Sampson, and H. M. Barr. "Neurobehavioral dose-response effects of prenatal alcohol exposure in humans from infancy to adulthood." *Annals of the New York Academy of Sciences* 562 (1989): 145–158.

A. Streissguth et al. , "Understanding the Occurrence of Secondary Disabilities in Clients with Fetal Alcohol Syndrome (FAS) and Fetal Alcohol Effects (FAE)," University of Washington School of Medicine, Department of Psychiatry and Behavioral Sciences, Fetal Alcohol and Drug Unit. *Final Report.* August 1996.

Tenbrinck S., and S. Y. Buchin. "Fetal alcohol syndrome: Report of a case." *Journal of the American Medical Association* 232 (1975): 1144–1147.

U.S. Department of Health and Human Services. *Report No. 1.* Washington, DC: Government Printing Office, 1997, 5.

Werner, Emmy E., and Ruth S. Smith. *Overcoming the Odds: High risk Children from birth to adversity.* Ithaca, NY: Cornell University Press, 1992.

White, Nancy. "Michael Dorris: A messenger of hope, prevention." *Iceberg* 7, 1 (1997): 3, 5.

Wolin, Steven J., and Sybil Wolin. *The Resilient self: How survivors of troubled families rise above adversity*. New York: Villard Books, 1993.

Index

About the first book...

FANTASTIC ANTONE SUCCEEDS! EXPERIENCES EDUCATING CHILDREN
WITH FETAL ALCOHOL SYNDROME
edited by Judith Kleinfeld and Siobhan Wescott

*Fantastic Antone Succeeds! Experiences Educating Children with
Fetal Alcohol Syndrome* describes in concrete, specific ways
how to educate children with fetal alcohol syndrome/effects
(FAS/E). It communicates an optimistic message that is both true
and appealing: with the right education, delivered by a nurturing
individual in the home or in school—many children with FAS/E
thrive.

The book consists of separate chapters written in a popular
and accessible style by psychologists, teachers, and birth and
adoptive parents of alcohol-affected children. It includes lists of
important resources, organizations to contact, and descriptions
of effective classroom practices for teachers.

Without minimizing the seriousness of FAS/E and the first
priority—prevention—*Fantastic Antone Succeeds* provides
practical tools and strategies that can help alcohol-affected
individuals and their families lead happier, more productive
lives.

1993, paper, ISBN 0-912006-65-X, $20.00
381 pages, 6 x 9, b/w and color illustrations

*Please contact the University of Alaska Press (toll free in
the U.S. 1-888-252-6657) for more information!*